Yale
Publications
in the
History
of Art

Walter Cahn,

Editor

Michael Lobel

Image Duplicator

Roy Lichtenstein and the Emergence of Pop Art

YALE UNIVERSITY PRESS   NEW HAVEN & LONDON

Designed by Richard Hendel.
Set in New Baskerville and Gill types by Eric M. Brooks.
Printed in China by C S Graphics.

Library of Congress Cataloging-in-Publication Data
Lobel, Michael.
Image duplicator: Roy Lichtenstein and the emergence of pop art / Michael Lobel.
p. cm.—(Yale publications in the history of art)
Includes bibliographical references and index.
ISBN 0-300-08762-4 (alk. paper)
1. Lichtenstein, Roy, 1923–1997—Image duplicator.
2. Lichtenstein, Roy, 1923–1997—Criticism and interpretation.
3. Pop art. I. Title. II. Series.
N6537.L5 A68 2001
759.13—dc21 2001045347

A catalogue record for this book is available from the British Library.

The paper in this book meets the guidelines for permanence and durability of the Committee on Production Guidelines for Book Longevity of the Council on Library Resources.

10 9 8 7 6 5 4 3 2 1

Illustrations on chapter opening pages:

p. xii, detail of fig. 8: first page of "Is He the Worst Artist in the U.S.?" from *Life* 56, no. 5 (January 31, 1964)

p. 16, detail of fig. 11: *Look Mickey,* 1961. National Gallery of Art, Washington, D.C.

p. 40, detail of fig. 19: *Spray,* 1962. Staatsgalerie Stuttgart

p. 74, detail of fig. 53: *Torpedo . . . Los!,* 1963. Simonyi collection

p. 104, detail of fig. 75: *Emeralds,* 1961. Private collection

p. 126, detail of fig. 93: *In the Car,* 1963. Scottish National Gallery of Modern Art, Edinburgh

p. 158, detail of fig. 103: *Yellow and Green Brushstrokes,* 1966. Museum für Moderne Kunst, Frankfurt.

Yale Publications in the History of Art are works of critical and historical scholarship by authors formerly or now associated with the Department of the History of Art of Yale University. Begun in 1939, the series embraces the field of art historical studies in its widest and most inclusive definition.

Series logo designed by Josef Albers and reproduced with permission of the Josef Albers Foundation.

TO THE MEMORY OF MARY RISLEY

Contents

Acknowledgments

I could not have completed this project without the professional, institutional, and personal support I received throughout. This book began as a dissertation for the History of Art department at Yale University. I am indebted to Jonathan Weinberg, my primary advisor at Yale, for his crucial support and encouragement; his incisive comments on my early work gave shape to the project. Romy Golan and Bryan Wolf provided substantive critical feedback on the text. Thomas Crow not only responded to my written work but also offered invaluable advice and support as the project developed.

Research for the book was made possible by grants from the History of Art department at Yale University, the Hagley Museum and Library, and the Henry Luce Foundation/American Council of Learned Societies. A postdoctoral fellowship at the Getty Research Institute for the History of Art and the Humanities afforded me the time and resources necessary to finish the book. My colleagues in the Scholars and Seminars program at the Research Institute provided a stimulating environment in which to work; I particularly want to acknowledge Malcolm Baker, Dorinne Kondo, Sherrie Levine, Maria Loh, Rani Singh, and Anne Wagner for their support and comments on my project. During the final stages of writing my work benefited from frequent—and lively—conversations with Alastair Wright. The staff at the Research Institute offered much-needed support, and my research assistant, Rebecca Epstein, provided invaluable help with photographic rights and reproductions. I would also like to thank Andrew Perchuk, who offered feedback with customary good humor and insight. My time at the Getty brought me into contact with a vibrant community of scholars in Los Angeles, and I am grateful for the advice and encouragement I received from David Joselit, Juliet Koss, and Steven Nelson.

My work benefited from access to a wide range of archives and libraries, including the Archives of American Art, the Museum of Modern Art library, and the

Whitney Museum of American Art library. The following individuals provided substantial assistance with my research: Allan Duffy, Leo Castelli Gallery; Dave Smith, Walt Disney Archives; Kristine Kaske-Anthony, National Air and Space Museum, Smithsonian Institution; Molly Donovan, National Gallery of Art; Marla Hand, Robert B. Mayer Memorial Loan Collection; Charles Simonyi and Karen Lambright; Allan Asherman, DC Comics; and Anita Duquette, Whitney Museum of American Art. I would especially like to thank Roy Lichtenstein's friends, colleagues, and family members who generously offered insights and historical details about the artist's work, including Bob Adelman, Bruce Breland, Allan Kaprow, Dorothy Lichtenstein, and Idelle Weber.

Both the Roy Lichtenstein Foundation and the Estate of Roy Lichtenstein were particularly helpful and supportive. The Foundation provided a much-needed grant to offset the substantive costs of permissions. Jack Cowart, Executive Director of the Foundation, offered encouragement, advice, and valuable criticism. Shelley Lee worked tirelessly to assist me with the enormous task of compiling reproductions of the artist's work. Cassandra Lozano patiently fielded my questions and allowed me access to Lichtenstein's studio on several occasions to photograph notebooks and source materials. She also arranged for me to interview the artist in March 1997. The course of my research—as well as my appreciation of the artist's work—was deeply affected by that interview. Roy Lichtenstein proved himself a gracious interviewee, and I was shocked and saddened when he passed away in October of the same year. There are many more questions I wanted to ask him. I hope that this book contributes to a greater understanding of the historical and theoretical implications of his practice.

My work has benefited from discussions with numerous colleagues, among whom I would particularly like to acknowledge Beth Handler, Richard Meyer, Sarah Rich, Kim Smith, and Cécile Whiting. I also received useful feedback from the participants and audiences at academic symposia where I presented earlier versions of the material in this book. I want to thank those who invited me to speak at the Department of Art History, University of Southern California; the Hagley Museum and Library; the "Popism" symposium sponsored by the History of Art department at Yale; the Rhode Island School of Design; and the "Media Pop" symposium co-sponsored by the Getty Research Institute, University of California, Irvine, and UCLA. An earlier version of Chapter Three ("Technology Envisioned: Lichtenstein's Monocularity") originally appeared—under the same name—in the Spring 2001 issue of the *Oxford Art Journal*.

Walter Cahn generously offered funds from the Yale Publications in the History of Art series to help offset reproduction costs. As duplication is one of the major themes of this book, perhaps it is fitting that its life at Yale University Press has been marked by a certain degree of doubling. Judy Metro initially acquired the manuscript for the Press. When Judy left Yale, Patricia Fidler stepped in and took over stewardship of the project. I am extremely grateful for the care with which she has guided the book through the production process. The manuscript was also split between two copy editors, and I want to acknowledge both Heidi Downey and Margaret Otzel for their careful attention to the text. Richard Hendel's design carefully and thoughtfully brings text and images together.

I owe a great debt of gratitude to my family and friends. My parents Adele and Sheldon Lobel and my brother Adam provided support throughout. My brother Richard, sister Marci Lobel-Esrig, and brother-in-law Marc Esrig sustained me with their good humor, insight, and thoughtful advice. The writing of this book would have been immeasurably more difficult without the numerous visits I made to my nephew, Caleb Esrig. I am deeply grateful to Linda Rosenberg for our conversations, which left a deep imprint on my work. Martin Berger, Bruce Hainley, Nancy Marshall, Arikha Moses, and Paul Young offered their support and saw me through all that it took to complete this project. Uli Baer contributed to this book in innumerable ways; he provided invaluable feedback on the manuscript and buoyed me with his friendship, advice, and constant encouragement. Finally, words cannot adequately express the strength and energy I draw from my friendships with Susan Beren and Vincent Fecteau, who challenge, inspire, and sustain me.

This book is dedicated to the memory of Mary Risley, an artist and teacher who was central to my intellectual and creative development. Mary was my undergraduate advisor at Wesleyan University, where I majored in studio art. It was she who, after my graduation from college, pushed me to pursue graduate studies in art history and provided constant encouragement through my early years in academia. During the time I studied with her at Wesleyan she taught me about the value of looking closely and critically, in an aesthetic sense but also in a moral, political, and ethical sense. As our relationship continued outside the classroom, my appreciation of her good humor, thoughtfulness, and honesty only grew. I miss her deeply, and wish she could have seen this book completed. I only hope that her spirit of critical thought, deep love of teaching, and commitment to artistic practice live on in my own work.

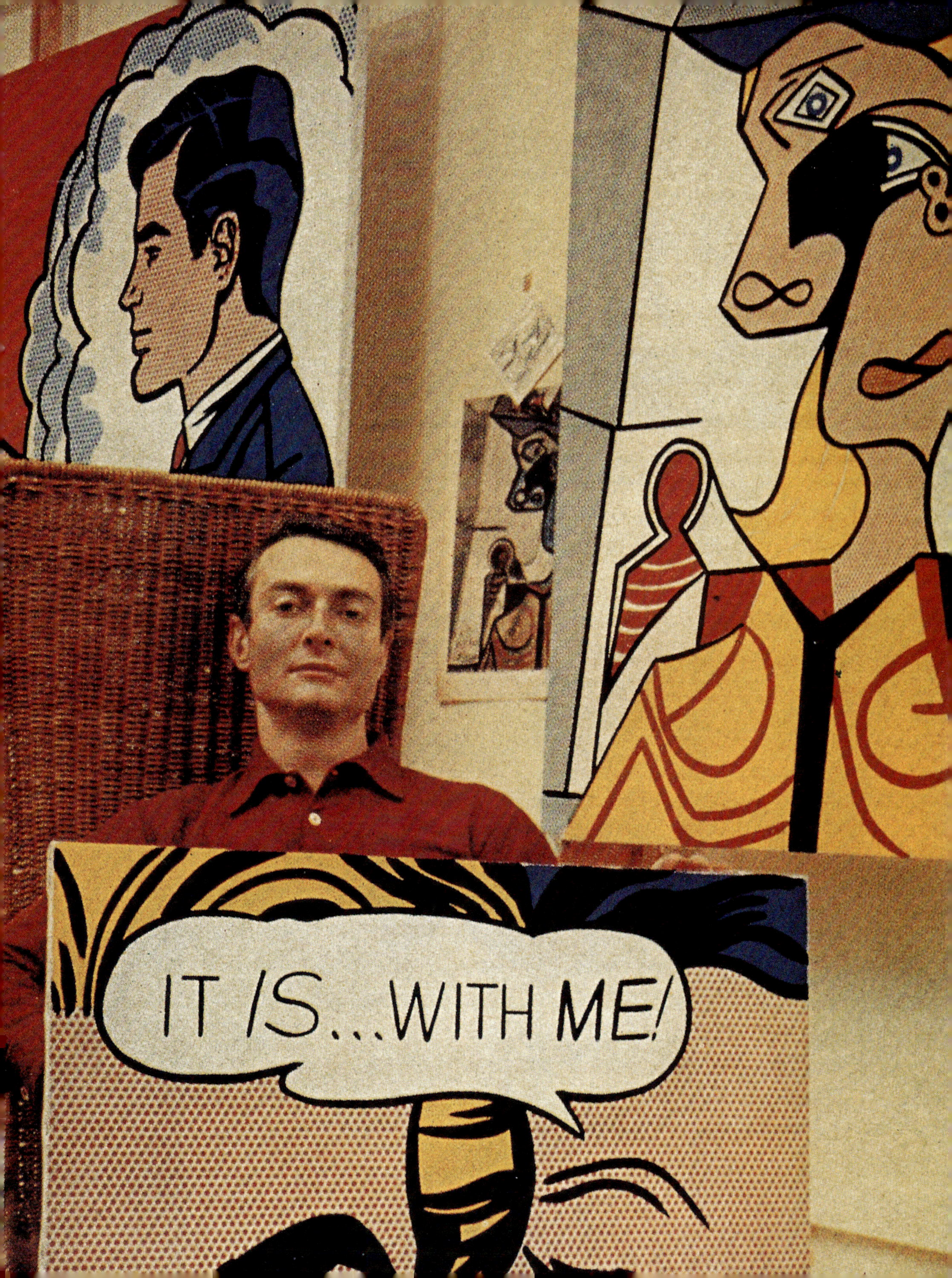
IT IS...WITH ME!

Introduction

"WHAT? WHY DID YOU ASK THAT? WHAT DO YOU KNOW ABOUT MY IMAGE DUPLICATOR?" These lines of text, aggressive and accusatory, almost fill the top half of a 1963 canvas by Roy Lichtenstein (fig. 1). With its thick black outlines, vibrant palette of primary colors, and regularized dot patterns, *Image Duplicator* is representative of Lichtenstein's work from the early 1960s. It also constitutes a response to some of the more hostile criticism the artist received during that period. The title of the painting makes reference to a basic component of Lichtenstein's practice, which saw him appropriating images from advertisements, the comics, and other printed sources and enlarging them into paintings. It is these works—which soon after their appearance came to be categorized within the larger movement known as Pop art—that concern me in this book.

The paintings Lichtenstein produced in the early 1960s, particularly the scenes derived from the romance and war comics of the period, are instantly recognizable to most contemporary viewers. They have been reproduced countless times in the decades since they were created, and their distinctive visual vocabulary—the magnified dots and stylized cartoon devices—has been absorbed back into the mass media from which it was derived.[1] That exaggerated comic book style has been put to such wide use that even the many viewers who would be unable to identify the artist by name are familiar with the idiom in which he executed his work. Yet one of my major contentions in this book is that, in spite of the sheer recognizability of the pictorial vocabulary developed by Lichtenstein, the artist's early Pop practice has never been sufficiently analyzed and interpreted. Perhaps it has been precisely the ubiquity of these images that has led us to overlook them as the products of a sustained artistic project. Ironically, it may be their very success—and afterlife in countless reproductions—that has led them to be undertheorized. This is precisely the problematic that structures Lichtenstein's work and provides the focus of my analysis: the relation between the work of art and its

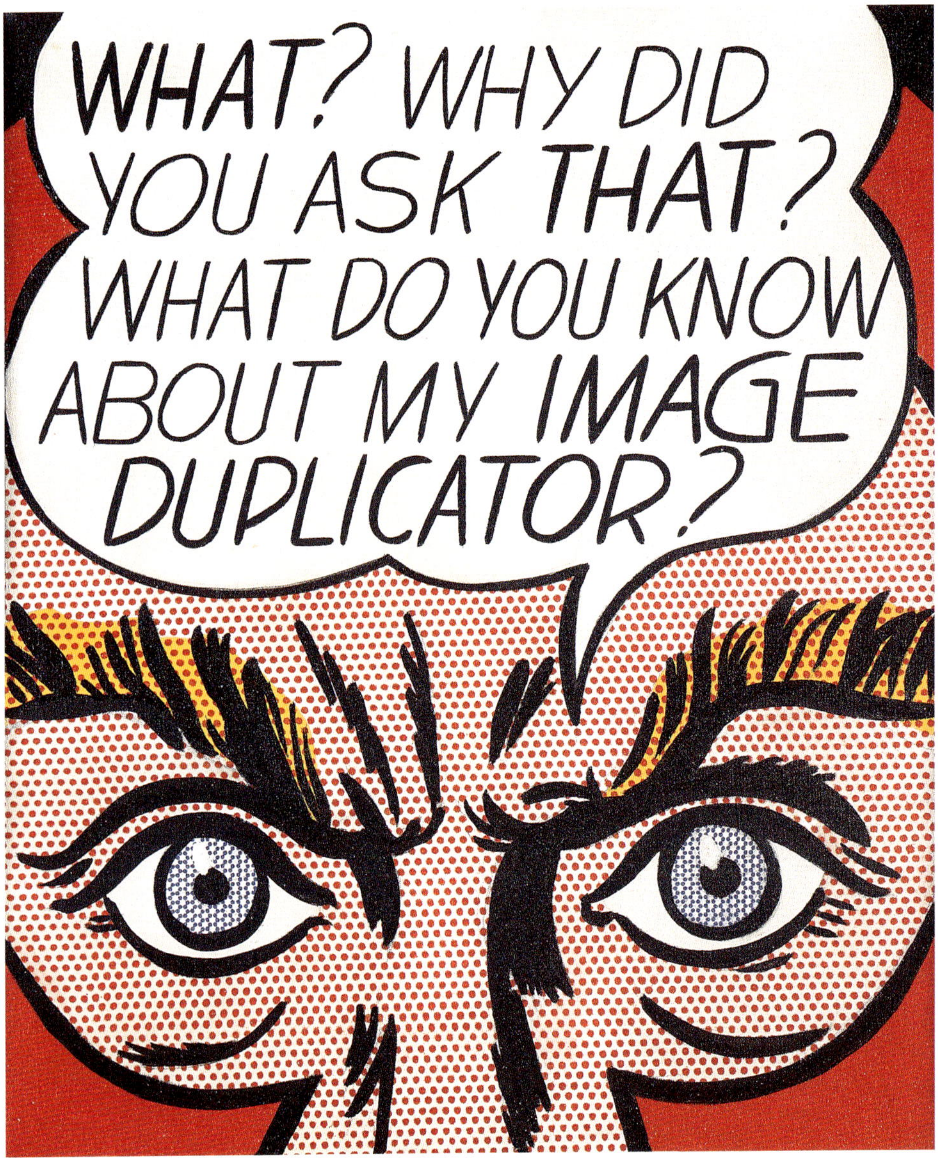

Figure 1.
Image Duplicator,
1963.
Magna on canvas,
24 × 20 in.
(61 × 50.8 cm).
Simonyi collection

reproductions, between the artist and the machine, between the terms of originality and repetition.

This is not to say that there has been a dearth of criticism on Lichtenstein's imagery; since Pop art's explosion on the cultural scene his work has been examined for its formal relationship to the history of painting, analyzed in relation to the development of mechanical printing techniques, and contextualized within the Pop movement as a whole. His approach to popular imagery was no isolated instance; the history of art since at least the late nineteenth century is replete with myriad approaches to the representation of cultures of entertainment and consumption. In the early- to mid-1950s the artists affiliated with the Independent Group confronted images of American consumer culture filtering into postwar Britain, while at about the same moment Jasper Johns and Robert Rauschenberg were incorporating common objects and vernacular idioms into their work. The early 1960s in the United States, particularly in New York, saw the appearance of a wide array of artistic projects that treated the products of mass-produced consumer culture; within a short time these came to be grouped within the category of Pop art. That category included such artists as Jim Dine, Robert Indiana, Claes Oldenburg, Marisol, Ed Ruscha, James Rosenquist, Andy Warhol, and Lichtenstein himself. But it is precisely this kind of categorizing that we need to interrogate; if the examples of historical antecedents—and the work of contemporaries—has helped contextualize Lichtenstein's approach to mass cultural imagery, the tendency to group such practices under larger headings like Pop art may also serve to occlude specific concerns and problems Lichtenstein confronted in his work. This is certainly true of the tendency to consider Pop as a movement solely concerned with the status of objects. Critical texts have often linked the Pop artists by concentrating not on their specific practices but on the broader categories of objects depicted in their work.[2] Such an approach certainly has its merits for those attempting a historical understanding of the movement, but what may be lost in the process is the recognition that these artists—who often refused the umbrella labeling of their work as part of a larger movement—took radically different approaches to the imagery of a mass-produced consumer culture.[3]

My analysis is intended to shift the terms of the critical approach to Lichtenstein's work—to focus not on the question of the object but on that of the subject. Because the artist's imagery appears relatively straightforward and uninflected, it lends itself to being read as an almost neutral presentation of printed images from the mass media and advertising. In order to counter such a tendency we will analyze the artist's works not as straightforward presentations but as *representations* that manipulate, reorganize, and reframe appropriated images in strategic ways. Lichtenstein's work poses questions about the individual's relation to a mechanically reproduced culture by restaging the viewer's mode of address to media imagery. To wit: What models of identity are offered—and problematized—by the centrality of the trademark and brand name in a consumer society? What effect do visual technologies have on the subject's relation to embodied perception? And, centrally, what threat does mechanical repetition pose to traditional notions of artistic originality and agency? Although any treatment of Lichtenstein's imagery—as of Pop in general—will always of necessity deal with objects and their depiction, our discussion will always return to questions of subjectivity.

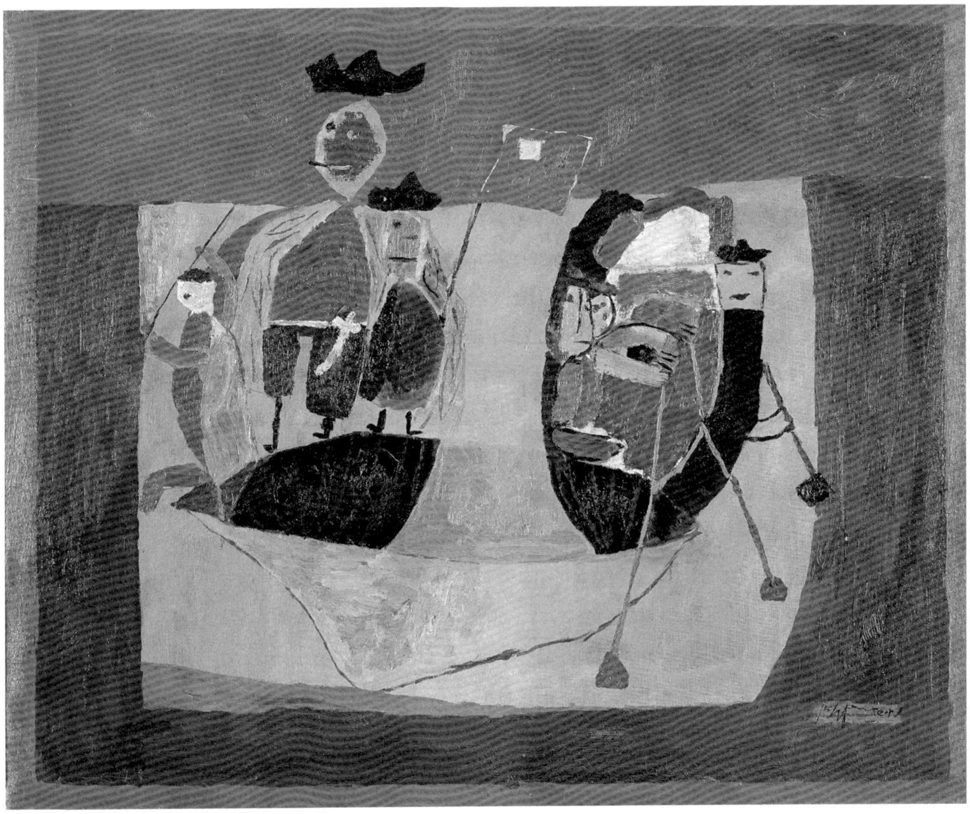

Figure 2.
Washington Crossing the Delaware I, c. 1951.
Oil on canvas, 26 × 32 in. (66 × 81.3 cm).
Private collection

What might have brought the artist to a confrontation with such issues in his work? In 1961, the year in which his distinctive Pop mode emerged, Lichtenstein was by no means an emerging artist. Rather, he was thirty-seven years old and had been producing mature work for at least a decade. In an important study entitled *Roy Lichtenstein: Das Frühwerk, 1942–1960,* Ernst Busche carefully documented the formal and iconographic development of Lichtenstein's pre-Pop imagery.[4] The artist's career prior to the 1960s had been marked by a great deal of experimentation; his work had ranged from figurative scenes to mechanical diagrams to abstract compositions. Nevertheless, as Busche points out, it was also marked by certain consistencies. Although it may seem that it was only with his move into Pop that Lichtenstein consigned himself to being a veritable image duplicator, he had utilized appropriated imagery in his work since the early 1950s. He consistently borrowed motifs from printed reproductions: grandiose American history paintings like Emmanuel Leutze's *Washington Crossing the Delaware* (fig. 2); French Rococo imagery from such painters as François Boucher and Jean-Honoré Fragonard; even anthropomorphic cartoon characters like Bugs Bunny and Mickey Mouse, which toward the end of the 1950s began to appear in fields of otherwise abstract,

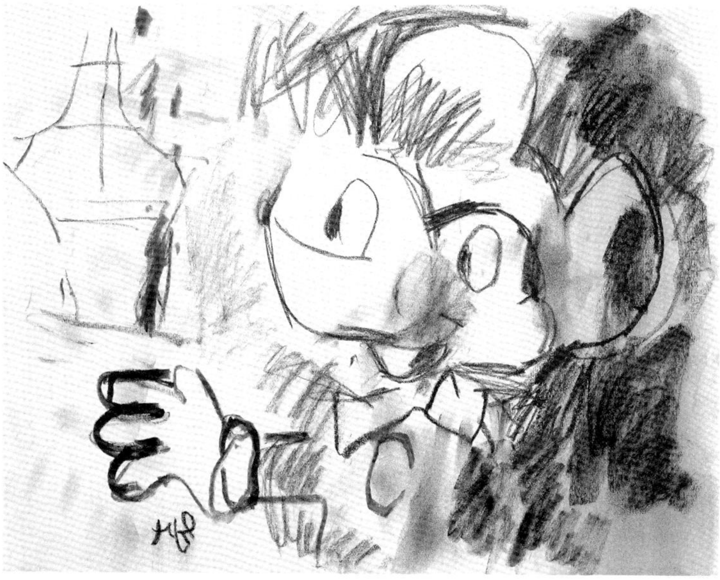

Figure 3.
Mickey Mouse I,
c. 1958.
India ink and
colored pencil
on paper,
19⅛ × 25 in.
(48.6 × 63.5 cm).
Private collection

gestural markings (fig. 3). Although the Pop artists' collective move into figuration—when viewed against the background of American painting in the 1950s—has typically been interpreted as a profound renunciation of abstraction, Lichtenstein himself came to abstract painting rather late. He began to experiment with the form in about 1958, producing a body of all-over, gestural canvases rendered in thick bands of striated pigment juxtaposed with calligraphic markings (fig. 4). He retained that mode for three years at the most.

Lichtenstein's move into Pop was motivated in part by his geographic and professional circumstances, which changed in about 1960. In that year—after almost two decades spent in Ohio and upstate New York—he moved to Highland Park, New Jersey, to teach at Douglass College, then the women's college of Rutgers.[5] This move put him in closer contact with the New York art world at a time when the examples of Jasper Johns and Robert Rauschenberg loomed especially large; critics have long emphasized that their so-called neo-Dadaist work exerted a profound influence on the artists who would, in the early 1960s, come to be identified with Pop.[6] But he also found himself in the midst of a circle of artists who played an equal—if not even more decisive—role in influencing his approach to art making. When asked by the critic John Coplans in a 1963 interview, "Did the work of Johns or Rauschenberg provide you with any insights at that time?" Lichtenstein responded: "Although I recognize their great influence now, I wasn't as aware at that time. I was more aware of the Happenings of Oldenburg, Dine, Whitman, and Kaprow. I knew Kaprow well; we were colleagues at Rutgers. I didn't see many Happenings, but they seemed concerned with the American industrial

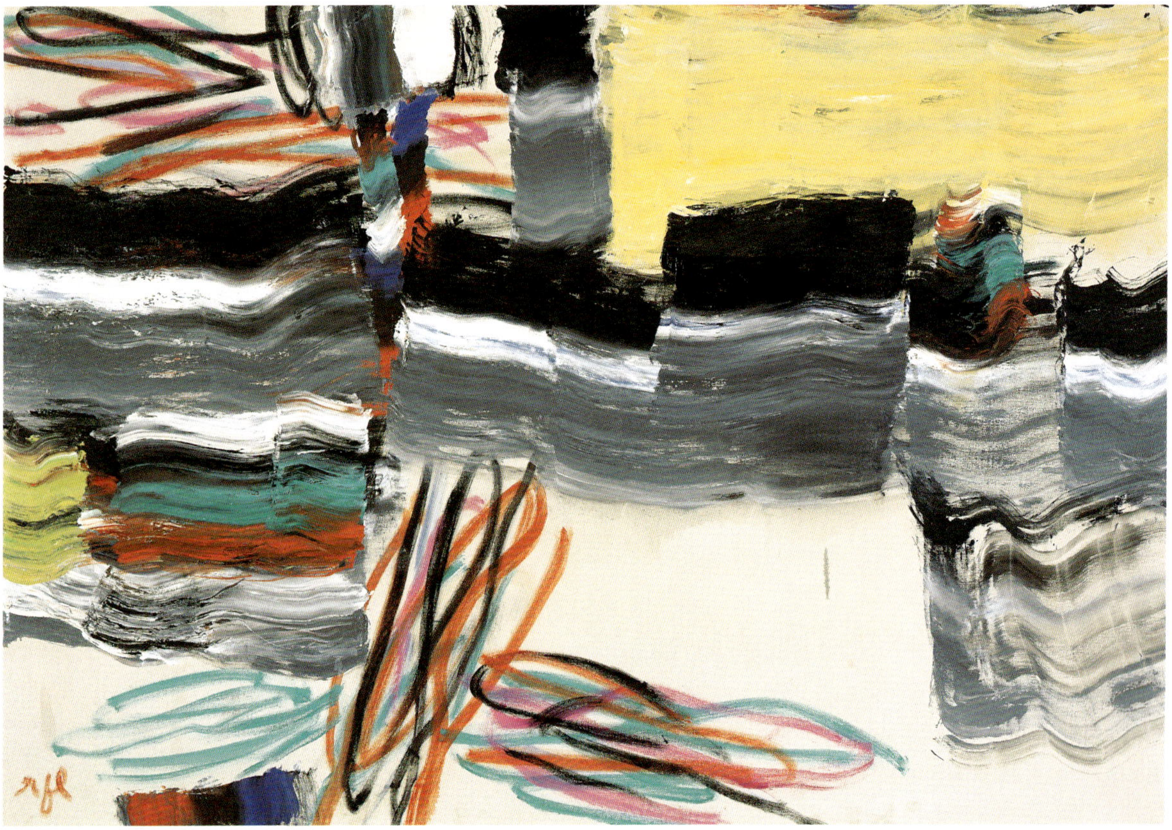

Figure 4.
Untitled, 1960.
Oil on canvas,
48 × 70 in.
(121.9 ×
177.8 cm).
Private
collection

scene. They also brought up in my mind the whole question of the object and merchandising."[7] Along with the examples of Oldenburg and Dine, Lichtenstein here cites two artists—Robert Whitman and Allan Kaprow—who were part of a larger group affiliated with Rutgers University in the late 1950s and early 1960s. This circle included George Segal (who would also come to be identified with Pop), Robert Watts and George Brecht (both of whom would become involved in the Fluxus movement), and Lucas Samaras. As a group they were engaged in an array of activities that included performances, Happenings, sculptural environments, and approaches to assemblage.[8] Their activities were informed by the examples of such figures as Marcel Duchamp, whose development of the concept of the readymade earlier in the century had radically reframed the relation between the work of art and the common object, and John Cage, whose experiments with musical composition allowed for the incorporation of randomness and chance—and the viewer's participation—into the production of the work of art.[9]

Kaprow, with whom Lichtenstein would forge a close friendship, was a charismatic member of the Rutgers group and a major figure in the development of the

Happenings movement.[10] In 1958 he published a veritable manifesto entitled "The Legacy of Jackson Pollock," in which he called for an art that celebrated the everyday, particularly by directing attention to the common object:

> Pollock, as I see him, left us at the point where we must become preoccupied with and even dazzled by the space and objects of our everyday life, either our bodies, clothes, rooms, or, if need be, the vastness of Forty-Second Street. . . . Objects of every sort are materials for the new art: paint, chairs, food, electric and neon lights, smoke, water, old socks, a dog, movies, a thousand other things that will be discovered by the present generation of artists. Not only will these bold creators show us, as if for the first time, the world we have always had about us, but ignored, but they will disclose entirely unheard of happenings and events, found in garbage cans, police files, hotel lobbies, seen in store windows and on the streets, and sensed in dreams and horrible accidents. An odor of crushed strawberries, a letter from a friend or a billboard selling Drano; three taps on the front door, a scratch, a sigh or a voice lecturing endlessly, a blinding staccato flash, a bowler hat—all will become materials for this new concrete art.[11]

Kaprow's text gives us a sense of his interest in an ephemeral art of performance that would be realized in his Happenings. It also highlights his emphasis on the common object, which has often been taken to prefigure the Pop artists' interest in the products of consumer culture. In the face of the bravura enthusiasm evident here, and in light of the excitement that the activities of the Rutgers group seem to have generated, it is tempting to view Lichtenstein's move into Pop as an almost logical development that merely involved the incorporation of such concerns into his painterly practice. In other words, one is inclined to suggest that he simply took certain neo-avant-garde strategies available to him at this time—particularly the embrace of the readymade and an interest in the ephemeral culture of the everyday—and extended them to painting.[12]

Such an assessment is accurate to a certain extent, but what is missing from it is the recognition that such a process was by no means uncomplicated. This is particularly evident when we consider Lichtenstein's prior development as an artist and his continued commitment to painting. As Diane Waldman has succinctly put it, "Lichtenstein was a relative latecomer to the avant-garde."[13] Unlike Kaprow, Watts, Samaras, and Segal—who all began their careers as painters but were impelled, through their experimentation, into other areas of artistic practice (whether performance-oriented Happenings, object-constructions or sculptural tableaus)—he doggedly stuck to painting throughout this period (and after), remaining committed to a resolutely aesthetic view of the painter's craft. For years his work consistently looked back to earlier models (particularly that of late synthetic cubism), and when he used appropriated images in his paintings it was in order to remake them according to a principle of organizing form rooted in the artist's unique aesthetic capabilities. These beliefs do not seem to have fundamentally changed or shifted with his move into Pop art. In other words, his commitments as a painter (to the transformative power of the artist's creative vision and the concomitant valorization of the work of art) were in some ways incompatible—or at least in profound tension—with the approach to the readymade image and the adoption of mechanical facture taken up in his Pop work.

If Lichtenstein's development of a Pop idiom necessitated the acceptance of a certain degree of contradiction within his practice, our analysis of the tension this produced in his work will not merely be a speculative diagnosis but will come through a close examination of the images he produced in this period. One of the difficulties of interpreting Lichtenstein's imagery is that its meaning is often considered to be as straightforward and uninflected as the seemingly unmodulated surfaces of his paintings. For that reason we will have to find new ways to think about the form of his work, and to reconsider his approach to his chosen subject matter. Further, treatments of his work often implicitly suggest—almost by default—that his selection of scenes from comic books and advertisements was almost random or arbitrary, above and beyond such generalized categories as images of romance, war, or consumer advertising. At best, when there is some strategy of selection posited for his work it is usually ascribed to questions of aesthetics, or to an image's potential for irony or parody. It is undeniable that these are components of Lichtenstein's approach to his subject matter, yet they do not tell the whole story. In fact, we will see how he selected scenes and images that foregrounded specific issues and concerns, particularly as related to problems of vision, technology, and artistic identity.

With my approach I reject that of traditional monographic treatments in two important ways. If I argue for a certain consistency in Lichtenstein's practice, we will see that any such consistency in the artist's work lies in its failure to resolve the tensions it attempts to work through. In short, Lichtenstein's art does not magically resolve contradictions; rather, it is structured by its ultimate inability to do so. In this way I reject the developmental account so often proffered in monographic treatments—that is, the linear narrative of the artist's work evolving over time, heroically solving problems along the way—for what I think is a more interesting model, and one far more adequate to the evidence presented in the work. For, as noted, Lichtenstein's approach to Pop seems less to have represented an evolution (which suggests an ineluctable movement forward) from a prior mode than to have operated in the tension between two modes of practice that were in large part incompatible. One could describe this tension as that between a more conventional, pictorializing modernist aesthetic and an emergent, object-oriented anti-aesthetic. Or as that accruing between two very different conceptions of the artistic act: on the one hand, a belief in the painter's mark as a fully expressive, humanist gesture; on the other, a sense of it as the product of a purely mechanical act. However, any attempt to analyze such structural tensions must also take into account that the artist's project was articulated within a particular set of historical conditions. I will return to those conditions—which relate to the status of mechanical reproduction, developments in consumer culture, and the uses of visual technologies—throughout the book.

Image Duplicator provides a fitting point to begin a close consideration of Lichtenstein's work because it brings together many of the concerns central to his project in the early 1960s. For one, his imagery consistently returns to issues of vision and visuality; for this reason it is hard to overlook the fact that the painting offers a scene of intense—and decidedly aggressive—looking. The figure's gaze is made all the more powerful by the symmetrical placement of the eyes, framed by the eyebrows above and the arcs of the red masklike element below. This formal intensification of the figure's eyes raises an issue to which I will repeatedly return: the relation between the artist's work and its so-called sources. In the critical literature it has become a commonplace to juxtapose Lichtenstein's paintings with the printed images from which they were derived; early on, hostile critics used this method to demonstrate the supposed lack of artistry in his work.[14] As the years progressed such juxtapositions were increasingly used to obtain the opposite effect, most often to demonstrate the artist's profound formal transformations of his sources.[15] My reading will rely on such comparisons, even though they must be approached cautiously, for we must be careful not to reduce the meaning of the artist's work to its relation to prior imagery. That being said, a careful comparison of Lichtenstein's images with their presumed sources is warranted in light of the nature of his project, which consistently foregrounds its reliance on the strategy of appropriation. Those sources are not simple keys that unlock the final meanings of his work. Nevertheless, they can be used to shed light on the development of finished works just as, in another artist's practice, an initial study or sketch can help illuminate the process by which a completed picture was produced. Lichtenstein pored through the pages of newspapers and comic books until he isolated an image—or even a fragment of an image—that provided him a suitable motif; this would be worked through a number of stages into a finished work. Meaning can be located in the sometimes subtle changes he made during this process.

Image Duplicator provides us the opportunity to track such changes, because a

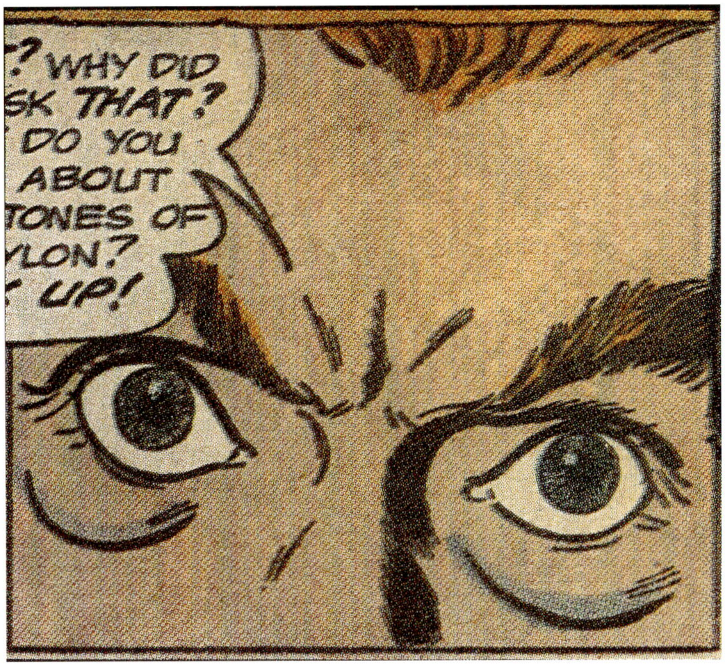

Figure 5. Unidentified comic book panel, source for *Image Duplicator,* from *Life* 56, no. 5 (January 31, 1964)

1964 *Life* magazine article that profiled the artist juxtaposed the painting with a portion of the panel on which it was presumably based (fig. 5).[16] Although it is only a fragment of the original panel—and the comic book from which it was taken is not identified—it demonstrates the significance of the changes that Lichtenstein effected in the process of appropriation. For one, he vertically lengthened the overall composition to relocate the word balloon directly above the figure's arched eyebrows. This emphasizes the visual force of the text, which contains the reference to an "image duplicator" that was entirely added by the artist.[17] While the face in the original panel seems to have been depicted slightly askew, Lichtenstein centered and balanced it, adding to the intensity of the figure's gaze. He further altered the image by adding the masklike form below the figure's eyes. If that mask adds visual emphasis to the figure's glaring eyes, it also references a set of concerns—relating to the interaction between the human body and machines—central to the artist's project at this time. Lichtenstein seems to have derived the mask from one worn by a character in the contemporaneous *X-Men* comic book (fig. 6).[18] The aggressiveness of the figure in Lichtenstein's painting is in keeping with the character's role in the comics as evil villain. This correspondence extends even further, for in the comics that character—Magneto—can control the forces of magnetism; his affinity with the mechanical is emphasized by his name, which is the term for a type of mechanism found in internal-combustion engines. This is not an incidental connection: Lichtenstein's work in this period would consis-

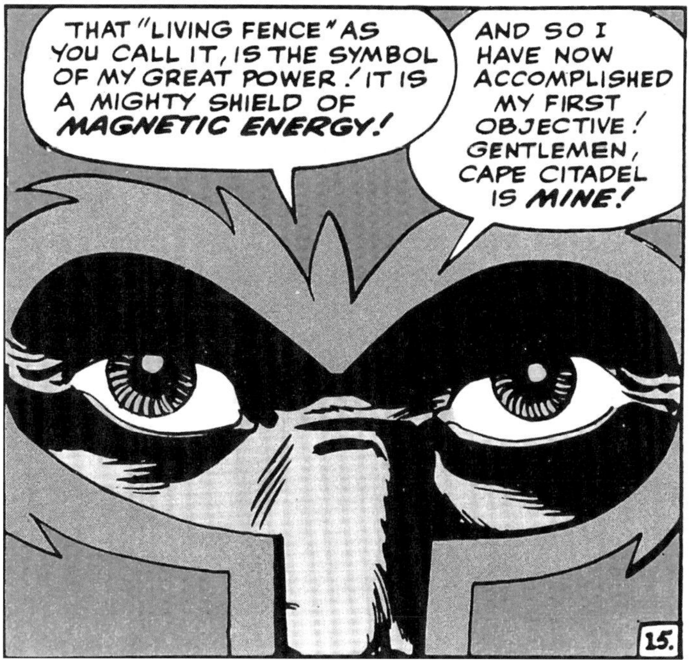

Figure 6.
Jack Kirby and Paul Reinman, panel from *X-Men* no. 1 (September 1963)

tently return to the interaction between bodies and machines, particularly in the context of historical developments in visual technologies.

The comic book villain is not the only referent for the figure depicted in *Image Duplicator*, for the work may also refer to the artist himself. Such an interpretation was offered as early 1968, when Albert Boime referred to the painting as Lichtenstein's "presumed 'self-portrait.'"[19] This reading is given further force in relation to the artist's earlier work: in a circa 1951 self-portrait Lichtenstein had depicted himself in knight's garb at a time when he was producing numerous scenes of helmeted knights. Viewed in this light, the mask in *Image Duplicator* recalls the type of helmet found on many suits of armor.[20] The painting's self-reflexiveness seems clear enough from the text, which aggressively challenges the viewer's understanding of Lichtenstein's project. Nevertheless, that text reveals a subtle inflection in the artist's approach to the process of image reproduction. With the telltale pronoun "my" functioning as a sign of ownership or possession ("WHAT DO YOU KNOW ABOUT MY **IMAGE DUPLICATOR**?"), the painting entertains the fantasy of a subject who *has*—rather than *is*—an image duplicator. As noted, the tension between those two possibilities underlies much of Lichtenstein's early Pop work. He was an artist committed to certain principles of originality and authenticity, yet he had developed a painterly practice that depended on the use of borrowed images as veritable readymade compositions for his paintings.[21]

Image Duplicator is also significant because Lichtenstein staged its production as

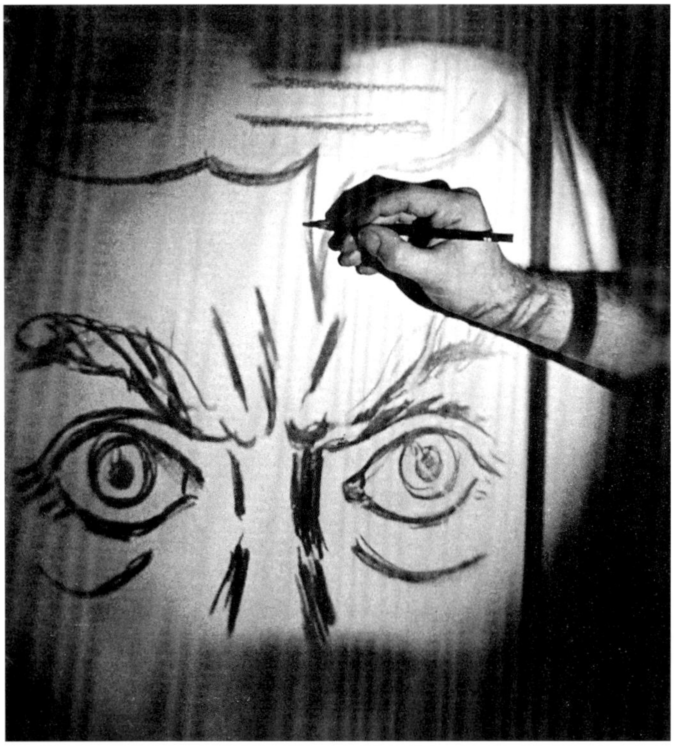

Figure 7.
John Loengard, photograph documenting the artist's working process, from *Life* 56, no. 5 (January 31, 1964)

a veritable performance for the *Life* magazine photographer. The resulting article not only contains reproductions of the painting and its comic book source but also includes two photographs of a hand (perhaps the artist's, perhaps that of an assistant) using a toothbrush to stencil a dot-screen onto the surface of a work. There is further documentation on a following page: the artist's hand, holding a pencil, is shown poised before a canvas as if tracing the projected image of his drawing (fig. 7). The accompanying text reads: "Starting with a scene from a science fiction comic book, Lichtenstein made a small sketch of the composition. Then he used a machine to project the sketch to the size he wanted and traced it onto his canvas."[22] Taken in the context of the *Life* article, the painting—like much of Lichtenstein's work from this period—represents a conflicted engagement between the artist's creative abilities and the work of the machine. Consider the complexity of the process: Lichtenstein begins with a comic book panel (that is, a mechanically reproduced image); makes a small sketch of that motif by his own hand; magnifies that handmade sketch using a machine (in this case an opaque projector); and finally traces that projected image, again by his own hand, onto the canvas. It is as if there is a tug-of-war here, a repeated back and forth between the artist's body and the machine. It is fitting, then, that the painting makes reference to the problem of reproducing images in a decidedly ambiguous way. For inasmuch as the "image duplicator" is not depicted in the work—it appears only as a textual reference—we are ultimately left unsure of the nature of such a device, and what its relation to the figure might be.

Image Duplicator was a public statement by the artist. Produced by Lichtenstein to demonstrate his working process, it angrily confronts the viewer's understanding of his art. In the end, the *Life* article offered a mixed message about his work. The textual description of the artist's working method, and the full-page photograph of his hand poised before the projected image of his own drawing, provided clear evidence that Lichtenstein was not merely tracing a mechanically enlarged comic book panel. However, it is not difficult to imagine that this subtle distinction might have been lost on many readers. The article's title—"Is He the Worst Artist in the U.S.?"—was an even unkinder cut (fig. 8). It is not that the claim for ranking him the worst artist (a suggestion first made by Brian O'Doherty in a 1963 *New York Times* article) is so severe; after all, it has long been a badge of honor for artists claiming avant-garde status to be judged harshly by critics and the public.[23] The question is no doubt posed ironically. At the same time, however, it makes Lichtenstein into little more than the debased repetition of an earlier artist, for it repeats the title of the better-known *Life* article that had asked: "Jackson Pollock: Is He the Greatest Living Painter in the United States?"[24]

Lichtenstein would not have known the eventual title of the *Life* article when he produced *Image Duplicator*, yet the painting's tone is not altogether surprising considering the criticism that his work received in the years following the emergence of Pop. Because his imagery is derived from the comics it is often viewed as merely lighthearted and amusing, in contrast to the more explicit—and photographically presented—violence of such contemporaneous Pop works as Andy Warhol's *Disaster* paintings. Take Dorothy Seiberling's reading of *Image Duplicator* in the *Life* article: "The finished picture shows how Lichtenstein altered the cartoon by centering the face and balloon, adding a red helmet and turning the comic strip's question into a joke about his own art."[25] Seiberling can describe the painting as humorous only by overlooking its decidedly aggressive tone. Even if Lichtenstein's work may at times appear as a mere joke, there are unrealized and even unsettling aspects of the artist's practice that merit close attention. To understand Lichtenstein's project, then, we have to take his jokes seriously. Rather than view his work as merely another instance of deadpan appropriation, we have to consider it as a complex and conflicted engagement with a particular type of subject matter and a pictorial vocabulary embedded in modes of mechanical reproduction. In short, Lichtenstein's paintings must be read in a thorough, consistent manner; in order to do so we may take a cue from art historian Michael Fried, who has offered the following observations on the work of Gustave Courbet:

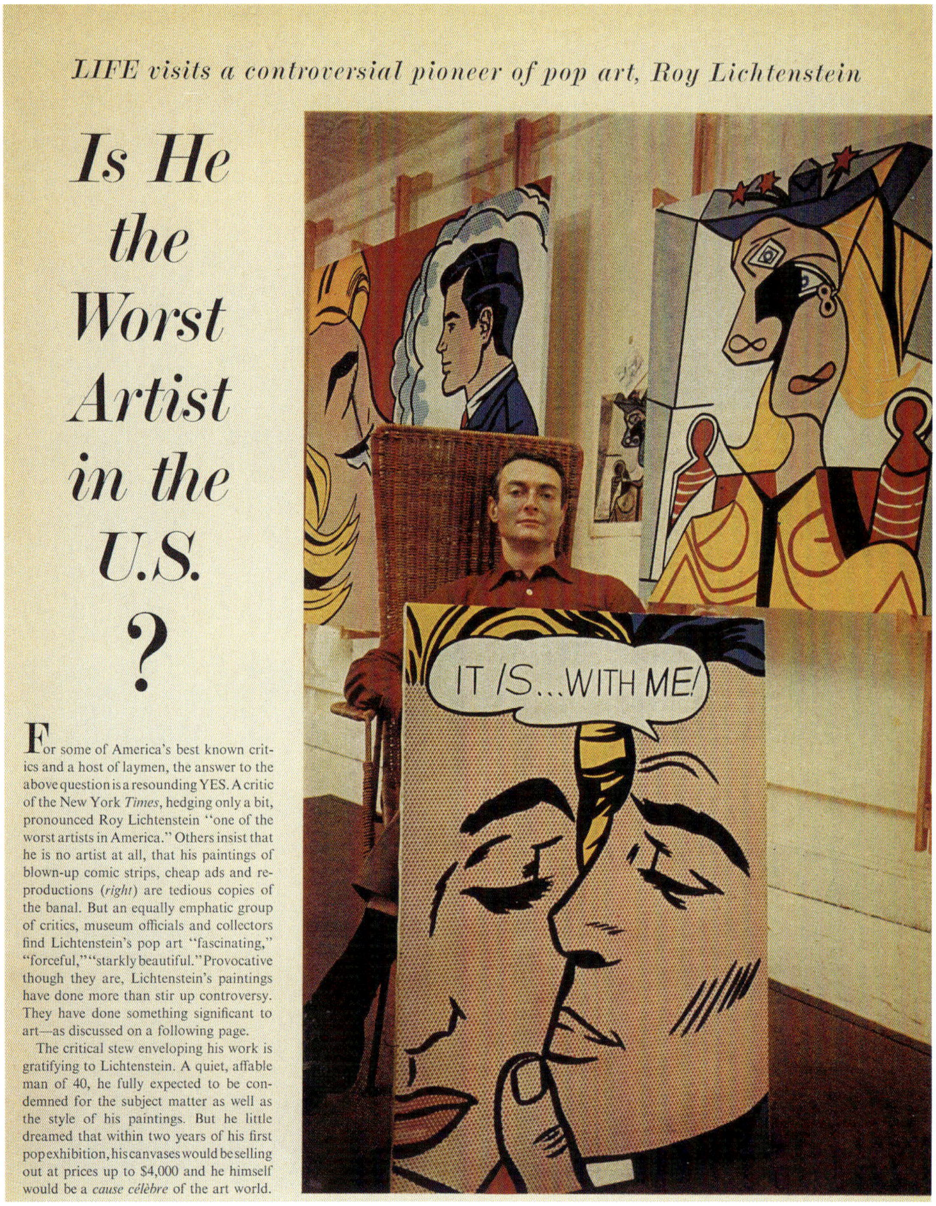

LIFE visits a controversial pioneer of pop art, Roy Lichtenstein

Is He the Worst Artist in the U.S. ?

For some of America's best known critics and a host of laymen, the answer to the above question is a resounding YES. A critic of the New York *Times*, hedging only a bit, pronounced Roy Lichtenstein "one of the worst artists in America." Others insist that he is no artist at all, that his paintings of blown-up comic strips, cheap ads and reproductions (*right*) are tedious copies of the banal. But an equally emphatic group of critics, museum officials and collectors find Lichtenstein's pop art "fascinating," "forceful," "starkly beautiful." Provocative though they are, Lichtenstein's paintings have done more than stir up controversy. They have done something significant to art—as discussed on a following page.

The critical stew enveloping his work is gratifying to Lichtenstein. A quiet, affable man of 40, he fully expected to be condemned for the subject matter as well as the style of his paintings. But he little dreamed that within two years of his first pop exhibition, his canvases would be selling out at prices up to $4,000 and he himself would be a *cause célèbre* of the art world.

Figure 8.
First page of "Is He the Worst Artist in the U.S.?" from *Life* 56, no. 5 (January 31, 1964)

I think it is fair to say that art history as a discipline has tended to view realist paintings of any period as if they were nothing more than accurate transcriptions of a reality outside themselves, or at any rate as if their "reality effect" (Roland Barthes's *effet de réel*) were simply a function of the painter's skill in representing more or less exactly what lay or loomed before his eyes. Practically speaking, this has meant that commentaries on Courbet's art, as on that of other realist painters . . . , have often focused on questions of subject matter, either narrowly or broadly construed. And it has also meant that discussion has tended to proceed on the unexamined assumption that a realist painting's representation of a given scene was to all intents and purposes determined by the "actual" scene itself, with the result that the features of the representation that ought to have been perceived as curious or problematic, as calling for reflection or analysis, have either been made invisible (the usual outcome) or, if registered at all, have been attributed to reality rather than art.[26]

What use can we make of Fried's observations? For one, Pop art is a realist mode (in fact, the Pop artists were initially identified as New Realists).[27] And Lichtenstein's work has been particularly open to charges that it is a mere transcription of a preexisting reality because its formal qualities emphasize its proximity to a presumed original (namely the printed imagery that it imitates). In fact, in his role as a critic Fried was antagonistic to Lichtenstein's project early on; in a 1963 review he deemed the artist's work "trivial" and "irrelevant," comparing it unfavorably with the work of none other than Courbet.[28] However, I want to treat Fried's comments in much the same way Lichtenstein treated printed images: I will appropriate and strategically reuse them for my own purposes. They have a great deal of relevance for—and may offer profound insight into—the project at hand. In the chapters that follow we will scrutinize precisely those "curious or problematic" elements in Lichtenstein's imagery that have been largely overlooked, and analyze their meaning in relation to a set of concerns—with the effects of mechanical reproduction, the relation between vision and technology, and the possibility of articulating artistic identity and agency—that appear consistently throughout his work.

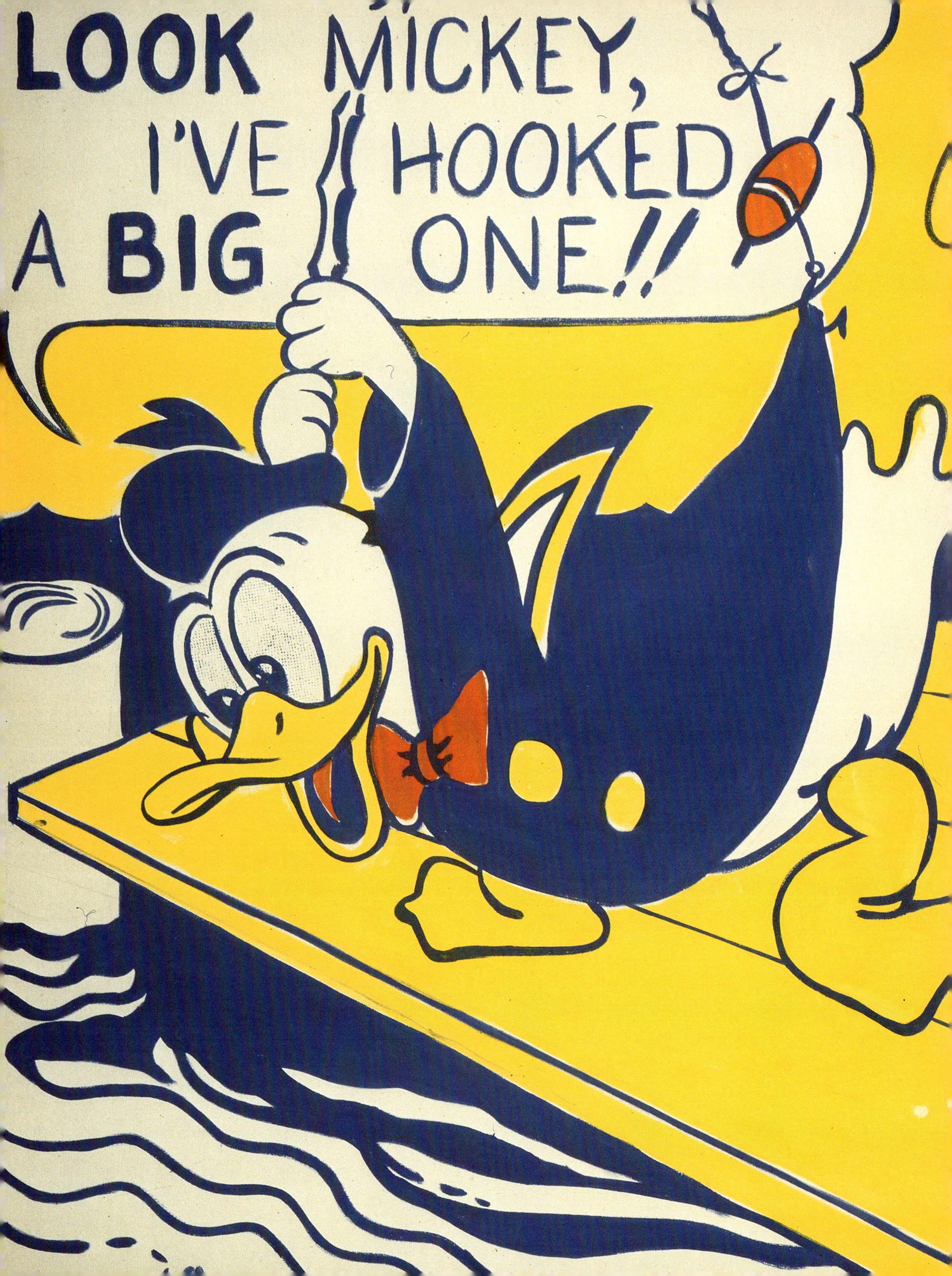
LOOK MICKEY, I'VE HOOKED A BIG ONE!!

1 The Emergence of Pop Art

To more fully understand Lichtenstein's practice we must attend to the critical apparatus that has developed over the years to describe his work. Critics have often returned to a common set of themes to frame the artist's project, as evidenced in this 1989 account by Carter Ratcliff:

> Andy Warhol's esthetic required him to be ubiquitous. Lichtenstein's makes the opposite demand. Warhol invented his esthetic at ground level, where the image-traffic is always jammed. The meanings of his art appear at tense intervals, through gaps in the culture's shifting surfaces. To get Lichtenstein's point, one must look upward to a distant zone where the artist, in serene and solitary control, keeps the traffic patterns in order. Imagery migrates through his oeuvre in patterns calm and arbitrary enough to fade from recollection even as they're tracked, yet details reach ground level in crystal-sharp focus. No clouds, no static, no disturbing signals from Lichtenstein's persona disrupt the transmission.[1]

It is not surprising, even in the midst of a sustained analysis of Lichtenstein's work, that the critic turns to Warhol as a point of comparison. As Pop art emerged in the United States in the early 1960s, Warhol and Lichtenstein came to be linked as inseparable yet distinct focal points around which the meanings of the movement could be articulated. In order to analyze Lichtenstein's practice, then, we must confront the ways that the relationship between the artists has been defined. This will not only lay the groundwork for an examination of Lichtenstein's imagery but will also provide insight into the wider significance of Pop art.

We must also attend to the point made in the final sentence of the above passage: "No clouds, no static, no disturbing signals from Lichtenstein's persona disrupt the transmission." This reading, which presents the vision of a completely untroubled artistic oeuvre, is undoubtedly based on the seemingly impersonal form of Lichtenstein's paintings. Yet even in the 1960s the artist made clear that he would never claim a complete absence from his work: "Personally, I feel that in my own work I wanted to look programmed or impersonal but I don't really believe I am being impersonal when I do it. . . . My work looks as if it is thought out beforehand to such a degree that I don't do anything but put the color on. But these are appearances and they are not what I really feel about it. I don't think you can do a work of art and not really be involved in it."[2] In spite of such statements by the artist, claims like that made by Ratcliff above have had great currency among the critics. Why is there a need to see nothing of the artist in his work, and to see that work itself as the outcome of a project unmarred by "disturbance" or "disruption"? Perhaps we could ascribe this assertion to the inevitable codification of an artist's reputation in the later years of his career, especially one who, like Lichtenstein, came to be read as the consummate detached formalist. I would argue, however, that there is something else at work here, additional factors that have motivated this rather circumscribed view of the artist's project. To begin countering this approach to Lichtenstein's work we will examine the image identified as his first Pop painting. As we will see, a close analysis will place its presumably unproblematic meaning—as well as its status as the putative origin point for Lichtenstein's Pop art—utterly in question.

WARHOL'S EXPOSURE, LICHTENSTEIN'S COMPOSURE

> When Ivan [Karp] brought Leo Castelli up to my studio, the place was a mess, with the big canvases strewn around the living room—painting was a lot messier than drawing. Leo looked my stuff over, the Dick Tracys and the Nose Jobs in particular, and then said, "Well, it's unfortunate, the timing, because I just took on Roy Lichtenstein, and the two of you in the same gallery would collide." Ivan had warned me that Leo was going to tell me, "The two of you in the same gallery . . ." so I can't say I wasn't prepared, but still I was really disappointed.[3]

In this passage from his 1980 book *POPism: The Warhol Sixties,* Andy Warhol describes something of an originary moment in the development of Pop art in the United States, a meeting of almost mythic dimensions. Ivan Karp, assistant director of the Castelli Gallery, had brought the dealer to Warhol's studio to inspect the artist's paintings of imagery culled from advertisements and comic strips. By this time Warhol already knew of Lichtenstein's work, having seen it on at least one occasion during a visit to the Castelli Gallery. Yet his account suggests that, in spite of the similarity of their work, he still held out some hope for an offer of gallery representation. That hope was not to be fulfilled: Lichtenstein had effectively beaten him to the punch. In 1961, at the very moment Pop was emerging as a movement on the New York art scene (encouraged by dealers like Castelli), Warhol was preempted by Lichtenstein.

Latter-day viewers might be surprised to learn that at an early stage Lichtenstein had trumped Warhol, since at some point in the years that followed the tables seem to have turned. Certainly both artists achieved a degree of fame they never would have thought possible in 1961, and each has been celebrated in an extensive monographic literature and in countless gallery and museum exhibitions. Nevertheless, over time Warhol emerged as the emblematic Pop artist for the public at large, particularly because of his highly visible public persona. Consider, for example, the opening lines of Lichtenstein's 1997 obituary in *Time* magazine, written by the critic Robert Hughes: "Roy Lichtenstein, who died at 73 last week of complications arising from pneumonia, was not quite the most famous of the American Pop artists. That honor belonged to Andy Warhol, who made it somewhat dubious."[4] Although Hughes' estimation of Lichtenstein's secondary status is not intended as a slight—his criticism of Warhol lies precisely in the artist's interest in the trappings of fame—it is telling that he chooses to highlight it in the first line of his piece. His assessment was not entirely off the mark. For one, Warhol's reach had always extended more broadly than that of the other Pop artists, whether in his involvement with the Factory scene in the 1960s, his repeated forays into filmmaking, or his publishing of *Interview* magazine. He also consistently publicized his career and persona in texts like *The Philosophy of Andy Warhol* and *POPism: The Warhol Sixties*. After his death in 1987 the attention paid to his life and work only increased, with numerous museum exhibitions, the spectacular auction of the Warhol estate, and the opening of the Andy Warhol Museum in the artist's hometown of Pittsburgh.

It is not merely that Warhol achieved the highest degree of recognition as a Pop artist to the public at large, for the years after his death also saw a veritable explosion of art historical and critical writing on his work. In addition to the biographical treatments by Warhol's friends and associates and the publication of the Warhol diaries, numerous academic treatments of the artist and his project appeared.[5] This extensive literature has provided profound insight into the critical, theoretical, and historical significance of the artist's work. Yet, when taken alongside Warhol's standing in many quarters as the emblematic Pop artist, it has had a significant impact on our understanding of Pop. Just as the term Pop art cannot be understood within the limited context of its American adherents in the early 1960s (for it must also be extended to the experiments of the Independent Group in Britain, to cite just one example), it is equally misleading to consider Warhol's project as somehow representative of the diverse approaches at work in the movement. Lichtenstein's practice, for one, exemplifies an approach to Pop imagery that is incommensurable with—if not antagonistic to—that adopted by his colleague. Which begs the question: if Warhol has, to a large extent, come to stand as the epitome of the Pop artist, what critical purpose might that serve? What kind of meanings (critical, historical, political) are secured by framing him as the most representative Pop artist, particularly when we contrast him with an artist—like Lichtenstein—whose work may approach the imagery of mass culture in a very different way?

Lichtenstein himself must have considered his relation to Warhol, particularly in regard to his colleague's higher degree of public visibility. We can find evidence for this in an unlikely place. In 1965, Lichtenstein and his future wife, Dorothy Herzka, attended a Halloween party at the home of their friends Idelle and Julian Weber. Years later the artist recounted the details of his masquerade that night:

> My wife, Dorothy, and I went to a Halloween costume party . . . dressed as Andy Warhol and Edie [Sedgwick]. Andy looked somewhat different then—leather jacket, blue jeans, funny sunglasses, and funny shoes that were all broken up . . . silver paint on them. Easy to imitate. I sprayed my hair with silver paint and I powdered my face to look very pale. When people said anything to me at the party, I said "Oh, wow!" or "How glamorous!" Even though Andy can be unusually articulate, I reduced his repertoire to those two expressions. . . . Andy does exactly what I don't do. *He* was his art. His studio was his art. Edie was part of his art, and a lot of other people. I was an old-fashioned artist compared with him. When I looked at Andy, I looked at him as a tourist would, I guess . . . with wonderment. How glamorous. How strange.[6]

Photographic documentation of the Webers' party survives: a contact sheet of grainy black-and-white photographs (the negatives have since been lost) depicts Lichtenstein and Herzka dressed as Warhol and his Factory superstar Edie Sedgwick (fig. 9).[7] In one shot (not shown) the couple is dancing; in others they are chatting, or leaning against a wall with various art works—including a Warhol *Flowers* painting—behind them. Although it would be easy to dismiss this as a mere lark, a fun Halloween joke, there is something terribly compelling about Lichtenstein's masquerade, in large part because his performance is so convincing. It's not that he's merely replicated the details of Warhol's costume—the sprayed silver hair, the sunglasses, the black leather jacket—but that he's also working to imitate the finer points of his colleague's studied pose: the expressionless face; the arm akimbo with thumb hooked into pocket or belt loop; even the cocked head with chin thrust forward, an uncanny evocation of Warhol's 1964 self-portrait (fig. 10).

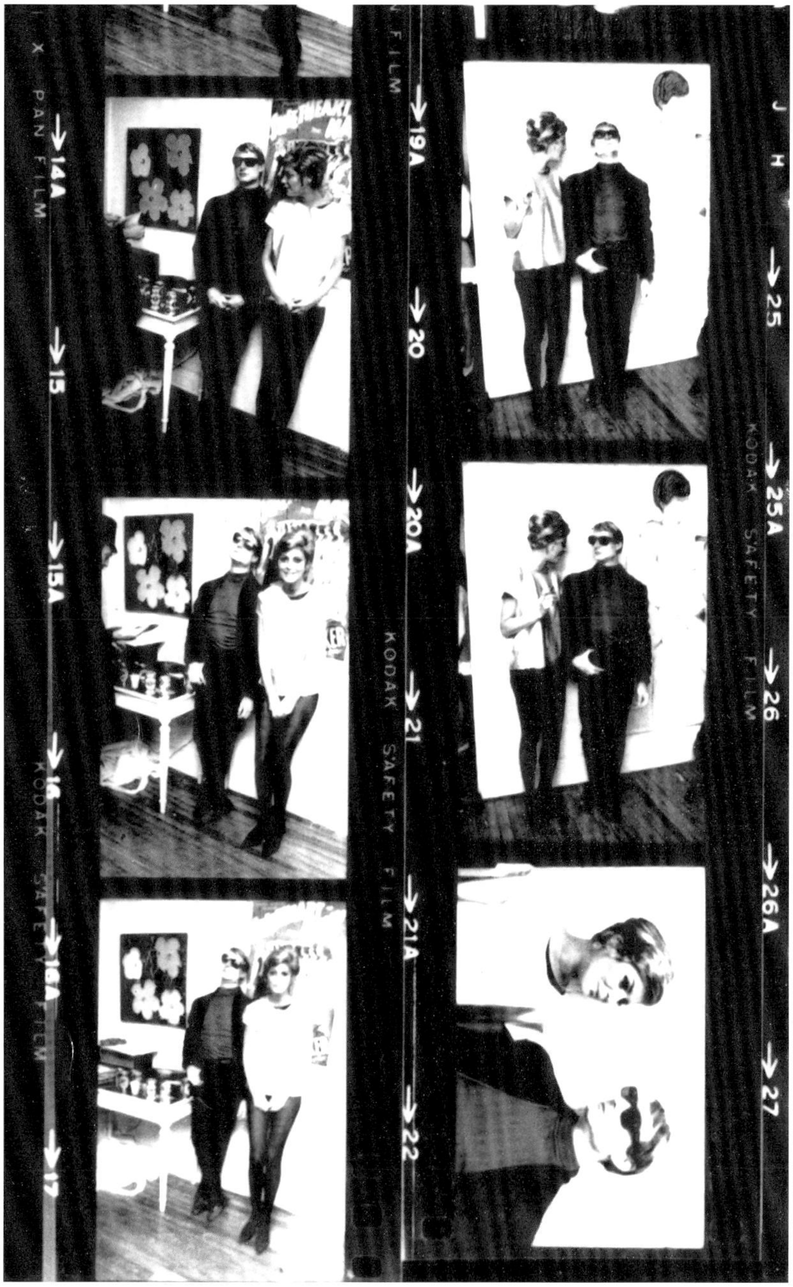

Figure 9.
Roy Lichtenstein and Dorothy Herzka dressed for Halloween as Andy Warhol and Edie Sedgwick, October, 1965

Lichtenstein's verbal account is equally telling, in his recognition of the distance between Warhol's project and his own. For Warhol, there is no operative distinction between the artist's studio practice and his construction of a public persona, one that mimics and even ironizes the concept of celebrity. By 1965, Lichtenstein had recognized the significance of this aspect of Warhol's project and would pro-

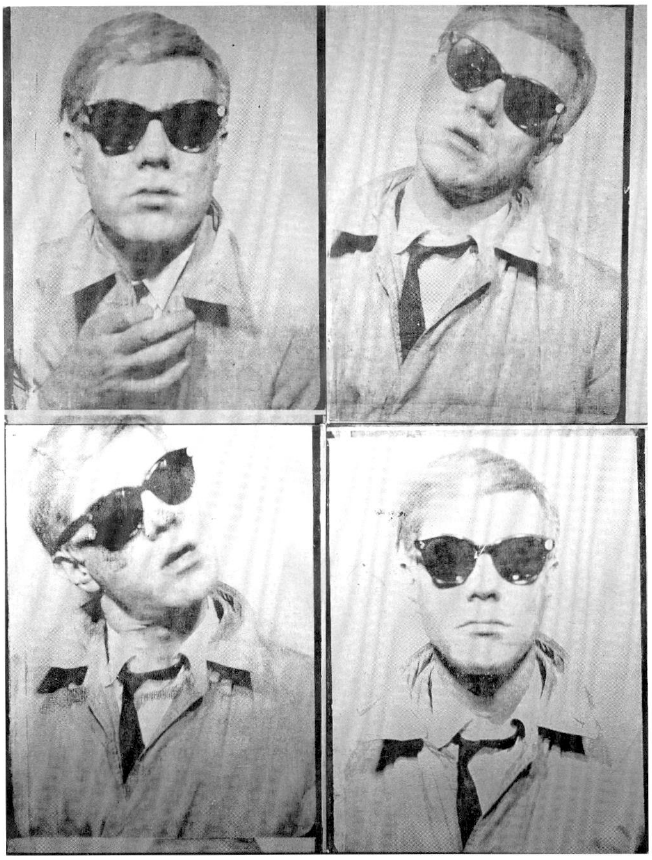

Figure 10.
Andy Warhol,
Self-Portrait, 1964.
Synthetic polymer paint and silkscreen ink on canvas, four panels, each 20 × 16 in. (50.8 × 40.6 cm).
Private collection

fess to feeling like an "old-fashioned artist" in relation to it, perhaps because he knew he lacked such a carefully constructed public face (one cannot imagine Warhol going to a Halloween party dressed as Roy Lichtenstein).[8]

Warhol was willing to make studio practice a public spectacle, thus connecting it with the world of entertainment and celebrity. This is something that Lichtenstein would not do; for him, elements of mass culture were brought into the studio to be transformed into fine art. I would propose, then, that the difference between the two artists can be summed up in one term: capitulation. That word is useful in describing the sense that Pop might represent the artist's utter subsumption in the spectacular excesses of a media culture. Despite the wide variety of critical approaches to Warhol's work, most critics would agree that on some level his practice is characterized by just such a capitulation, whether it is viewed as the means to a deconstructive critique or as a sign of the artist's uncritical immersion in the rituals of mass culture.[9] The term is also useful because it describes a quality that no longer seems to be ascribed to either Lichtenstein or his work. While the earliest hostile critical responses to his Pop art—and there certainly was no dearth of these at the time—charged him with a slavish, uncritical appropriation of imagery from newspaper advertisements and comic strips, that evaluation does not seem to have stuck for very long. What emerged instead, after the shock of Lichtenstein's apparently banal subject matter wore off, was a sense of the artist as a consummate aesthete who could recast any appropriated image according to his impeccable sense of form. Take, for instance, Robert Hughes' assessment on the occasion of the artist's 1993 Guggenheim Museum retrospective:

> Time has done its annoying work, converting Lichtenstein into a historical figure remarkable for his taste, his dependable virtuosity and his pictorial manners. He has become the great academician of the Pop movement. . . . You can't imagine people asking themselves with bated breath, "What will Lichtenstein do next?" You know the answer, although the exact image he will do it to is as yet unknown. It will be done very well, probably on a huge canvas, with perfect decorum and an unfaltering sense of design, every black line in its right place, not a slippage in the stripes and Benday dots.[10]

Even though Hughes describes as "annoying" the process by which an artist's reputation congeals over time, his account accomplishes much the same thing: his repeated references to the artist's presumed "taste," "dependable virtuosity," and "perfect decorum" only serve to reiterate the received view of the untroubled nature of Lichtenstein's practice.

The seeds for this view seem to have been planted rather early. In fact, they were already evident in an early film that provides us further insight into the ways that Lichtenstein and Warhol were cast, respectively, as the good boy and bad boy of Pop art. Entitled *Andy Warhol and Roy Lichtenstein,* this 1966 television documentary treats the subject of Pop art through interviews with the two artists and through documentation of their lives and working practices.[11] Despite the shared subject matter of their work, the distinctions between the two are immediately apparent. After a series of opening titles superimposed over shots of urban billboards, the film presents us with a clean-cut, youthful-looking Lichtenstein in his studio. Throughout the first half of the film he articulately presents his views on the chosen subject matter of his work, issues of form, and the problem of industrialized culture. He appears amid the conventional trappings of the artist's studio: at one point an assistant is shown working in the background; at another the camera pans over shelves of paints and materials. The artist's sketches are shown juxtaposed with their printed sources. We are given no indication of the presence of an interviewer, and Lichtenstein is allowed to talk at length about his work. This is in marked contrast to the second portion of the film, in which Warhol (in typical fashion) turns the interview on its head, deftly exposing the conventions of the form. During the Warhol scenes the first voice we hear is that of the off-camera (and unidentified) interviewer. He is not only heard but eventually seen, in large part because of Warhol's growing refusal to abide by the conventions of the situation. The artist short-circuits his role as passive interviewee; at certain moments he provides incomplete or partial answers, at others he professes to not understand the interviewer's questions. He goes on to suggest, finally, that Alan Solomon (the unnamed interviewer) provide him with questions *and* answers: "Oh, you should just tell me the words and I could just repeat them. . . . Why don't you just tell me the words and they'll just come out of my mouth."[12] The interview devolves even further, with Warhol repeating verbatim the questions posed to him.

If Warhol's deconstruction of the interview is in stark contrast to Lichtenstein's obedient, articulate responses, a similar distinction arises between the studio spaces in which they are filmed. Lichtenstein had been shown surrounded by the traditional trappings of the artist's studio, while Warhol's milieu is entirely different. Warhol, who is interviewed at the Factory, does not work at paintings on easels; rather, he and his unnamed assistant (Gerard Malanga) are shown pulling a squeegee across a silkscreen, thereby transferring a photographic image to a length of canvas laid out on the floor. The fact that this is not an ordinary studio is also indicated by the cast of hangers-on, including Edie Sedgwick, who talks about the artist in voice-over. The film gives us shots of Warhol with a film projector (registering his interest in, and move into, filmmaking), the artist and his assistant inflating one of his silver Mylar *Cloud* sculptures with helium, and a practice session of the band the Velvet Underground. If all of these elements were not enough to index Warhol's general resistance to the traditional terms of artistic studio practice (in contrast to Lichtenstein's demonstrated commitment to painting), it is made explicit in the artist's own statement: "I don't believe in painting because I hate objects and uhh . . . I hate to go to museums and see pictures on the wall because they look so important and they don't really mean anything."[13] The film articulates a clear distinction between the two artists; not only do they correspond roughly to aesthetic and anti-aesthetic positions, but on a more popular level Warhol in his leather jacket and sunglasses is the delinquent to Lichtenstein's wholesome achiever. It is almost as if the scenes with Warhol and the denizens of his Factory are a direct fulfillment of Max Kozloff's early response to the appearance of Pop art: "The truth is, the art galleries are being invaded by the pin-headed and contemptible style of gum chewers, bobby soxers, and worse, delinquents."[14] Lichtenstein is the one who—despite his engagement with similar subject matter—recuperates the traditional role of the artist in the face of the spectacular culture that seems to have produced Warhol's unapologetic delinquency.

The film, then, explicitly plays one artist against the other. Warhol is presented as subsumed by the spectacle, repetition, and excess of media culture, while Lichtenstein is offered as resisting or refusing such a condition. But what does this accomplish? Lichtenstein may very well provide the critics—and us—the example of an artist whose work might seem to bear no trace of desire for the banal, mechanically reproduced imagery that he insistently reconstituted in his artistic practice. This is a compelling possibility, for it would allow us to imagine an artist who, at the very moment his work became utterly immersed in the languages of advertising and mass entertainment, refused to be seduced by their powerful lure. This would be an artist, in fact, very much like the Roy Lichtenstein the critics have fashioned over time. But if this view of the artist as maintaining an utterly controlled distance from his chosen subject matter has set in so completely over the years, how might we begin to deconstruct or interrogate it? In large part, Lichtenstein's imagined refusal to capitulate to the effects of mass culture has been based on his seeming distance—and Warhol's contrasting proximity—to the machine. It would not seem that we could imagine an artist who seems to capitulate more completely to the mechanical than Andy Warhol. He was, of course, the one who offered that now-famous pronouncement "I want to be a machine."[15] Yet if we examine the evidence and compare Warhol's approach with that of Lichtenstein, a literal reading of that statement is no longer quite so simple. For a case can be made that Warhol's practice provided him a measure of distance from the work of mechanical reproduction.

Soon after Pop emerged as a movement in the United States (shaped as much, if not more, by critics and art dealers than by the artists themselves), hostile critics attacked the Pop artists for imitating techniques of mechanical reproduction and jettisoning the emphasis on the artist's touch that had played such a central role in the rhetoric of Abstract Expressionism. The work of artists like Warhol and Lichtenstein seemed to bear no trace of the artist's hand, providing instead the look of machine-produced artifacts. Yet I would suggest that Warhol frequently used techniques that distanced his body from machine-like labor. Even as a commercial illustrator in the 1950s, before his entry into the field of fine art, Warhol developed a technique in which he hinged together two sheets of paper in order to transfer the blotted impression of an ink drawing from one sheet to the other: this was a primitive mechanism—but a mechanism nonetheless—for image reproduction. When he finally turned to painting, in about 1960, he consistently used such simple mechanisms to perform the repetitive act of image duplication for him. For example, while he could have attempted (like other Pop artists, such as Lichtenstein and James Rosenquist) to manually copy and enlarge source imagery, he chose instead to use an opaque projector to project an image and trace it onto a canvas.[16] Warhol's use of such devices only multiplied at this point: he used various stamps and stencils to produce works like the *Campbell's Soup Can* paintings, and in 1962 he developed his signature silkscreen technique. With that process he was able to have a photograph made into a silkscreen, which was then used to transfer the image to canvas.

These techniques certainly required a degree of repetitive labor; to produce his paintings of repeated images Warhol had to lay down a stencil or silkscreen, apply pigment through it, and then repeat the process to create a serial arrangement on the canvas. Yet for the most part he stopped short of manually copying images, which requires that the artist corporeally mimic the rote, mechanical act of image duplication. It was Lichtenstein who became well versed in this activity, while Warhol developed techniques that could be (and many times were) delegated to others. This included not only the fabrication of his silkscreens—which he sent out for manufacture by commercial printers—but also their use in the production of paintings, a task that could be performed by assistants at the Factory. It is in this way that Caroline Jones has categorized the administrative or managerial sensibility of Warhol's stance in the 1960s.[17] One could argue, then, that Warhol could make the statement "I want to be a machine" precisely because his administrative role already provided him a measure of ironic distance from the rote, bodily reenactment of machine-like copying.

Now contrast Warhol's simple machines for reproduction (stamps, stencils, silkscreens) with Roy Lichtenstein's practice of image duplication. It is often thought that from the very beginning Lichtenstein used an opaque projector (or similar type of mechanical device) to transfer his source images onto canvas, yet he did not initiate that practice until two years or so after he had begun painting in the Pop mode. In the early years of Pop, then, Lichtenstein was tackling the problem of magnifying and transferring a two-dimensional image onto canvas by hand. Even when he finally began to use an opaque projector in his work, in about 1963, he always took pains to emphasize that he projected not the appropriated image itself but his own small drawing after the source. In other words, he wanted his interlocutors to understand that his source imagery would always be recircuited through the manual activity of drawing, and thus through his own body. When asked in 1967 by critic John Coplans "How do you do your paintings?" Lichtenstein responded:

> I just *do* them. I do them as directly as possible. If I am working from a cartoon, photograph or whatever, I draw a small picture—the size that will fit into my opaque projector—and project it onto the canvas. I don't draw a picture in order to reproduce it—I do it in order to recompose it. Nor am I trying to change it as much as possible. I try to make the minimum amount of change.

> Although sometimes I work from two or three different original cartoons and combine them, I go all the way from having my drawing almost like the original to making it up altogether.[18]

This statement provides a concise description of Lichtenstein's working process. At the same time it offers the grammatical convolutions of that central sentence ("Nor am I trying to change it as much as possible"), which contains a strange kind of doubled denial that gets to the heart of Lichtenstein's project. The artist locates his work at an unknowable point between two opposing possibilities: that of changing the image *as much as possible* (which would require the act of artistic invention or creation) and *as little as possible* (which would constitute the rote, mechanical process of copying). Certainly Lichtenstein never copied an image wholesale, and occasionally he even combined motifs from several sources to arrive at a final composition. Moreover, he soon began to use stencils to produce the regularized screens of dots that would become his trademark. Nevertheless, the above account of his practice points to the ambiguous status of manual copying in his work, an activity from which Warhol seemed more able to distance himself.

This point allows us to see Warhol's practice at a remove from that of other Pop artists like Lichtenstein, or for that matter James Rosenquist, whose work also required him to copy and enlarge printed imagery. Rosenquist's training as a billboard painter had provided him abundant experience with taking a tiny image and enlarging it to enormous scale; preliminary collages for his early Pop paintings reveal the regularized grids he inscribed onto his printed sources to help him scale them up to size for his large canvases.[19] This manual labor—which itself reiterates the machine-like process of image reproduction—again provides a contrast to Warhol's quasi-managerial deployment of stencils, silkscreens, and the like.[20]

As we've seen, the critical literature has often emphasized Lichtenstein's distance from his chosen subject matter, as if he had somehow resisted the mechanical processes that seem to have subsumed his colleague Warhol. Yet a close reading of the critics' accounts demonstrates that they often register—albeit obliquely—a sense of Lichtenstein's capitulation to the machine. Here is Calvin Tomkins, in a 1987 profile of the artist: "Although Roy Lichtenstein's work is not even remotely autobiographical, the same combination of authority and ironic distance that characterizes the work also applies to his personal life. People who feel they are close friends of his often say that they do not know him very well. Lichtenstein himself sometimes says he has no real life outside the studio."[21] Tomkins' account provides a version of the artist, much like we have seen above, as one who maintains a relation of authority to and utter distance from his work, although now that quality is—somewhat strangely—extended to his personal life as well. A similar assessment appears in a 1993 *Vanity Fair* profile, which quotes an unnamed Italian art dealer on Lichtenstein: "Everything is a bit like his painting—extremely well-organized and thought-out and intellectual. And no passion. I don't know if there *is* a passion, but it's not to be seen. He seems to me like someone untouched and untouchable."[22] Citing Lichtenstein's "strict discipline," the writer of the piece comments that "at this late date there's little likelihood that he will depart from an obsessive routine of hard work and repetitive recreation," and then quotes the artist himself: "'I do work every day, pretty much, and all day, essentially,' says Lichtenstein, who went to his studio even on the day after his mother's death."[23] Is this last anecdotal observation—that the artist continued to work in the face of his mother's death—intended to describe a kind of personal coldness and detachment, or an utter allegiance to a predetermined, repetitive schedule obeyed like clockwork? (Or perhaps both, since these two options are not mutually exclusive.) The issue of Lichtenstein's "humanity" is raised yet again—and in similar terms—in Peter Schjeldahl's *Village Voice* obituary for the artist: "Lichtenstein was so little screwed up, so efficiently an art-making critter, that he could seem barely human. He apparently had a deal with perfection, which served him faithfully on the condition that he take neither it nor himself too seriously."[24]

We could simply ascribe Schjeldahl's assessment of Lichtenstein's "perfection" to an understandable tendency toward hyperbole in the wake of the artist's death. But if taken in the larger context of the existing critical discourse outlined here, quite another picture emerges. In the course of a seeming celebration of the artist, for which the critics construct a picture of Lichtenstein as the disciplined, hard-working creator, they return time and again to a particular descriptive language: that of the machine. We need only consider the language used in the above accounts—the talk of "efficiency," of "distance," of the "repetitive," and of "perfection"—and look back to the description by Carter Ratcliff with which I began this chapter: "No clouds, no static, no disturbing signals from Lichtenstein's persona disrupt the transmission."[25] At the very moment in which the critics aim to distance Lichtenstein from the industrial facture of his work by describing him as a cool, detached formalist, they come closest to describing him as a machine. They return—unintentionally, I believe—to a central problematic around which his work circulates but which has been symptomatically overlooked in their accounts: the machine as a threat to creative or aesthetic practice.

The critical articulation of Lichtenstein and Warhol as representing divergent possibilities for the figure of the Pop artist is also inflected by the issue of gender. Cécile Whiting has discussed the gendering of various critical discourses around Pop in the 1960s, highlighting the "central role played by the overwhelming number of objects in Pop art associated with what was ostensibly the sphere of women—household fixtures, consumer goods, and fashion."[26] Whiting's text constitutes a significant point of entry into a topic that requires more analysis. For example, no recent critic or historian seems to have made much of the fact that the name of the movement itself is gendered: in the United States "Pop" is, of course, a colloquial term for the father.[27] If latter-day critical accounts seem to have overlooked the gendered significance of that term, it was not lost on certain participants in the movement in the 1960s. For instance, Andy Warhol had this to say when critic Gene Swenson asked him (in a 1963 interview) "Is 'Pop' a bad name?": "The name sounds so awful. Dada must have something to do with Pop—it's so funny, the names are really synonyms. Does anyone know what they're supposed to mean or have to do with, those names?"[28] The import of that name must also have registered with Joan Kron and Audrey Sabol of the Philadelphia Arts Council, who played off of it in the title of their 1967 benefit exhibition, the "Museum of Merchandise." That show, which showcased consumer goods designed by such artists as Warhol, Nancy Graves, and Allan D'Arcangelo, was featured as MOM ART in *Home Furnishings Daily,* thus making explicit the ironic acronym embedded in the exhibition's title.[29] These examples resonate with yet another invocation of the paternal in the context of Pop; in the same series of published interviews in which the above quote by Warhol appeared, Robert Indiana provided this answer to the question "What is Pop?": "Pop is everything art hasn't been for the last two decades. It is basically a U-turn back to a representational visual communication, moving at a break-away speed in several sharp late models. It is an abrupt return to Father after an abstract 15-year exploration of the Womb."[30] Indiana's response is significant precisely because the relationship between Abstract Expressionism and Pop is so often considered in exactly the opposite terms: the masculine persona of an artist like Jackson Pollock is contrasted not only with the ostensibly feminized imagery of Pop art but also with Warhol's putative homosexual identity (as well as that of Rauschenberg, Johns, and Indiana).[31]

Clearly, even these few examples demonstrate the complexity of the issue, and they point to the need for continued investigation into the gendered meanings of Pop. The issue of gender is raised here to suggest that it may be present in the divergent critical appraisals of Lichtenstein and Warhol that I have been discussing. In short, Warhol's reputation as the representative or emblematic Pop artist seems at times connected to his sexual identity, inasmuch as he is often seen as the consummate dandy whose camp sensibility underlay much of his artistic practice. Even though Warhol himself left the details of his sexuality suitably ambiguous, the identification of his homosexuality has become part and parcel of the latter-day critical reception of his work.[32] Aside from the fact that Warhol provides a useful figure for recuperation by the field of lesbian and gay studies, the strength of this identification may also be related to the question of capitulation discussed earlier. The artist's distance from traditional models of masculinity may allow him to be seen as more effectively bearing the feminizing weight of the products and effects of consumption. In other words, the sense of Warhol's submission to consumer culture dovetails with the issue of his sexual identity, for it underscores the camp quality of his work, the identification with feminine glamour (as in the portraits of Marilyn Monroe, Elizabeth Taylor, and others), and the often melancholic tone of his work.

Lichtenstein, then, might prove for the critics a useful corrective to this example. He can be seen as the masculine counterpart to Warhol's feminized dandy; in the face of Warholian excess Lichtenstein provides the figure of the hard-working artist who dutifully returns to the quiet, painstaking work of the studio. In other words, he provides the convenient example of an artist whose masculinity might be preserved in the face of a wholesale immersion in the processes, products, and effects of consumer culture. We have already seen, however, that this requires maintaining a distance between the artist and his chosen imagery. Cécile Whiting has suggested a similar reading in arguing that Lichtenstein, in contrast to the type of masculine persona presented by an artist like Jackson Pollock, offered the critics a new model for the masculine artist. She suggests that the formalist defense of Lichtenstein—in which the artist turns his aestheticizing gaze on consumer culture but never falls victim to its powerful seductions—helped to remasculinize the figure of the artist:

> Lichtenstein's persona as the white-collar professional and affable father recalled the description of the typical middle-class man, of the potentially emasculated American male. Yet Lichtenstein's performance in the role of the cool and disciplined artist could also allay fears that his domestic responsibilities or profession effeminized him. The cerebral and detached artist could be seen to reinfuse the normative male with a cool, masculine veneer. Likewise, his paintings, defended in formalist terms that abandoned some of the precepts of Abstract Expressionism, could demonstrate the masculine control that the professional artist exerted over his medium.[33]

Whiting's analysis correlates with my own, although her account privileges the category of gender. I would suggest that in Lichtenstein's case the role of gender becomes inextricably intertwined with other issues, particularly those pertaining to technology and vision. Moreover, her account suggests that Lichtenstein's work was able to resolve or suture certain cultural tensions, particularly in the historical negotiation of gender roles.[34] My argument is that such tensions are never resolved in the artist's work, and that a close analysis of his imagery only highlights the contra-

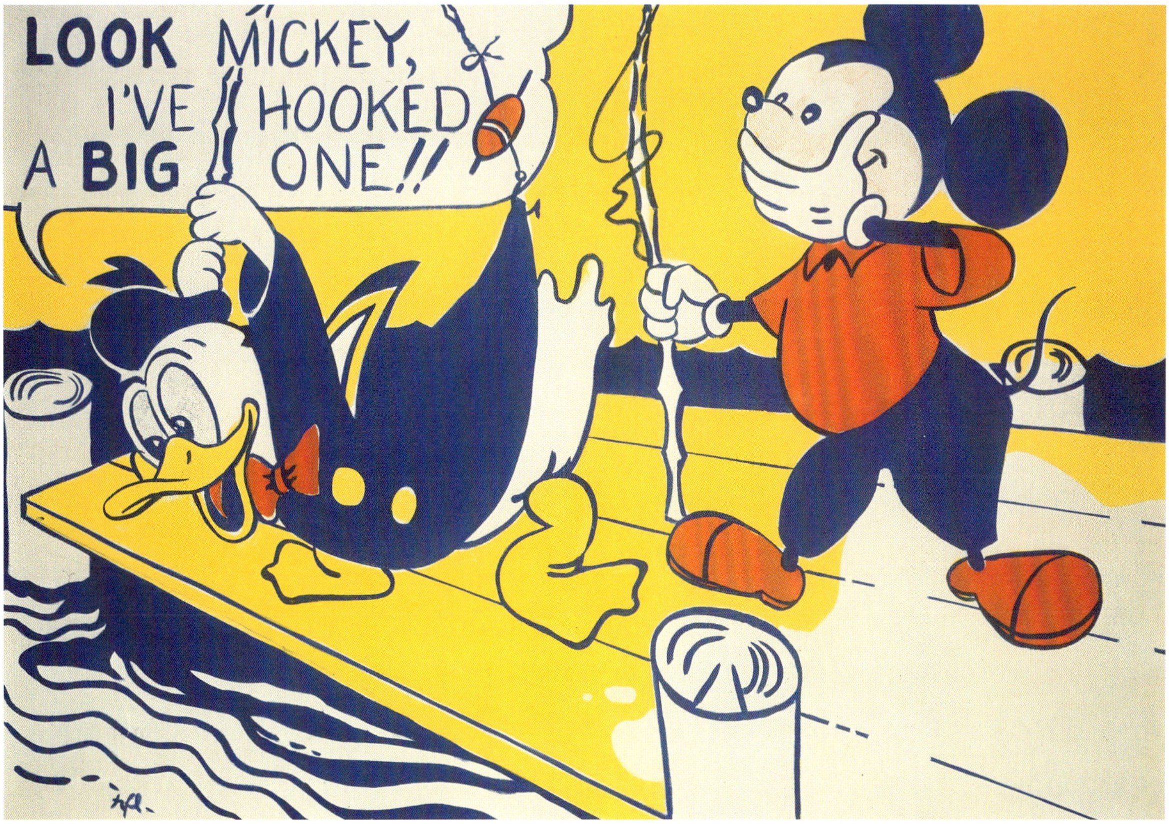

dictions embedded within his practice. In fact, we can begin to better understand those contradictions by looking at a critical work by Lichtenstein from the early 1960s, one that has long served as the fictive point of origin for his turn to Pop art.

Figure 11. *Look Mickey,* 1961. Oil on canvas, 48 × 69 in. (121.9 × 175.3 cm). National Gallery of Art, Washington, D.C. Partial and promised gift

THE ORIGIN WITHOUT AN ORIGINAL

Even though *Look Mickey* (fig. 11) is routinely identified as Lichtenstein's first Pop painting, it has proved resistant to critical interpretation. Its humorous, even childish subject matter makes it seem at first unworthy of extended analysis. There are some things we know for certain about the work: it measures 48 by 69 inches and is executed in oil on canvas, its palette limited to red, yellow, and blue laid down over a white ground. Various pencil lines—traces of Lichtenstein's sketching of the motif onto the canvas—are visible on the surface of the canvas alongside and under the painted areas. The painting depicts the Walt Disney cartoon characters Donald Duck and Mickey Mouse standing on a pier that juts out from the

Figure 12.
Donald Duck,
1958.
India ink
on paper,
19¾ × 24½ in.
(50 × 62 cm).
Private
collection

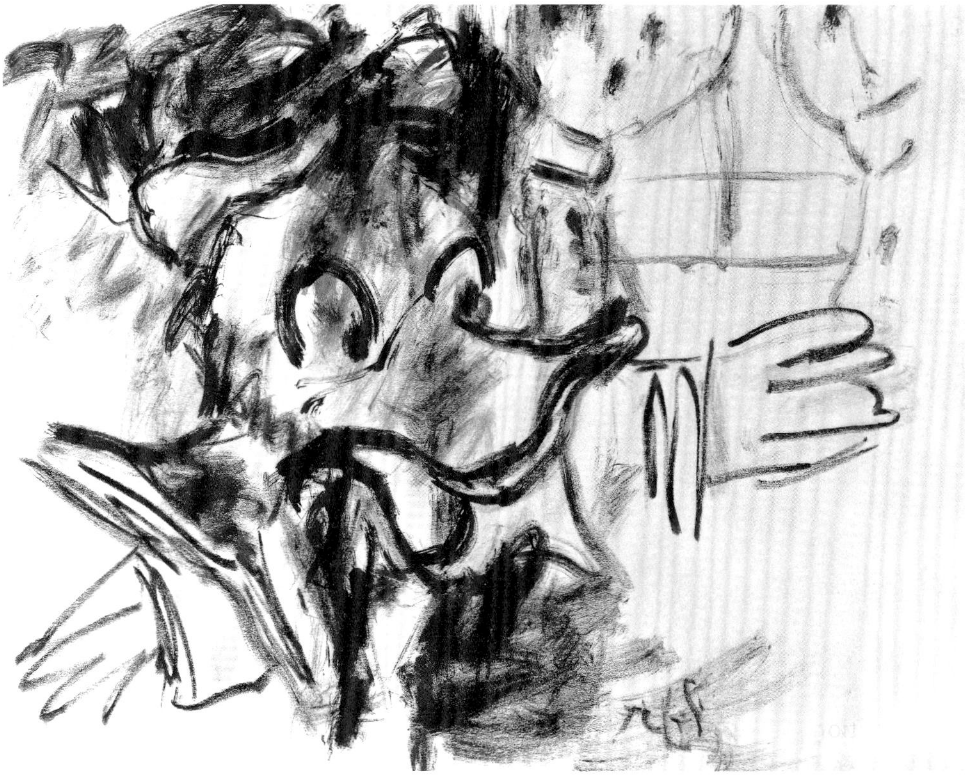

lower right-hand corner of the composition above an area of water denoted by a series of undulating curves limned in blue. To the left, Donald peers down at the depicted surface of the water, his hands grasping a fishing pole above his head. The arc of his pole is interrupted by the upper edge of the canvas; to the end of the pole are affixed a line, sinker, and a hook, which is snagged on the back of Donald's shirt. The text in the word balloon above his head reads "LOOK MICKEY, I'VE HOOKED A **BIG** ONE!!" The figure of Mickey Mouse stands just to the right, a fishing pole in his hand. He looks toward Donald, his left hand covering his mouth in a gesture that signifies a stifled laugh.

How did the artist arrive at this imagery? We know that Lichtenstein painted this work during—or just after—a period of experimentation with an abstract, painterly idiom derived from the example of Abstract Expressionism, in which he had used various modes of application (often wide bands of striated color applied alongside linear, calligraphic markings) to distribute paint over the surface of the canvas.[35] At a certain point during that period, in fact, he had experimented with placing images of cartoon characters (Mickey Mouse, Donald Duck, Bugs Bunny) within fields of otherwise abstract, gestural marks, although unlike those in the later *Look Mickey* these figurative elements had been articulated through an expressive painterly vocabulary. The dating of these works is somewhat imprecise (they were produced in about 1958) because Lichtenstein destroyed the canvases, and only a small number of preliminary drawings remain (fig. 12).

In large part, then, our understanding of *Look Mickey* as the ostensible origin of Lichtenstein's Pop art can be ascribed to the artist's own intention to have it seen in that way; his destruction of what could have been viewed retrospectively as transitional works makes this singular canvas seem even more to mark an abrupt break with anything he had done prior to that point. In fact, his desire to make a decisive break with the direct precedents of his Pop work may explain the peculiar method by which he chose to destroy those gestural cartoon paintings. As Lichtenstein explained to an interviewer in 1991, "I used all those other paintings—the abstract ones—as mats. I was painting in the bedroom and I put them on the floor so I wouldn't get paint on the floor. They got destroyed. It's too bad that I didn't keep them, because they might have been interesting to me now. I just walked on them and let paint drip on them from other paintings. Then I threw them away—about a dozen or so."[36] This is a compelling account. An account, perhaps, of a violent renunciation of abstraction, but also of an artist intentionally editing his own oeuvre by erasing his tracks. On another level this could be seen as another instance of repetition in Lichtenstein's practice: the dripping evokes Jackson Pollock's painterly drip technique, while the destruction of canvases recalls Jasper Johns' own destruction of his early work several years prior.[37] Ernst Busche has done a great deal of work in outlining the most significant points of continuity between Lichtenstein's early work and his Pop practice, yet I am less interested in the terms of such continuity—or, for that matter, of a possible break—than in calling attention to the artist's investment in defining the terms of his career for the critics.[38] That also meant providing a narrative about the genesis of *Look Mickey*. When asked in a 1964 interview how he came upon his Pop imagery, Lichtenstein replied:

> I had about a three year period, just preceding this, in which I was doing only abstract work. At that time I began putting hidden comic images into those paintings, such as Mickey Mouse, Donald Duck and Bugs Bunny. At the same time I was drawing little Mickey Mouses and things for my children, and working from bubble gum wrappers, I remember specifically. Then it occurred to me to do one of those bubble gum wrappers, as is, large, just to see what it would look like. Now I think I started out more as an observer than as a painter, but, when I did one, about halfway through the painting I got interested in it as a painting. So I started to go back to what I considered serious work because this thing was too strong for me. I began to realize that this was a more powerful thing than I had thought and it had interest.[39]

Although the artist asserts here, as he did in a number of interviews, that he derived *Look Mickey* from a cartoon on a bubble gum wrapper, this particular claim seems apocryphal at best. For one, it was exceedingly rare for the figures of Mickey Mouse and Donald Duck to appear together in the same comic strip. There were also no bubble gum companies licensed to use the Walt Disney Company's "standard characters" at this time.[40] There are any number of possibilities, then, to account for how Lichtenstein arrived at *Look Mickey*'s particular imagery: he might have transcribed the image wholesale from a panel in a comic strip or comic book; he may have found the structure of the visual joke itself in some other context (for example, enacted by two different comic strip characters) and then inserted Mickey and Donald into the scene; or he may have constructed the image wholesale. This last option is the least likely, considering the consistency with which Lichtenstein would rely on appropriated imagery in his work of the following years; yet it remains possible as long as a direct source for the painting remains unlocated.

Whatever the exact nature of the appropriation involved in the production of the work, there is another significant element in Lichtenstein's account, namely the claim that he produced the image for his children. This is yet another component of the myth of the painting's origins. Ivan Karp, who was among the first to see—and respond to—the artist's Pop paintings when Lichtenstein brought them to the Leo Castelli Gallery in 1961, provides this account: "'I did some paintings for my kids,' Roy told me. 'They asked me if I could paint a cartoon if I had to. And I said I probably could. So I did this giant, oversize cartoon. And they were very impressed by it.' "[41] In spite of Lichtenstein's strong denial of the accuracy of this story when interviewed by the author ("I know that's gotten to be a story of how I got into it, it sounds nice but it just isn't true"), this particular account of the genesis of *Look Mickey*—the artist making an image for his two young sons—has had remarkable tenacity, reappearing in various forms over the years.[42] And in spite of his denial, it seems likely that Lichtenstein himself was responsible for relating elements of this story to various interviewers and interlocutors. For instance, as early as December 1961 (quite some time before Lichtenstein's work, and Pop in general, had reached a wide audience) a short profile in the *St. Louis Post-Dispatch* noted that "when he began this style, his two young sons said: 'Now we know daddy can really draw.' "[43] There is a similar and even more extended account in Hans Richter's 1965 text *Dada: Art and Anti-Art.* Richter claims to have met the artist, and he relates the humorous anecdote with which Lichtenstein explained the origins of his Pop art:

His little son's schoolfellows asked him what his father was. An artist? What kind of artist? An abstract expressionist! Oh, said the children, somebody who paints abstracts because he's no good at drawing. Lichtenstein Junior came home crying and told his father he couldn't draw. Lichtenstein Senior assured him that this wasn't true and drew him a great big Mickey Mouse, just like in the comic strips. This didn't satisfy him; his father had to prove he could draw people too. So Papa L. drew him a big George Washington in comic-strip style. That satisfied him![44]

At first blush this line of investigation might seem frivolous. Even if Lichtenstein did provide the above account to Richter, wouldn't he have done so only in jest, poking fun at his interviewer's gullibility? Moreover, the signature in the lower left of the canvas makes it unlikely that *Look Mickey* was made for the artist's two sons, because it seems to provide clear evidence that Lichtenstein intended this as an easel painting like any other. Yet there are elements in Richter's account that ring true. One is the opposition it sets up between painting and drawing, with the suggestion that the abstract expressionist painter was being challenged in his ability to draw. In fact, Bernice Rose has called attention to the ways that Lichtenstein's Pop mode represented the artist bringing elements of drawing—including the separation of line and color—into his painting practice.[45] And there is something further, a detail about the painting, that sheds light on a certain type of meaning that *Look Mickey* may have held for the artist. The above accounts suggest that the painting was produced for the artist's two sons, David and Mitchell—let us refer to them, for the sake of abbreviation, as "D" and "M." Returning to the canvas, we note that it depicts a humorous interaction between two well-known anthropomorphic figures named Donald and Mickey; we can call them "D" and "M" for short.

Is this more than just a trivial detail? For one, it calls attention to the fact that the names of the figures in Lichtenstein's painting are the products of repetition, not just "D" and "M" but "DD" and "MM"—Donald Duck and Mickey Mouse. Lichtenstein's Pop practice would consistently return to issues of mechanical repetition, and *Look Mickey* is only one example of repetition entering the artist's work on the textual level as well. Soon after there would be the "IT'S . . . IT'S NOT AN ENGAGEMENT RING, IS IT?" of *The Engagement Ring*, followed by the 1962 canvas *Takka Takka* and the stammered repetition of *M-Maybe* in 1965. *Look Mickey*, then, highlights an effect in which textual repetition underscores the larger issue of duplication within the artist's working practice. Further, the embedding of the names—or at least the initials—of Lichtenstein's sons into the work may explain in part why the above accounts have had such staying power. For on some level the painting may very well have compelled him to recognize that the ostensibly anonymous images of an ephemeral mass culture might register personal meaning; or, in a slightly different formulation, that meaning could be located within—or inserted into—seemingly impersonal imagery. And the significance of appropriated imagery would in no way be limited to personal meanings, as he would put borrowed images to profound formal and theoretical uses as well. In this way Lichtenstein's approach to found imagery might be compared less with the model of the readymade developed by Marcel Duchamp than with the concept of the *trouvaille*, or found object, pioneered by the surrealist André Breton. Unlike Duchamp's objects the trouvaille was chosen for its psychological significance, usually associated with the discarded or ephemeral, and often selected for its aesthetic qualities. According to Henry Okun, Breton was, in 1927, "in the habit of collecting odd objects and searching for them in junk shops, flea markets, and country fairs. . . . Breton collected these objects throughout his life and used them in his work, referring to them in his writings, supporting his arguments with some of them, and illustrating his books with them."[46] In his own work Lichtenstein never toyed with the Freudian rhetoric of desire rooted in the unconscious that served as the basis of Breton's practice. Nevertheless, his project is related to Breton's inasmuch as both artists came to recognize that meaning could be located in material otherwise considered anonymous and ephemeral. The same case could be made for other Pop artists as well.[47]

If *Look Mickey* served as a vehicle for meaning in Lichtenstein's practice, in what other ways might it have done so? For one, the painting is fundamentally concerned with vision. The depicted scene foregrounds a complex circuit of various acts of looking, a property only emphasized by the title of the work. Donald's gaze is directed toward the surface of the body of water below him; in other words, the painting depicts a figure looking at a flat surface, an activity much like the one in which we as viewers are engaged. However, we are refused access to the object of Donald's gaze; he seems to see something, or perhaps more accurately misreads what he sees, but in either case we have no access to the object of his look. Moreover, in looking so intently at the water below he fails to see that he has hooked himself on his own fishing line. In so doing he has put himself in a humiliating position, revealing his posterior to Mickey behind him.

Look Mickey, then, is something of a vulgar joke.[48] In categorizing such jokes Sigmund Freud mapped out the pyramidal or tripartite structure of relations necessary for their telling: "Generally speaking, a tendentious joke calls for three people: in addition to the one who makes the joke, there must be a second who is taken as the object of the hostile or sexual aggressiveness, and a third in whom the joke's aim of producing pleasure is fulfilled."[49] Lichtenstein's painting instantiates just such a tripartite relation: Mickey takes the position of the teller of the joke, inasmuch as he is posed looking at Donald's exposed posterior; Donald is clearly the object of the joke's aggression, as he is unaware of his own self-exposure; and the viewer takes up the third point as the intended recipient of the joke's humor. The painting's humor derives not only from Donald's self-exposure—he has been made, quite literally, the butt of the joke—but also from his failure to see what he's done to himself. Further, it is motivated by Mickey's presence in the scene as the viewer of Donald's predicament. The painting presents us with a pair of figures occupying very different positions: one bent over and failing to see, one upright and seeing. In fact, Freud postulated the very origin of civilization as the moment at which humans progressed from that first state to the second: from the hunched or horizontal posture of the animal to an upright, erect gait. Further, he argued that this move shifted attention from the body's nether regions (the buttocks and genitals) and placed new emphasis on sight as a primary mode of relatedness to the world.[50] This may remind us that one of the basic characteristics of anthropomorphic cartoon characters like Mickey Mouse and Donald Duck is that they have been made more human precisely by raising them, vertically, into an erect human posture. In contrast to Mickey's upright stance, then, Donald has been lowered back down to the animal's crouching posture. And it is precisely in that horizontal position that his vision fails him, while it is the verticalized figure of Mickey who is ascribed the power of authoritative vision. Taken in the context of Lichtenstein's project, those two figures—one raised up and one lowered down—could be seen as standing in for the relation between so-called high and low forms of culture. There is a longstanding tradition in the West of mapping the body according to social topographies: the cultural forms of the lower classes are seen as aligned with the body's lower regions (including belly, genitals, and buttocks), while those of the upper classes come to be identified with its upper regions (particularly head, face, and eyes).[51] In light of this we might contrast Donald's open mouth and raised posterior with Mickey's covered mouth and fully clothed form.[52] This relation is embodied by the painting on another level as well. This is a cartoon joke—a form utterly identified with low culture—that has been made into an easel painting, perhaps the epitome of the high cultural form.

It is tempting, in light of this analysis, to suggest that the scene offers a straightforward reading: as viewers we identify with Mickey in witnessing Donald's debasement. This would imply that the painting unproblematically asserts the authority of high over low. But such a reading would ignore the fact that the tripartite structure of the joke allows for the possibility of shifting or multiple identifications: the listener or viewer might identify as much with the object of the joke's aggression as with its teller. In other words, the painting also offers the possibility of the viewer's identification with Donald. Such a possibility provides us with a suggestive interpretation, particularly when taken in the context of Lichtenstein's investment in defining *Look Mickey* as the veritable origin of his Pop practice, and hence of his very notoriety as an artist. For the painting presents a scene in which a seemingly momentous discovery comes at the price of an equally profound degradation; or, to use the term I adopted above (to describe the relation between Lichtenstein and Warhol), a capitulation. In a 1991 interview Lichtenstein noted: "Even the quote in the painting, 'Look Mickey, I've hooked a big one!!' seems so appropriate in retrospect. But I didn't realize it at the time."[53] At the time, no, but perhaps sometime later he recognized that even in that pose of degradation (perhaps precisely because he was in that very pose) Donald Duck might serve as a figure of identification in the painting, his words seeming "so appropriate." Appropriate for an artist whose move into this distinctive mode represented both success and failure, an equal (and simultaneous) possibility for approbation and degradation. As the viewer's identification oscillates between the figures of Mickey and Donald, the image serves up both those possibilities in equal measure: to be both the teller of the joke and its intended victim.

This reading of *Look Mickey* is given more force when taken in the context of one of Lichtenstein's most oft-quoted statements about his intentions for his practice as it developed in the early 1960s. When asked by Gene Swenson "What is Pop Art?" Lichtenstein responded: "I don't know—the use of commercial art as subject matter in painting, I suppose. It was hard to get a painting that was despicable enough so that no one would hang it—everybody was hanging everything."[54] Lichtenstein's stated desire to paint a despicable painting has most often been taken as yet another instance of an artist wanting to shock his audience in the venerable tradition of the avant-garde. Yet why choose that particular adjective—*despicable*—over other, more commonly used terms, such as "vulgar" or "shocking"? For one, the word contains a reference to vision; it derives from the Latin root *specere,* meaning "to look." Moreover, it expresses—like *Look Mickey* itself—a degree of ambiguity. Although the term despicable most commonly refers to that which is "to be looked down upon or despised; vile, base, contemptible," an older form means precisely the opposite: "exhibiting or expressing contempt; contemptuous."[55] In short, it describes the very characteristic I have located in *Look Mickey:* not only the invocation of the act of looking, but an oscillation between positions of authority and debasement.

We can now better understand the wide range of possibilities for meaning that *Look Mickey* offered to Lichtenstein and that led him to frame it—retrospectively—as the decisive origin of his practice. It provided a set of formal strategies that, while allied with figuration, nevertheless maintained a connection to modes of abstraction. It suggested an alternative to what the artist perceived as the dominant and academicized painting idiom of the time. And it offered a category of imagery through which the artist could represent issues of particular concern at the time. In short, it condensed these possibilities into a conveniently mythic—yet humorous—form with which to mark the emergence of Pop art.

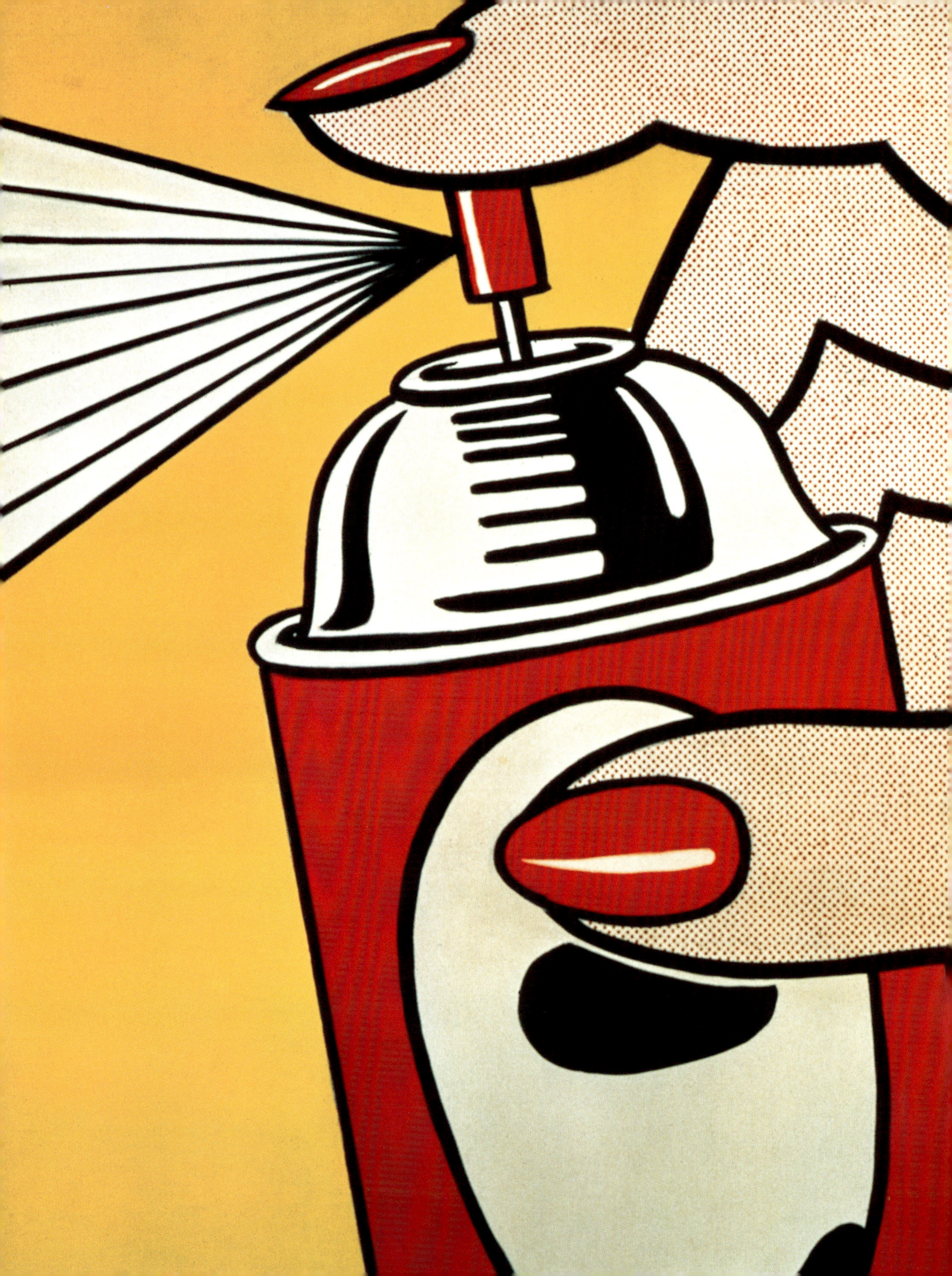

Trademark Lichtenstein

If Lichtenstein set out, in the early 1960s, to depict appropriated imagery using the facture of the machine, how would he attach his name to it? What are the historical possibilities and limits of articulating an identity as an artist when one's work is so intertwined with the languages of advertising and mechanical reproduction? We may begin to glean answers to these questions by looking to one particular area of Lichtenstein's practice. If comic-derived images like *Look Mickey* comprised a substantial portion of his work in the early 1960s, at the same time he was also engaged with the problem of imaging the common object. *Golf Ball* (1962)—just one of his many images of consumer objects—is a painting reduced almost to its simplest components: a field of arcs contained within a circle is centered on the canvas, described only by the laying-down of black pigment on a white ground (fig. 13). Along with his comic strip paintings it was through works like *Golf Ball* that critics aligned Lichtenstein with other practitioners of Pop art such as Warhol, Oldenburg, and Tom Wesselmann. Early exhibitions featuring the work of these artists (such as "New Paintings of Common Objects" and "Six Painters and the Object") often emphasized the movement's orientation toward the object.[1] As I noted in my introduction, this shared emphasis has often complicated the critical discourse around Lichtenstein's work, leading to a general lack of differentiation between his project and those of his fellow Pop artists. In order to more fully understand his distinctive treatment of the object we need to consider the imbrication of brand name, trademark, and signature—all emblems of ownership and identity—in his work. Lichtenstein's adoption of formal devices that mimicked modes of mechanical reproduction has often been interpreted as a clear-cut removal of any claim to authorship. However, analysis of his work from this period, particularly his images of consumer objects, demonstrates something quite different: that he was confronting the tensions involved in bringing together divergent strategies of authorship and identity from commercial culture and fine art practice.

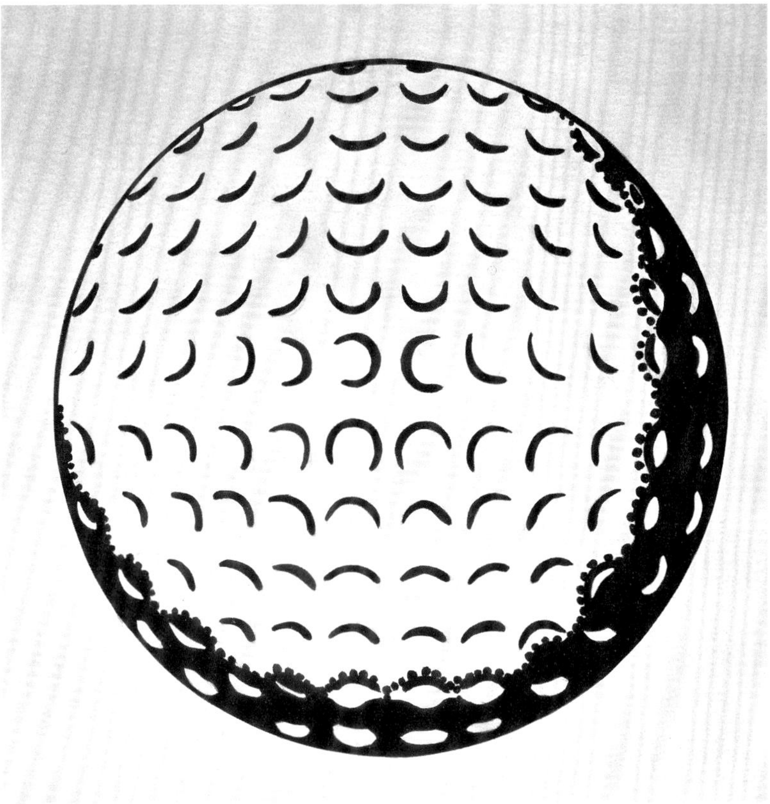

Figure 13.
Golf Ball, 1962.
Oil on canvas,
32 × 32 in.
(81.3 × 81.3 cm).
Private collection

EFFACING THE BRAND NAME

There's something about brand names that I don't care for.

—Roy Lichtenstein, in Alloway, *Roy Lichtenstein*

Could we imagine more prosaic images of everyday consumption than those presented in Lichtenstein's paintings? A kitchen range, its door open, displays a variety of meat and baked goods; a woman's hand sprinkles detergent into a washing machine; an automobile tire hangs suspended in an airless void (figs. 14–16). In the face of such paintings one is tempted to view Lichtenstein's work as nothing more than the neutral transcription of consumer and advertising images. However, closer scrutiny reveals that he approached this type of imagery in a distinctive way. In contrast to such Pop images as Andy Warhol's *Green Coca-Cola Bottles* (fig. 17) or Ed Ruscha's *Standard Gasoline Station*—both of which foreground the importance of brand names in consumer culture—Lichtenstein's paintings proffer an array of generic objects removed from the world of product logos and trademarks. In short, the brand name is consistently effaced in his work.

At the very beginning of his experimentation with Pop imagery Lichtenstein

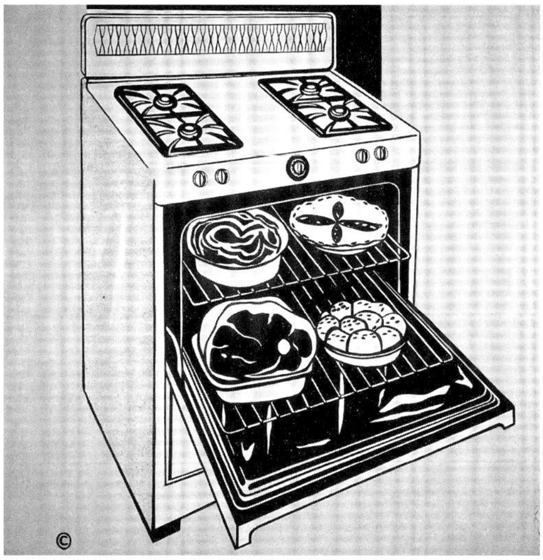

Figure 14. *Kitchen Range,* 1961.
Oil on canvas,
68 × 68 in. (172.7 × 172.7 cm).
National Gallery of Australia, Canberra

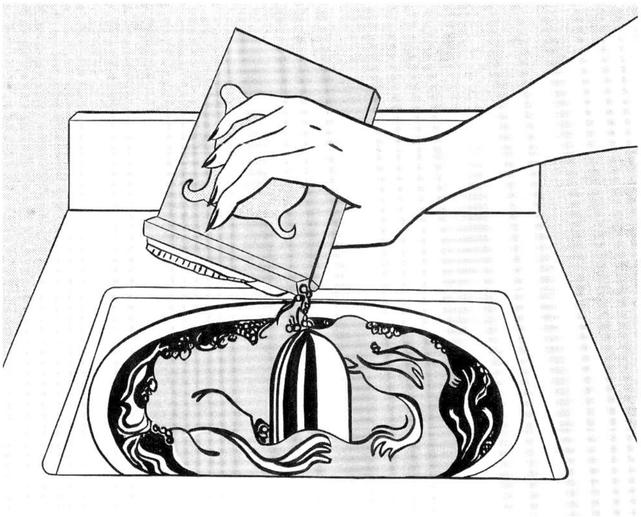

Figure 15. *Washing Machine,* 1961. Oil on canvas,
56½ × 68½ in. (143.5 × 174 cm).
Yale University Art Gallery, New Haven.
Richard Brown Baker Collection

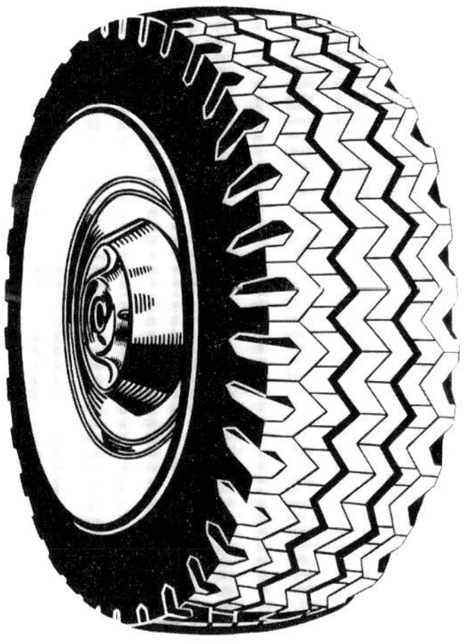

Figure 16.
Tire, 1962. Oil on canvas,
68 × 56 in. (172.7 × 142.2 cm). Private
collection

Figure 17.
Andy Warhol,
Green Coca-Cola Bottles,
1962.
Oil on canvas,
82½ × 57 in.
(209.6 × 144.8 cm).
Whitney Museum
of American Art,
New York. Purchase,
with funds from the
Friends of the Whitney
Museum of American
Art

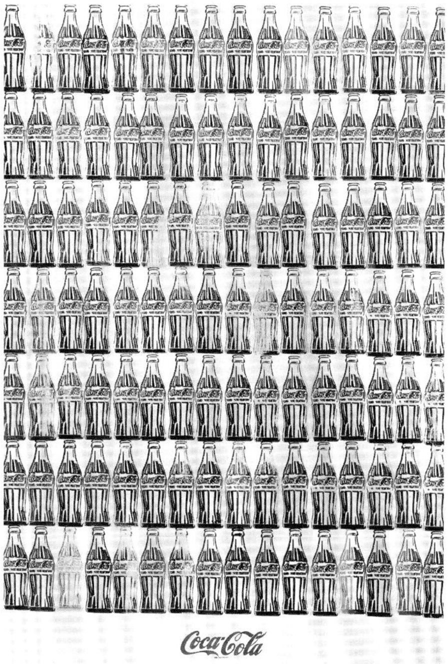

depicted one or two objects that retained their trademark or product logo, most notably *Roto-Broil*.[2] In that painting the titular object is displayed against a brilliant red background, its name emblazoned above the temperature knob on its front panel. Yet almost immediately Lichtenstein rejected the use of brand names in his work. This is particularly evident when we compare *Golf Ball* with its source image pasted into one of the artist's notebooks (fig. 18). His transcription of the image onto canvas involved a great deal of changes: he separated the object from its context and isolated it on a blank ground; lengthened many of the small arcs that describe the ball's dimples; widened the dark band of shading, especially along the ball's right edge; and applied dots (to indicate shading) where none were noticeable in the printed source. Yet such ostensibly formal adjustments to the image have tended to overshadow a no less significant alteration, namely the removal of the brand name from the golf ball's depicted surface. Lichtenstein directly addressed this issue in an early interview, when he commented, "I very rarely put any brand name on anything, or any identifiable product, which some people do. The only one I think that I can remember I've done is Roto Broil, actually keep the name of the product or an airplane, or keep a type of airplane identifiable. I do like to make more general types and not advertise . . . any product.[3]

Lichtenstein effected this erasure of the brand name in a variety of ways. In some works he simply deleted it from his painted version, altering the object in order to obscure the brand name's elision (in *Golf Ball* he accomplished this by extending the dimple-marks into the ball's center). In paintings like *Washing Machine* and *Spray* (fig. 19) a feminine hand obscures a logo that seems to have been simplified and stylized—and stripped of any lettering—by the artist. In other cases, such as the drawings *Airplane* (fig. 20) and *Shock-Proof* (1963), we are treated to a more peculiar alteration. Lichtenstein retains a vestige of product logo or brand marking (whether on the airplane fuselage or the watch face), but alters the text to the point of unreadability. In the process he creates a strange lettering-system all his own. Whatever the means, this kind of alteration has profound significance in a society in which consumer activity is structured around the precision of brand names. It also highlights the extent to which Lichtenstein's depiction of the consumer object is radically different from Warhol's. If Lichtenstein tended to isolate a singular object against a blank ground, Warhol depicted rows and rows of nearly identical objects that fill the frame of the canvas, thus emphasizing the standardization and repetition of consumer products. Further, Warhol's focus, in such works as the *Campbell's Soup Cans, Brillo Boxes,* and *Coca-Cola Bottles,* is on the distinctive packaging of brand name goods. Even his star portraits, such as the *Marilyn* paintings, prompt our recognition that the celebrity's persona assumes many of the same characteristics as the packaged consumer object. Licht-

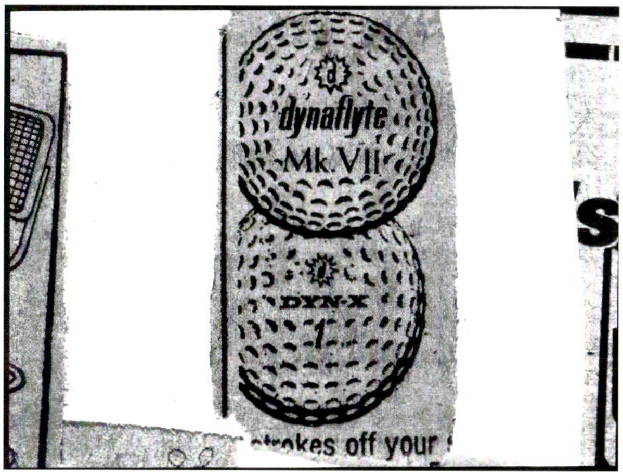

Figure 18.
Detail of page from Roy Lichtenstein's source notebooks, c. 1960s

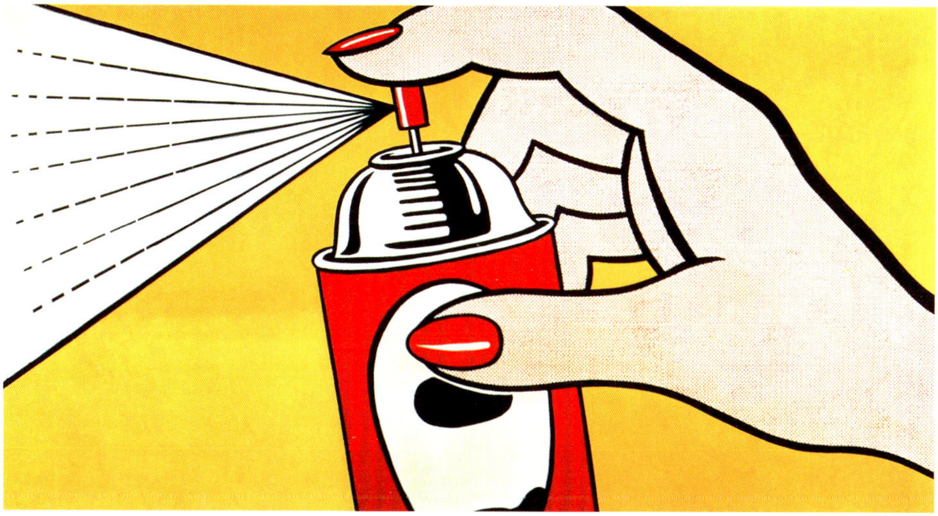

Figure 19.
Spray, 1962.
Oil on canvas, 36 × 68 in. (91.4 × 172.7 cm).
Staatsgalerie Stuttgart

enstein gives us something much different: the forced genericness of such works as *Kitchen Range, Hot Dog,* and *Cigarette.*

The artist's familiar comic strip images followed the same trajectory. We have already seen that he effectively initiated his Pop mode with *Look Mickey,* which depicts two of the most widely recognizable cartoon characters of the time. Mickey Mouse may well represent the most extreme case of a cartoon character that stands for a particular corporate identity (in this case, that of the Walt Disney Company). In other words, he is nothing more than a trademark.[4] Soon after, Lichtenstein produced two additional cartoon paintings that depicted identifiable characters: Popeye and Bluto in *Popeye,* and Popeye's hapless sidekick Wimpy in *Wimpy (Tweet).* Yet as his approach to Pop imagery developed, he quickly abandoned such characters and moved on to something else: his well-known comic-derived images depicting generic human figures.

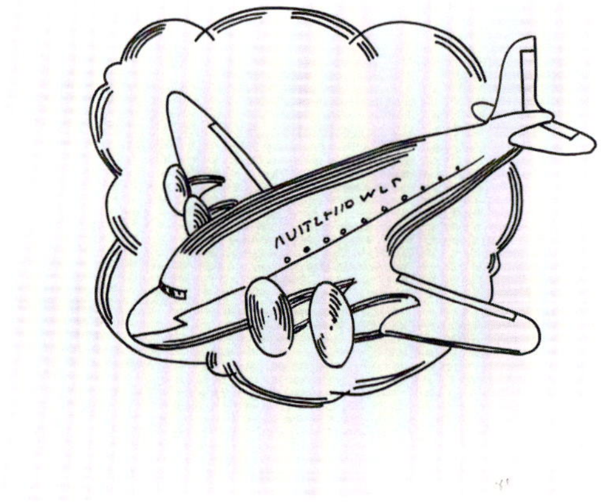

Figure 20.
Airplane, 1961.
Ink on paper,
20 × 23¾ in.
(50.8 × 60.4 cm).
Private collection

The term generic is of crucial significance here. A general classification of these works is certainly possible: they contain imagery culled from comic strips like *Winnie Winkle* and *Steve Roper,* or from romance- and military-themed comic books. Yet the figures depicted in the artist's paintings are generic not only because Lichtenstein had moved away from representing identifiable cartoon characters but also because he had made particular formal changes to his source imagery—changes that would soon become recognizable as components of his distinctive style. In other words, his departure from recognizable characters, and his removal of brand names and product logos from his paintings, occurred concurrently with the evolution of a set of highly structured pictorial codes in his work. The critical literature on the artist's work has consistently emphasized the formal differences between Lichtenstein's paintings and their sources, as evidenced in his rearrangement of compositional elements, elimination of incidental pictorial details, and simplification of color values. For instance, in their catalogue to the 1990 Museum of Modern Art exhibition "High and Low: Modern Art and Popular Culture," Kirk Varnedoe and Adam Gopnik reproduced five separate comic book panels that, combined, provided the source imagery for Lichtenstein's 1963 canvas *Okay, Hot-Shot.*[5] Such a comparison demonstrates how Lichtenstein condensed the work of two different comic book artists—Irv Novick and Russ Heath—into a single painting. He borrowed elements and motifs from various panels and reduced the complexity of hatching and color tones. Commenting on this process of painterly appropriation, Varnedoe and Gopnik noted:

> Ironically, [Lichtenstein] had to aggressively alter and recompose [his found images] to bring them closer to a platonic ideal of simple comic-book style. . . . The effects that make Lichtenstein into Lichtenstein involved not the aestheti-

cizing of a consistent style through mechanical displacements, but the careful, artificial construction of what appears to be a generic, whole, "true-folk" cultural style from a real world of comics that was by then far more "fallen" and fragmented. His early pictures work by making the comic images more like the comics than the comics were themselves.[6]

Varnedoe and Gopnik's account provides abundant information on the historical status of the comic books from which Lichtenstein drew his imagery, and it details the selections and alterations he made in producing his paintings. Moreover, it describes how the artist replaced the more illustrational style of the comics of the time with a simplified formal approach more in keeping with the cartoon genre exemplified by *Look Mickey.* Yet the authors' reference to a "platonic ideal" makes it seem that through his work Lichtenstein had somehow isolated the fundamental characteristics of the comics as a medium.[7]

Lichtenstein's project was in fact much more fraught, particularly in relation to the question of authorship. For it was not, as Varnedoe and Gopnik claim, that the artist made the comic images look "more like the comics," but rather the opposite: he attempted to make the comics look like *his* images. His distinctive treatment of appropriated imagery eliminated details that would otherwise have pointed to the previous authorship of these images. In other words, the fictively generic status of Lichtenstein's comic book imagery was arrived at by similar means as the genericness of his paintings of consumer objects. While illustrators like Russ Heath, Irv Novick, and Joe Kubert each has his own recognizable visual language (and those with experience in the field of comic book art can easily differentiate their work), by simplifying his borrowed imagery Lichtenstein effectively repressed that distinctiveness. Carter Ratcliff seems to have made this point most directly when he coined the term "Lichtensteinize" to describe the operation by which the artist altered appropriated imagery to make it his own.[8] In so doing, no matter how much he became a master appropriator he could still maintain the fiction that he was the central, authoritative subject of the aesthetic act.

Although it may seem that in the early 1960s Lichtenstein was involved in a veritable celebration of the work of comic book illustrators, he based his practice on the assumption that comic book art was merely a type of rudimentary, vernacular imagery. As he stated in an early interview, "the comics really haven't anything I would call art connected with it [*sic*]. They are really using a craft ability almost entirely and artistic sense only slightly. There's composition connected with comic strips, but in a very superficial way."[9] He maintained that his work as a fine artist involved taking such imagery and transforming it according to a principle of "unifying form" (an idea derived from his training in a Gestalt-oriented program of modernist aesthetics, which I will discuss at length in the next chapter). This type of approach was not new to him; he had appropriated imagery for years before the emergence of his more recognizable Pop idiom. In an early interview he noted that even before 1961 "reproduction was really the subject of my work."[10] What, then, had changed? Prior to the early 1960s he had presented appropriated imagery through a painterly vocabulary derived largely from the examples of earlier modernist painters like Klee and Picasso.[11] For example, a canvas like *The Explorer* (fig. 21) was based on a printed advertising image, yet its form—particularly the cubist-derived faceting of geometric color planes—signified that this was a work of art.[12] In other words, the formal vocabulary used in his paintings provided visual cues for the artistry of his work, in that it signified the artist's creative or aesthetic transformation of the preexisting image. Such was not the case as Lichtenstein's practice developed after 1961, for at that point his paintings took on the mechanical facture of the printed image as well. This was a conflicted strategy, because the work no longer provided clear evidence that the appropriated image had been subject to any process of transformation. Quite the opposite, in fact: his paintings resolutely clung to the look of mechanically reproduced imagery. But there was a countereffect to this: if the form of Lichtenstein's pre-Pop work could be ascribed to the influence of earlier painters (Picasso, Klee, and others), the machine-made look of his imagery after 1961 made his paintings seem radically new. Ironically, his very claim to originality (at least within the discourses of art history and criticism) resides in his having adopted the standardized facture of the machine in his work. Moreover, that facture came to be considered his own—that is, as identifiably "Lichtenstein." (Even though both artists borrowed from mechanical printing techniques, one can't imagine mistaking a Lichtenstein for a Warhol, or vice versa.) In the process, it is almost as if there is a shift from the conventional notion of signature style—a set of motifs and formal devices that identify the work of a particular artist—to something else: a kind of trademarking function.

This is not an arbitrary claim, for the formal operations adopted by Lichtenstein have significant correlations in the field of trademark design. In fact, if brands and product logos were repressed in his work on the level of subject matter, they nonetheless seem to have returned on the level of form. That is to say that the artist's chosen set of formal strategies (including the reduction of palette, elimination of incidental pictorial detail, and use of bold and highly legible outlines) was consistent with concurrent developments in trademark design. A 1960 industry research report entitled *The Language of Corporate Trademarks and Symbols* illustrated the evolution—under the aegis of modernist design principles—of ever more simplified trademark designs.[13] This tendency is demonstrated, for example, in a comparison of the Prudential life insurance company's product logos from

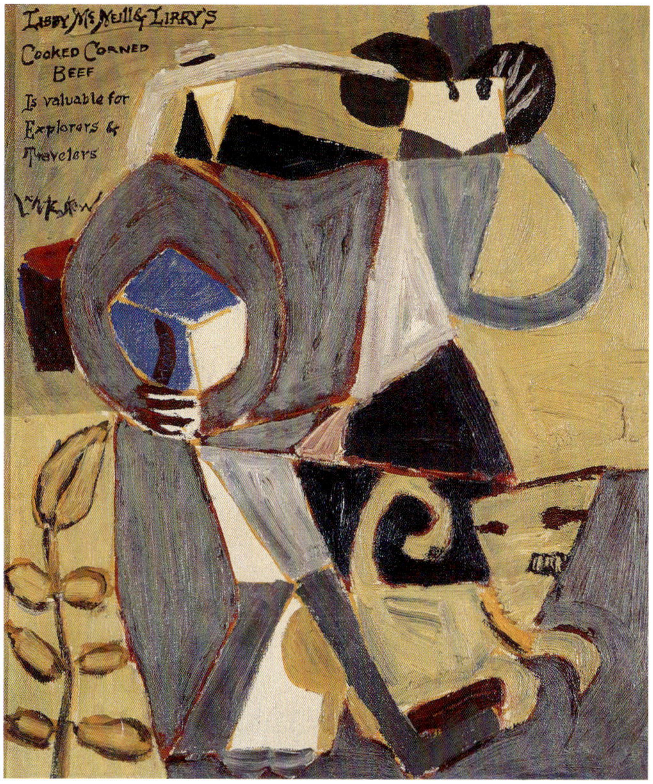

Figure 21.
The Explorer,
c. 1952.
Oil on canvas,
16 × 14 in.
(40.7 × 35.6 cm).
Butler Institute
of American Art,
Youngstown, Ohio.
Gift of Mr. and Mrs.
Robert Miller, 1960

1896 to 1984 (fig. 22). Trademarks and product logos from the late nineteenth and early twentieth centuries often employed narrative or illustrational devices; these include many of the marks that Barbara Capitman identifies as "trade figures," including Buster Brown, the Dutch Cleanser girl, and Psyche (the White Rock beverage muse).[14] However, as trademark design developed as a distinct field of practice and came under the influence of modernist design, the trademark became more simplified and graphic. This general inclination toward abstraction is evidenced in texts like Egbert Jacobson's 1952 *Seven Designers Look at Trademark Design*, in which various designers inveigh against narrative or illustrational trademarks. Instead, they value trademark designs that are as stripped down and bare as possible.[15]

Caroline Jones has made a similar claim relating to the development of the marketing brand, arguing that Frank Stella's abstract canvases of the early 1960s can be read as adhering to the logic of contemporaneous developments in corporate logo design. Describing a continuum between fine artist and commercial designer through this shared logic of branding, she suggests that "Stella's paintings of the period (1960 to 1967) thus aimed to function like brands in their insistent 'stamping out' on the retina, their assertive presence in the social field. The 1960s brand

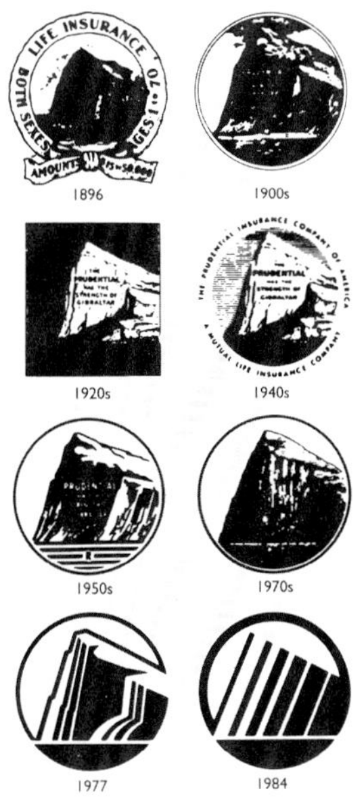

Figure 22. Development of the Prudential Life Insurance company logo, from Veronica Napoles, *Corporate Identity Design* (1988)

functioned as an icon, not a picture—there was no depth, merely visual information."[16] While Jones' account is suggestive, the connection between the work of art and the product logo is more self-evident in Lichtenstein's case; after all, he was directly confronting the problem of representing (or, more accurately, refusing to represent) the logo or brand in his work. Moreover, his project intersected with that of trademark designers on the level of technology. The same device used for years in consumer design laboratories to test consumers' reactions to package and logo designs had been used by Lichtenstein's teacher Hoyt Sherman to instruct his pupils in a Gestalt comprehension of "visual unity." Sherman employed the tachistoscope (a shutter-device that allows images and objects to be illuminated for controlled intervals of time) to flash images on a screen for fractions of a second. Those fleeting images were copied by his students, who sat at their desks in otherwise complete darkness. During the same historical moment in which Sherman employed the device to heighten his students' visual acuity, it was being used in advertising research to evaluate the effectiveness of package and logo design. A 1947 article entitled "Can Package Design Be Evaluated?" related:

> A measure of the recognition factor of the package may be obtained by employing the Tachistoscope. A Tachistoscope is an instrument which presents packages for brief, controlled periods of time, and is so constructed that the presentation periods may be held uniform or be varied at will. The package being studied, plus the competitive packages, are all placed in the Tachisto-

> scope at one time. In order to further control the conditions under which this measure is obtained, the letters which make up the brand name are converted into a meaningless pattern which retains the original configuration so that identification is based on recognition and not readability.[17]

Significantly, Sherman had employed the very same method in his program of art instruction; he would often create slides with letters and numbers arranged in unreadable configurations in order to place emphasis less on the meaning of the individual elements in a grouping than on their configuration as an overall form. Yet if his program—which exerted a profound influence on Lichtenstein—shared the same technology as that of consumer product designers, their immediate ends were somewhat different. Sherman used the tachistoscope to heighten his students' visual acuity, while advertising researchers used it to test the recognition of various design strategies. However, both projects proceeded from the same assumption: that the magnitude of sensory stimuli in an industrialized consumer culture required the development of new methods—and the use of new technologies—to test and train the individual's perceptual responses.

By the 1950s the burgeoning field of consumer product design was influenced not only by more generalized modernist design principles but also by perceptual psychology and Gestalt theory. This was part of a larger trend in advertising toward motivational research into the psychology of consumer behavior.[18] Evidence of this trend can be located in various texts of the time, including the aforementioned *Seven Designers Look at Trademark Design*. In his contribution to that book, editor Egbert Jacobson links the basic principles of visual communication to the Gestaltist notion of the figure/ground relation. He devotes much of his discussion to illustrations of figure-ground interactions and their effect on the viewer's perception of visual motifs, explaining that

> the object of this chapter is twofold: on the one hand to stimulate analysis of the designs collected here; on the other, to make the reader familiar with principles he may use in judging new trademark designs as they are being evolved. There are, of course, other criteria by which to judge trademark design: uniqueness, well-chosen symbolism, appropriate lettering, elegance of style, to name a few. All add character and associative values to a chosen *organization of figure and ground*.[19]

Jacobson's language was echoed by Lichtenstein in a discussion of the relation between Pop and commercial art. In a talk given at the 1964 meeting of the College Art Association, the artist offered his views on Pop's approach to the consumer object:

> The subject matter [of Pop], of course, is commercialism and commercial art; but its contribution is the isolation and glorification of "Thing." Commercial art is not our art, it is our subject matter and in that sense it is nature; but it is considered completely at odds with the major direction of art during and since the Renaissance and particularly at odds with our directly preceding movement—Abstract Expressionism. Commercial art runs contrary to a major art current in the sense that it concentrates on *thing* rather than *environment;* on *figure* rather than *ground.*[20]

Since Lichtenstein's training had relied heavily on the principles of perceptual psychology, it is perhaps unsurprising that the language he uses here resonates with that of Jacobson. His comments suggest, however, that he may have recognized the conjunctions between his own project and the work of commercial artists like trademark designers. At the same time they demonstrate his insistence on distancing himself from commercial art. Lichtenstein asserts here that commercial art was only his "subject matter," that he was as much removed from consumer imagery as earlier artists were ostensibly distant from nature itself. He maintains that there is an utter difference (above and beyond the material distinctions between painted canvas and printed image) between his formal language and that of commercial artists. Significantly, certain critics at the time interpreted his work in complete opposition to his stated aims; Robert Rosenblum, a sympathetic early critic of the artist's work, would assert that "Lichtenstein force[s] us to examine American commercial illustration in terms of its aesthetic potential."[21]

If Lichtenstein used the distinction between figure and ground to describe the function of commercial art, he used almost identical terminology to differentiate between his work and that of the Abstract Expressionists before him:

> In Abstract-Expressionism the paintings symbolize the idea of ground-directedness as opposed to object-directedness. You put something down, react to it, put something else down, and the painting itself becomes a symbol of this. The difference is that rather than symbolize this ground-directedness I do an object-directed appearing thing. There is humor here. The work is still ground-directed; the fact that it's an eyebrow or an almost direct copy of something is unimportant. The ground-directedness is in the painter's mind and not immediately apparent in the painting. . . . This tension between apparent object-directed products and actual ground-directed processes is an important strength of Pop Art.[22]

This quote contains a central description by Lichtenstein of his own practice, and it tells us something about his approach to problems of form. His language is somewhat ponderous; the reference to the property of ground-directedness is basically a recapitulation of the modernist notion of the canvas as a site for the attempted dissolution of formal distinctions between figure and ground. His account provides us evidence that his move into a Pop idiom did not so much represent a desire to deconstruct or overturn the modernist aesthetic project but rather may have provided what seemed a new possibility for reinvigorating it. He would attempt to instantiate a tension in his work between those object-directed products and the aesthetic, ground-directed form he imparted to them.

Critics have often noted that this visual tension between figure and ground is a major component of Lichtenstein's images of consumer objects. Many of them produce a veritable oscillation between the figural resolution of the object and its dissolution into a field of flat, abstracted marks. This is especially apparent in those paintings (including *Golf Ball, Tire,* and *Large Spool*) in which the object's surface bears a resemblance to a geometric abstraction (fig. 23). Lichtenstein was clearly experimenting with various means to this end; in some canvases he offset the object against a background of regularized dots, while in others he displayed it against the blank ground of the canvas. In a discussion of the artist's 1963 drawing *Ball of Twine* (fig. 24), Bernice Rose observes that "Lichtenstein expresses his

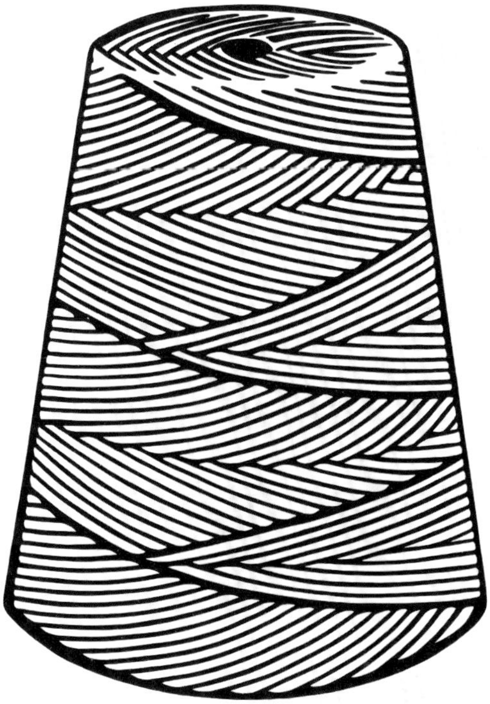

Figure 23. *Large Spool,* 1963. Magna on canvas, 40 × 36 in. (101.6 × 91.4 cm). Private collection

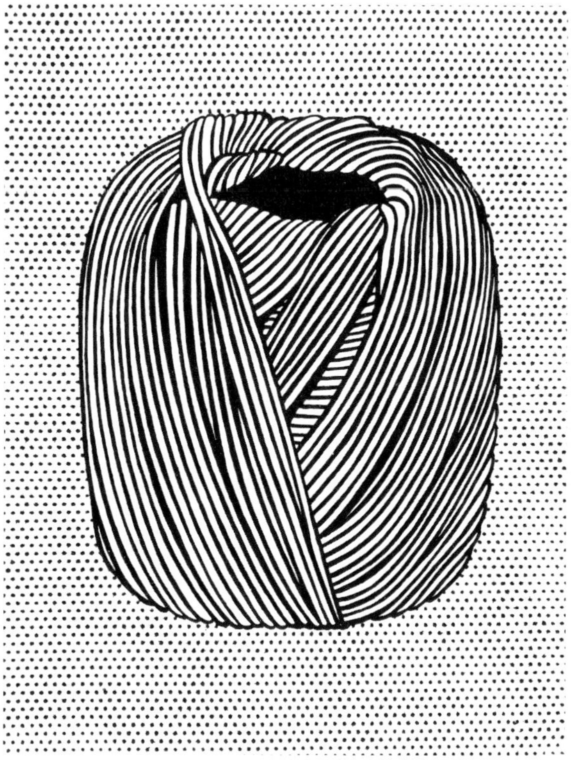

Figure 24. *Ball of Twine,* 1963. Pencil and tusche pochoir on paper, 15¼ × 12½ in. (38.8 × 31.8 cm). Private collection

attitude toward the object by refusing to integrate it with the field as [Jasper] Johns had done, and instead constitutes the object as its own field: all of the marks of the object are related to one another to create a closed system, clustered around the black form at the top center."[23] Rose suggests that even though the object is not integrated with its field, Lichtenstein attempts to reconcile figure and ground through a series of formal reversals, thereby producing the kind of visual oscillation I have already described. Diane Waldman has called attention to much the same effect:

> Because of the potential conflict between a representational figure and a neutral (abstract) ground, Lichtenstein was forced to find a solution that sacrificed neither but permitted a mutual coexistence. For him, therefore, the relationship of the object to the picture plane was of utmost importance. Far from denying the figure/ground relationship, he accentuated it. By emphasizing both the object's potentially three-dimensional character and the flatness of its depiction by means of a magnified screen of Benday dots, he established a dialectical tension between the subject and ground that is a major strength of his single-object paintings.[24]

This type of description of figure-ground relations has become an almost hackneyed trope in formalist discussions of modernist painting. Yet Lichtenstein's engagement with commercial culture forces us to expand its scope and to consider its relation to elements outside the ostensibly closed sphere of modernist fine art practice. If the tension between figure and ground is a major strength of the artist's paintings of consumer objects, it seems that he achieved it only through the sacrifice of a particular element, namely the trademark or brand.

The trademark is a powerful thing: its placement marks a surface as occupying a position in a complex system of exchange. Like Egbert Jacobson, other trademark designers recognized this effect, and it is often discussed in corporate trademark manuals from the period. Great care was expended to ensure the trademark's formal integrity; for example, a company manual on Du Pont's distinctive oval trademark instructs that "the Oval should never be reversed or printed on a small area of any shape—rectangular, round, triangular, etc., of another color. This might lead to the assumption that the background area was a part of the registered trademark."[25] Another manual from the period, issued by General Electric, devotes considerable space to instructing the user on the proper form of these brand marks. Careful attention is paid to size, positioning, color, and placement on background. In typical corporate language the manual emphasizes the significance of the company's brand:

The General Electric signature and monogram are two of the best known and most highly regarded trade-marks in the world, and they are two of the Company's most valued assets. . . . They have been developed to a high degree of public acceptance only through years of consistent use in connection with dependable products, and they represent an enormous advertising and commercial investment. Because the signature and monogram are so well known and accepted, it is to the General Electric Company's advantage to put them to work in every way possible to identify itself, its products, and its activities; and for the many distributors, dealers, and agents who handle the Company's products to use the trade-marks to further their sales of G-E products.[26]

Lichtenstein's removal of logos and trademarks from images of consumer objects was in part a response to the formal problems raised by his development of a Pop idiom. As I noted earlier, prior to the early 1960s he had employed various techniques to structure his compositions. For example, he would often break figures into interlocking planes arrayed across the surface of the canvas, a strategy largely derived from the example of synthetic cubism. Yet with his images of consumer objects he adopted a new approach to composition in which the figure was centered on the canvas and radically detached from the ground and framing edge. As he described in an interview, "I think that in these objects, the golf ball, the frankfurter, and so on, there is anti-Cubist composition. You pick an object and put it on a blank ground. The idea is contrary to the major direction of art since the early Renaissance, which has more and more symbolized the integration of 'figure' with 'ground.' "[27] He had begun to arrive at an approach that might provide an engaging visual tension between the figure and its collapse into flat abstraction, yet he had to sacrifice the logo and brand in order to achieve that effect. Although the trademark is a component of commercial culture, its effects are not necessarily neutralized when it is brought into the realm of fine art. The intended function of the brand is to separate figure from ground, to differentiate the individual object from the vast array of products circulating within consumer culture. If Lichtenstein had retained it in his paintings, it would not only have figured the object but would have pulled the image back into a system of corporate branding and identity. His work refuses this element in order to allow the artist some kind of claim—however tentative or provisional—to the object.

INDEXING THE SIGNATURE

In an *Artforum* review of Lichtenstein's 1963 show at the Ferus Gallery in Los Angeles, Doug McClellan critiqued what he saw as an inattentiveness to form, writing that the artist's paintings "are like an anonymous Letter-to-the-Editor, a default on the part of the author. The signature on the letter—the commitment through form by the artist—that gives substance to what is said is not there."[28] McClellan's account is significant on a number of levels. For one, it predicts a standard poststructuralist reading of Lichtenstein's work—and Pop art in general—as signaling what Roland Barthes called the "death of the author": the artist's subjectivity is presumed to have been utterly evacuated from the work.[29] Yet already with the example of Lichtenstein's repression of brand name and trademark we have seen how issues of identity—of naming, authorship, and ownership—were confronted in his practice. Could it be that his project represents less a "default on the part of the author" than a troubling—and shifting—of conventional notions of authorial presence?

It is significant that McClellan criticized Lichtenstein's work using the metaphor of a letter devoid of a signature, for by the time of his review the artist had effectively removed his signature from his paintings. Prior to the emergence of his Pop mode Lichtenstein had consistently signed his canvases. The form of his signature varied; paintings from the early- and mid-1950s bear his last name in a kind of jaunty, angular lettering (see, for example, fig. 21), but by the late 1950s he had adopted a signature composed of his three initials, RFL (for Roy Fox Lichtenstein), rendered in lowercase script (fig. 25). He certainly had the opportunity to recognize the degree to which an artist might become publicly identified with his signature: his distinctive monogram was featured in the publicity material for both of the one-person exhibitions held just before his turn to Pop. It appeared on the invitation to a 1959 show of Lichtenstein's untitled abstractions at the Condon Riley Gallery in New York, and it was reproduced on the cover of a brochure for his 1961 exhibition at the Douglass College art gallery.[30] It also appeared on some of his earliest Pop canvases, like *Look Mickey* and *The Engagement Ring*. Yet soon after he began his experimentation with Pop imagery that signature disappeared from the pictorial field of his easel paintings—left homeless, as it were.[31]

This decision to forgo the signature became increasingly common among postwar abstractionists (such as Mark Rothko and Ad Reinhardt), who most likely viewed it as a potential impediment to the play of fictively pure color and form in their canvases. Not only is this tendency reversed in Lichtenstein's case (he retained his signature in abstract canvases from the late 1950s and removed it only upon his turn to Pop figuration), but certain of his paintings directly thematize

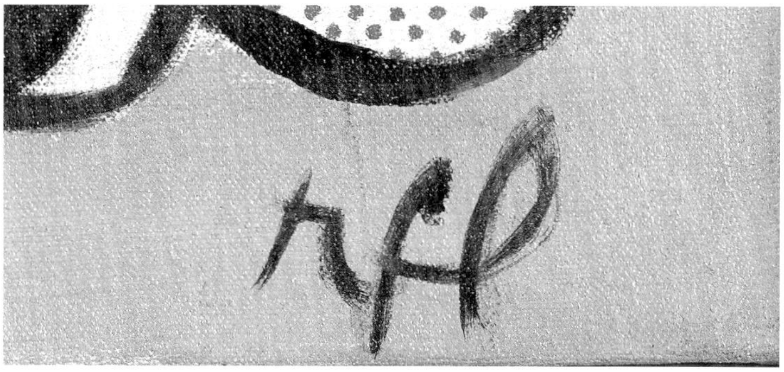

Figure 25. *Wimpy (Tweet),* 1961 (detail of fig. 52)

the signature's absence. This is especially true of the 1964 canvas entitled *Composition I,* a monumental rendering of the cover of an ordinary grammar-school notebook (fig. 26). Lichtenstein produced three versions of the image. Perhaps he returned to the motif several times because it brings together some of the most substantive issues confronted in his work. For one, it embodies the mediation between abstraction and figuration; it replicates the surface of a common, mass-produced consumer object while posing as a so-called all-over abstraction of the type most readily identified with the New York School. In other words, it makes a monumental abstraction out of—or finds abstraction in—a rather banal object from the everyday environment. In addition, the lettering on the object's face allowed Lichtenstein to insert an ironic title into the center of the painting: this is a common composition book transformed into a monumental canvas, and at the same time a painterly composition brought down to the level of a student's notebook. Yet in the context of our current discussion we must consider the implications of the word ("NAME") directly below, and those three horizontal lines which are intended—at least on the cover of an ordinary composition book—for the inscription of the owner's name. In leaving those lines utterly blank Lichtenstein has inscribed a signifying absence—one that circulates around the status of the proper name—into the very center of his painting.

In a 1993 essay Sarat Maharaj called attention to this particular aspect of the *Composition* paintings, citing two later instances in which the blank lines of Lichtenstein's composition books were "signed" or filled in with text (fig. 27).[32] Maharaj attends at length to one of those instances, in which a Spanish artistic duo appropriated Lichtenstein's own borrowed image, inscribing their name—"Equipo Crónica"—and other details into the space Lichtenstein had left blank:

> Literally "writing in" themselves to the empty spot, Equipo Crónica were not so much reversing the piece's stark anonymity with personal signature as inscribing it for the second time. They were spotlighting Lichtenstein's own invisible

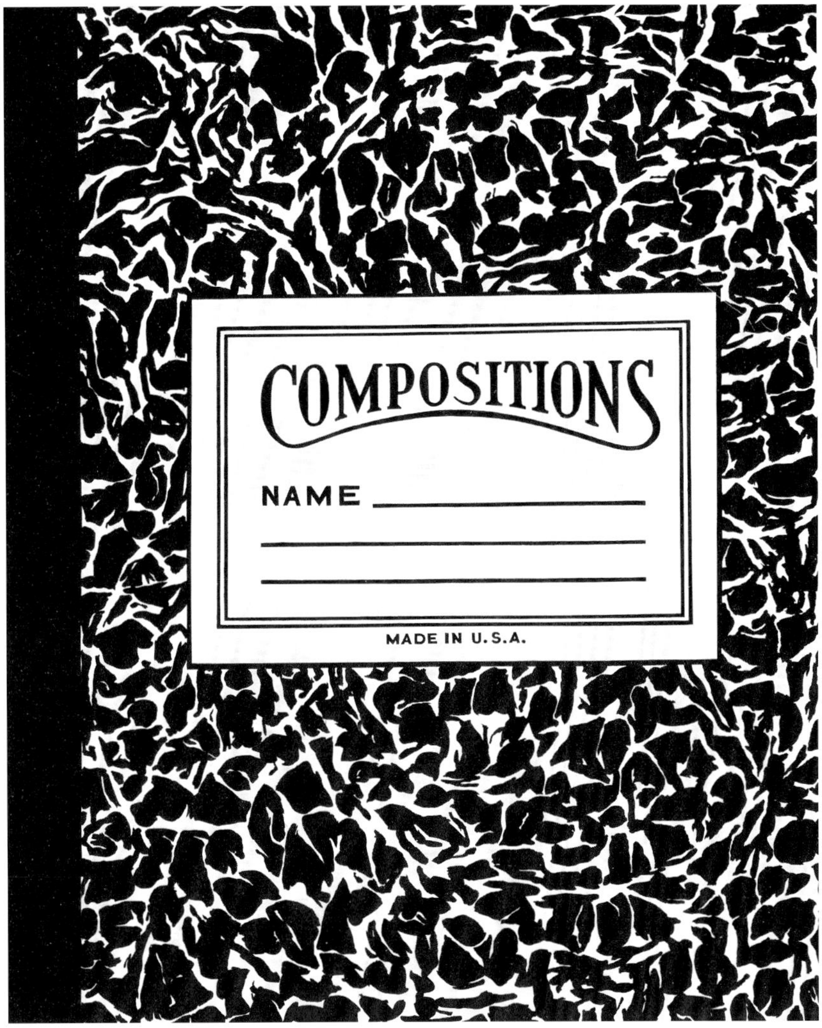

Figure 26.
Composition I, 1964.
Oil and Magna on canvas,
68 × 56 in. (172.7 × 142.2 cm).
Museum für Moderne Kunst,
Frankfurt

> signature—a double-mark in which he had stamped the composition book image with his unmistakable form of seeing, while holding on to its nondescript quality. . . . With each act of inscribing, even Lichtenstein's "own" images come to be lifted, cited and re-cast in fresh compositions and contexts. He appropriates the ready-made image, attaches to it his "proper name."[33]

This "stamping" of the composition book image to which Maharaj refers is precisely the trademarking logic I discussed earlier. Maharaj points out the connection between the removal of the signature and this trademark effect: it is no longer necessary to sign the image, in large part because the form of the work is now understood to be its signature.

However, Lichtenstein's removal of the signature from his canvases did not

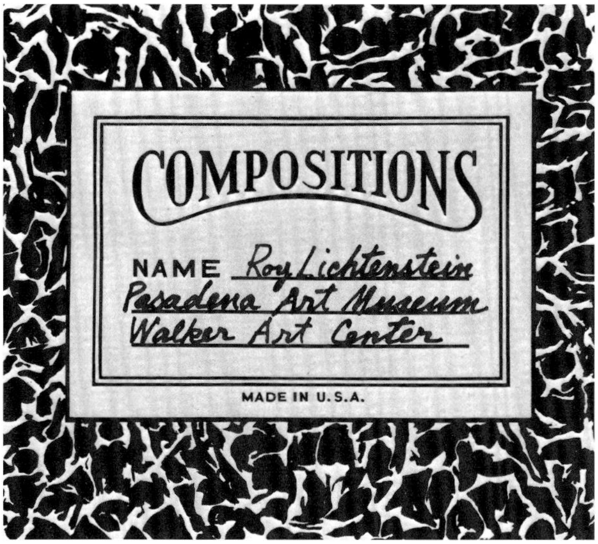

Figure 27.
Cover, *Roy Lichtenstein* exhibition catalogue, Pasadena Art Museum (1967)

occur without incident; it was shadowed by the appearance of another symbol of ownership ubiquitous in late twentieth-century consumer culture. In the lower left corner of *Popeye,* the artist's signature and the date are joined by another element: the distinctive copyright symbol (fig. 28). Here, at the very beginning of Lichtenstein's move into Pop (and before he discarded the signature altogether), he seems to have been searching for an appropriate way to mark the canvas, resulting in a veritable multiplication of marks of ownership. While this is the only instance in which such a conjunction would appear, the copyright symbol appears alone in several paintings, including *Kitchen Range* and *Keds* (fig. 29). At this early stage in his development of a Pop idiom Lichtenstein was attempting to find a motif with which to mark his work yet which would at the same time suggest a connection to commercial culture. However, it was the copyright symbol's very connection to commerce that made its use problematic; like the trademark, it signified a network of economic, social, and juridical relations that were carefully policed and controlled. It is thus unsurprising that Lichtenstein quickly rejected the use of that symbol, perhaps because he realized that the copyright status of his images might be in question.[34] A close examination of his paintings provides evidence that the very ambiguity of the artist's claim to authorship came to be embedded in his work in material form. This is certainly true of the *Composition* paintings, in which the unsigned lines in the center of the canvas serve as a reminder of the absent signature. This is also the case with *Popeye,* although here our attention is drawn not to an absent presence but to the uncanny repetition of marks of ownership. Look at the lower left-hand corner of the painting, just above the multiple marks of copyright, date and signature: the copyright symbol has been clearly reduplicated in the open lid of the can of spinach above it. Finally, *Keds* speaks as well to the irresolution of such marks in the artist's practice. While in most reproductions the circular motif on the sneaker seems devoid of any brand mark, a close examination of the surface of the painting reveals a surprising detail. Within the circle's decorative border an unreadable, ghostly marking is visible—perhaps inscribed by the artist in pencil, perhaps applied in paint and covered by a thin wash (fig. 30). Against the precise articulation of the rest of the painting this faint trace reads like the ghost of a trademark. Here, at a point at which the artist struggled with representing commercial imagery and its effect on the status of the proper name, signs of ownership and identity never seem fully resolved.

These issues are also at stake in Lichtenstein's contemporaneous appropriations of the work of so-called modern masters, specifically Mondrian and Picasso. It has gone unremarked in the critical literature that, among the substantive changes Lichtenstein made in the process of appropriation, he deleted the signatures that those earlier artists had consistently applied to their paintings. However, the logic of his appropriations is that these images are still recognizable as belonging to those earlier artists whether or not their signatures are present. In spite of the profound changes made to Picasso's imagery in a canvas like *Woman with Flowered Hat*—including the drastic reduction of color palette, linearization of composi-

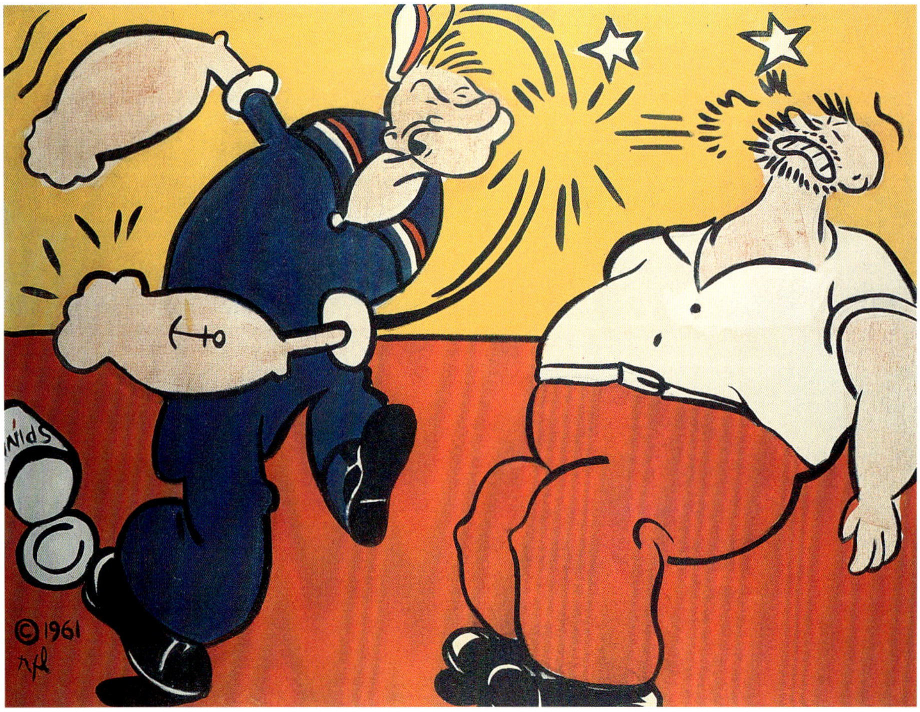

Figure 28.
Popeye, 1961.
Oil on canvas,
42 × 56 in.
(106.7 × 142.2 cm).
Private collection

tional elements, and application of regularized dot patterns (as well as the deletion of the signature and date that had appeared in the lower left of Picasso's painting)—the painting still reads as a "Picasso" (figs. 31, 32). This is in contrast to Lichtenstein's appropriation of comic images discussed earlier in the chapter, in which the recognizable styles of individual comic book illustrators were effectively repressed. But if the painting reads as a Picasso, it also reads simultaneously as a Lichtenstein. Although Diane Waldman has suggested that Lichtenstein's *Femme d'Alger* (another of the artist's Picasso appropriations) "was meant to look like an imitation or cheap reproduction of the original," such a claim is patently inaccurate.[35] Even the cheapest mechanically printed reproduction would look nothing like Lichtenstein's painting, in which Picasso's composition has been completely reorganized according to Lichtenstein's chosen pictorial syntax and aesthetic ma-

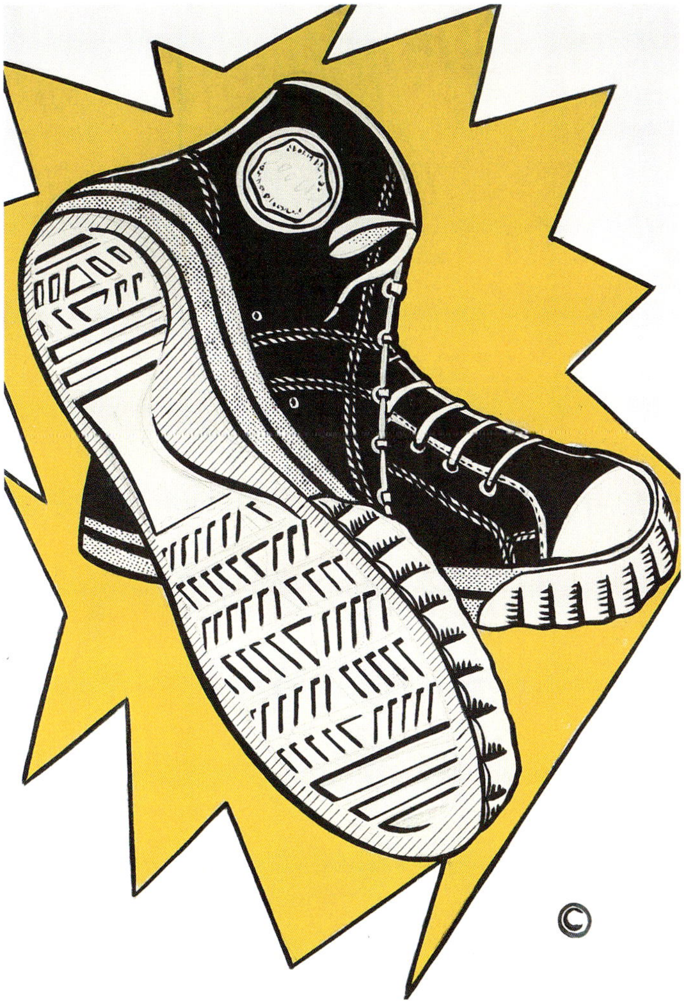

Figure 29.
Keds, 1961.
Oil on canvas,
48½ × 34¾ in.
(123.2 × 88.3 cm).
The Robert B. Mayer
Family Collection,
Chicago

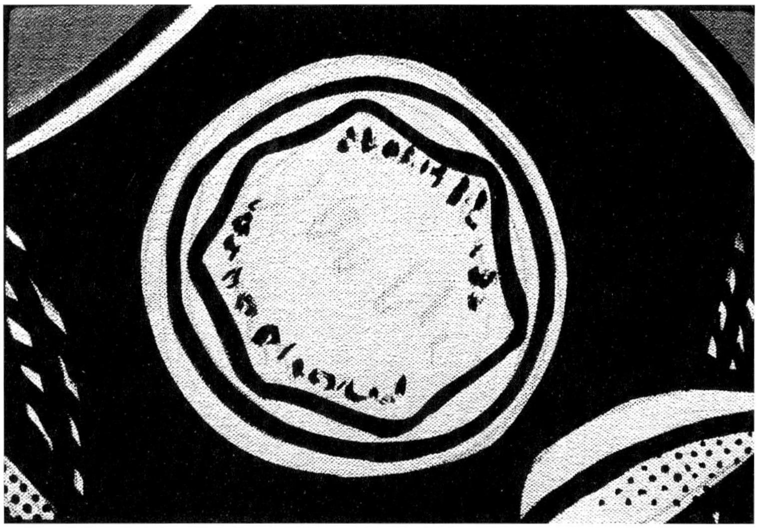

Figure 30.
Keds, 1961
(detail of fig. 29).
The Robert B. Mayer
Family Collection,
Chicago

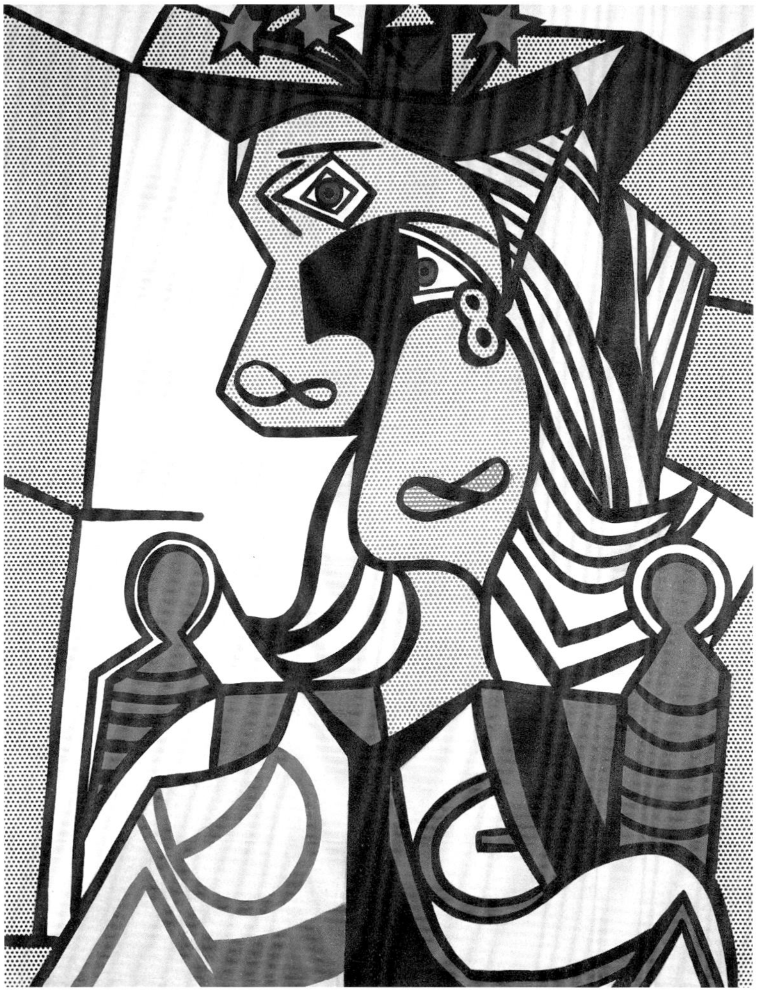

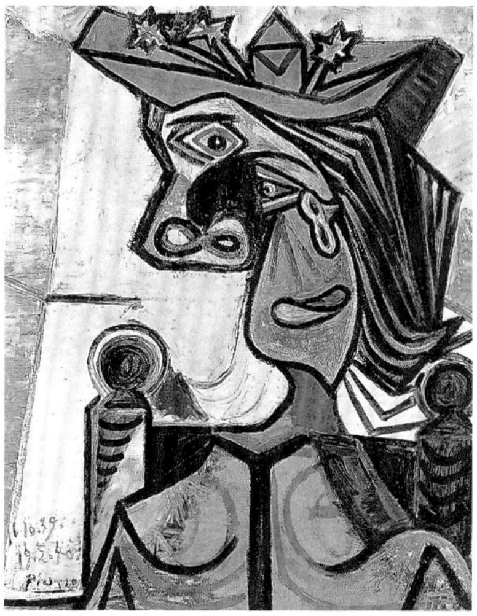

Figure 32.
Pablo Picasso,
Woman with Flowered Hat, 1939–40.
Oil on canvas,
28 × 23 in. (71.1 × 58.4 cm).
Morton G. Neumann Family
Collection

Figure 31.
Woman with Flowered Hat, 1963.
Oil and Magna on canvas,
50 × 40 in. (127 × 101.6 cm).
Private collection

nipulations. (A cheap copy would, of course, retain Picasso's signature as well.) Rather, Lichtenstein has come up with an admittedly provisional response to the age-old problem of artistic influence. The work fundamentally acknowledges the influence of the earlier artist but changes it so substantively that Lichtenstein may now make his own claim to the image. Yet it is a claim that, as I've been suggesting, remained decidedly ambiguous.

Lichtenstein's removal of the signature from his paintings may also signal his recognition of the proximity between, or even equivalence of, signature and brand name. Upon reflection, the artist's signature is something of a blind spot for modernist painting. For all the rhetoric espoused by many modernist painters about the supposed integrity of the picture plane and the purity of forms arrayed on the canvas surface, the viewer is often expected to overlook the signature even as it intrudes into the pictorial field. Some painters avoided this problem by purging the signature from their canvases. Others took quite a different route: they chose to make the signature into something distinct and unique. This was true of Mondrian, who placed his distinctive conjoined "P" and "M" in the lower left corner of one of the "plus-and-minus" paintings that Waldman has cited as a source for Lichtenstein's *Golf Ball* (fig. 33). At an early moment of experimentation with Pop, when Lichtenstein was caught up with the problem of the trademark—or more precisely, with removing it from his paintings—he may very well have recognized the unsettling similarity of trademark and signature. A veritable Derridean recognition *avant la lettre:* that the signature, while always taken as a token of the singularity and uniqueness of the individual's presence at the moment it is inscribed, is dependent on its very iterability.[36] If the engineered and stamped quality of the trademark reeked too much of endless repetition, then so did the signature *as* trademark—especially to an artist who had carefully crafted his own signature as a token of identity, yet who had begun to align his practice with the work of the machine.

Warhol's example again proves instructive, for he not only seems to have recognized the particular paradox of the signature but also proceeded to deconstruct it through various ironic gestures. His name itself is evidence that he recognized the importance of the brand name, even for an artist; in dropping the vowel from the end of his given name—Warhola—he not only anglicized it but made it more distinctive, one of the most important characteristics of a good brand name.[37] His deconstruction of the signature's authenticity occurred even before his move into Pop; throughout the 1950s Warhol had his mother, Julia, sign many of his commercial illustrations in her looping, folksy script. Later in his career he further distanced himself from the signature by having a stamp produced that could be used to "sign" his paintings. These various gestures served to highlight the contradictions inherent in extending the logic of the brand name to the practice of fine art.

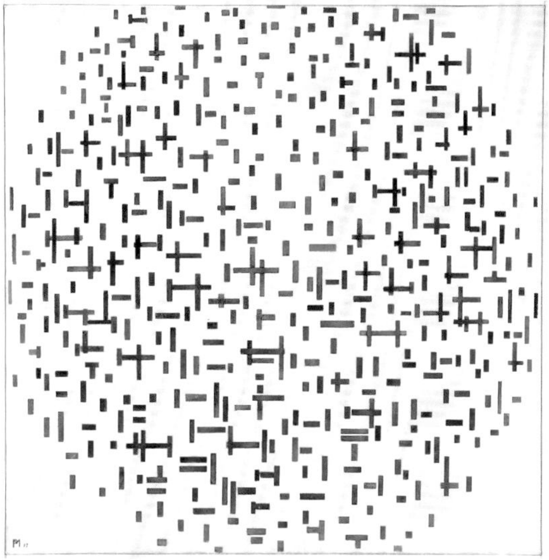

Figure 33.
Piet Mondrian,
Composition in Black and White, 1917.
Oil on canvas,
42½ × 42½ in. (108 × 108 cm).
State Museum Kröller-Müller,
Otterlo, The Netherlands

For in creating that signature-stamp Warhol was parodying the signature's function as proof of the artist's material contact with the surface of the art object. At issue here, then, is the semiological status of the painterly gesture, particularly its indexical component. Richard Shiff has described the trajectory of modernist painting as structured by the relation between index and icon. He argues that initially the aim of modernism was "to fuse iconic appearance to indexical performance."[38] According to Shiff, action painting represented a step away from that original goal, for it marked a moment in which the painter (de Kooning, Pollock, and so forth) attempted to redirect painting away from appearance and toward performance, a mode that captured the ostensibly unique movement of the artist's body. In contrast, says Shiff, Claes Oldenburg and the other Pop artists brought iconicity back to painting as a critical force; the "postmodernism" of the 1950s and 1960s was "an art that openly *represented* indexicality as an iconic sign. The painter's mark was revealed as a sign as unstable as any other, subject to appropriation, imitation, and decontextualization."[39]

For a long time such an analysis has been the basis for reading Lichtenstein's *Brushstroke* paintings as ironic parodies of Abstract Expressionism: they are understood to reveal the ostensibly unmediated indexical gesture of the painter's body as nothing more than an utterly iterable iconic sign (see, for example, fig. 100). Nevertheless, I would argue that in Lichtenstein's work the status of the index itself is as much in question as the shift from indexical to iconic functions. His images correlate the index not with free bodily gesture (as in the rhetoric of action painting) but with repetitive mechanical activity. For example, his 1961 ink drawing *Mail Order Foot* depicts an activity that would appropriately be described as indexical: a hand holding a pencil traces the outline of a foot onto a sheet of paper, while another hand holds a measuring device to assist with the act of tracing (fig. 34). Here, in this scene of rudimentary image making, indexicality is aligned with a kind of rote transcription. There are two other works from this period—*Tire* and *Keds*—that offer similar readings. Certainly, both of these images utilize common objects to comment ironically on the properties of geometric abstraction. In each, however, the identity of the object is expressed by a mark-making surface, whether sneaker print or tire tread.

The case of *Keds* is particularly instructive. We have already seen that the circular logo on the athletic shoe depicted in the painting contains the ghostly trace of a brand name. Within a year of executing the painting, Lichtenstein produced a drawing—also entitled *Keds*—that corresponds quite closely to the earlier painted depiction, although the image has been subjected to a veritable mirror reversal (fig. 35). Here, however, he incorporated a clearly visible name—"leeper"—into the circular logo. Initially, one might consider this a clear embrace of the brand name, and thus a counter-example to the rejection of product logos that we have viewed as a fundamental component of Lichtenstein's practice. However, we need only look to the source for *Keds* in a newspaper advertisement of the time to see that the situation is somewhat more complex (fig. 36). For one, we can see how profoundly he altered the image in order to put it to his own uses. Further, the brand name that serves as the title of both painting and drawing is something of a misidentification, for these were not Keds at all. Lichtenstein appropriated the image from an advertisement for Jeepers, an athletic shoe marketed by Sears Roebuck & Company. The name "leeper" that he inscribed on the shoes in his drawing, then, represents either a misreading of the original product logo or an intentional alteration (the latter is the more probable explanation). He also severed the depiction from the rest of its printed context, not only the graphic illustrations of boys playing at sports but also the advertisement's supporting text. But the most significant alteration is an unexpected one: the shoes have been repositioned, and the rear one (with its sole facing the viewer) has been relocated to the front. The resulting image places far greater visual emphasis on the shoe's sole. Why would Lichtenstein radically restructure the image in this way? If the patterned sole undoubtedly resembles certain geometric abstractions, there is more here than a wry reference to abstract painting. For in both versions of the motif (drawing and painting) Lichtenstein has fundamentally shifted the terms of the object's identity. We have already seen how in works of this period he examined the relation between fine art and commercial culture by comparing different strategies of marking (signature versus trademark) and naming (artist's name versus brand name). In light of this, we could say that the drawing plays on the tension between mark-

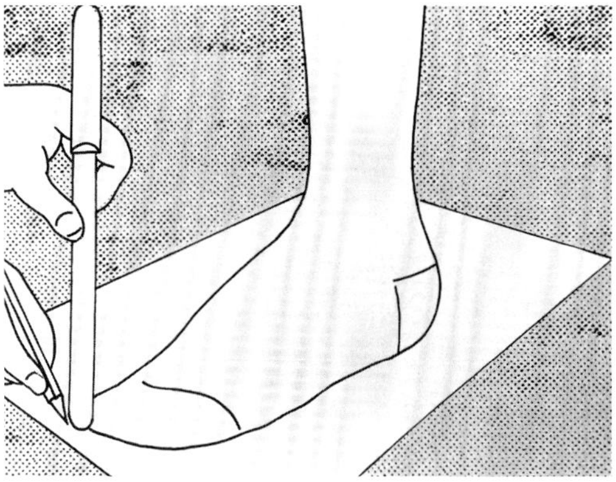

Figure 34. *Mail Order Foot,* 1961.
Ink on paper, 17⅞ × 27⅛ in. (45.4 × 68.9 cm).
Private collection

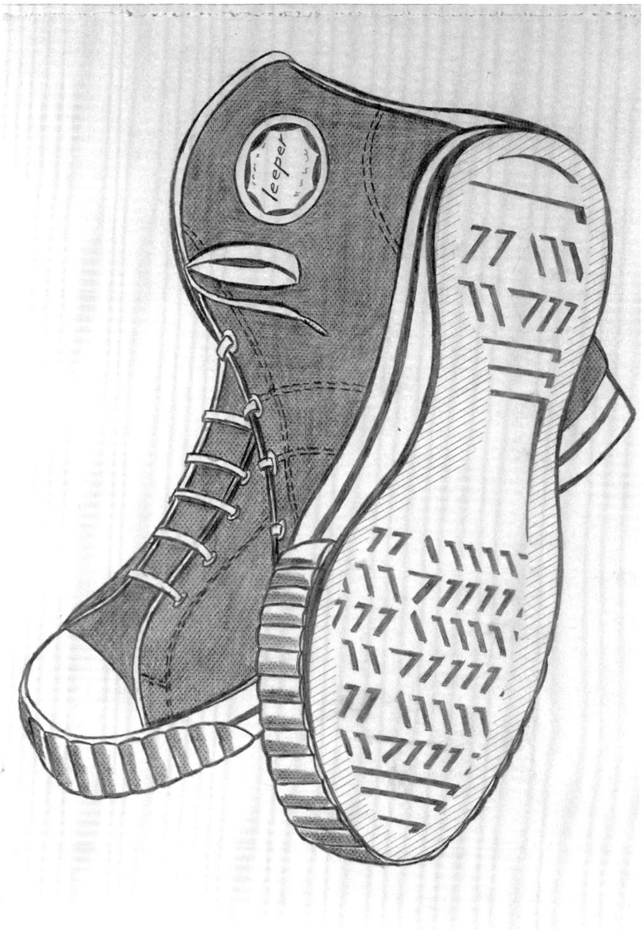

Figure 35. *Keds,* 1962. Pencil and frottage on paper, 22½ × 16½ in. (57.1 × 41.9 cm). Private collection

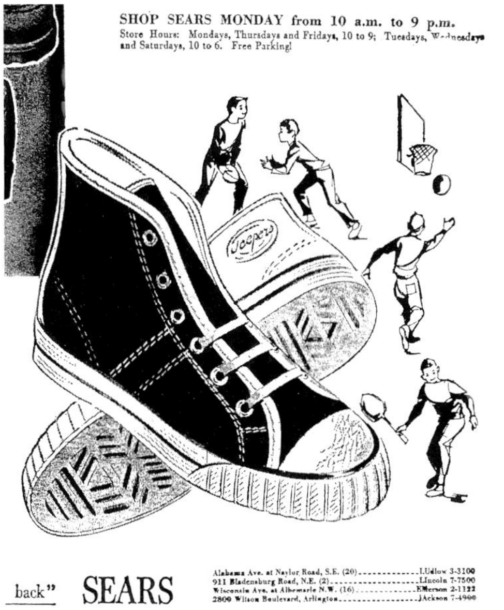

Figure 36. Detail, Sears, Roebuck & Company advertisement, *Washington Post* (April 9, 1961)

ing and naming set up by the consumer object itself: is the sneaker's identity located in the brand name, or in the distinctive print on its sole? Lichtenstein's formal manipulation of the image only draws attention to that patterned sole. Although the advertising illustration strove for a naturalistic depiction, he introduced a degree of naiveté into his drawing, inasmuch as the sneaker print now looks awkwardly aligned with—even pushed up against—the picture plane. Such a sneaker print—like the impression of a tire tread or an outline drawn around a foot—belongs in the category of the indexical mark.

At this time Lichtenstein's experimentation with producing fields of regularized dots had brought him to a set of techniques that directly incorporated indexical marking into his work. In drawings from this period he had begun to utilize frottage (in which the pattern of a raised surface is transferred to a sheet of paper through rubbing) to produce the regularized fields of dots he sought. In some instances, like the drawn version of *Keds,* the dots correspond to raised areas of the underlying surface; in other drawings, like *George Washington,* the dots represent areas in which the surface was perforated (and thus left untouched by the rubbing of the pencil) (fig. 37). There is even one instance in which he used a similar technique in a painting. In *Popeye* he had created the look of regularized dots by dragging a lightly loaded brush across the surface of the painting, thus picking up the weave of the canvas. In this way, if the dots used in his work are often erroneously referred to by critics as "Ben Day dots," their origin in the artist's working method also links them to the indexical interaction between the painter's hand and the surface of the canvas.[40]

Lichtenstein's work foregrounds the instability of the index as it had been deployed in the rhetoric of Abstract Expressionism. The movement of the brush not only captures the painter's gesture but also records the texture of the canvas beneath; thus at the same time the index registers the artist's presence it also signifies the obdurate materiality of the object—an object that leaves a regularized and repeatable mark, like that of a tire print or sneaker tread. Lichtenstein's engagement with such concerns can be placed within a larger historical shift in the status of the index in art-making practices. In analyzing this shift, Rosalind Krauss argued that in a substantial segment of abstract art from the 1970s "photography has increasingly become the operative model for abstraction."[41] She charts that development through the growing tendency for artists in that period to use modes of indexical signification in their work:

> The pressure to use indexical signs as a means of establishing presence begins in Abstract-Expressionism with deposits of paint expressed as imprints and traces. During the 1960s, this concern was continued although changed in its import in, for example, the work of Jasper Johns and Robert Ryman. This development forms a historical background for the phenomenon I am describing as belonging to 1970s art. However, it must be understood that there is a decisive break between earlier attitudes toward the index and those at present, a break that has to do with the role played by the photographic, rather than the pictorial, as a model.[42]

Lichtenstein's practice stands poised at the site of the very "break" described by Krauss; his work represents an uneasy intermingling between photographic and

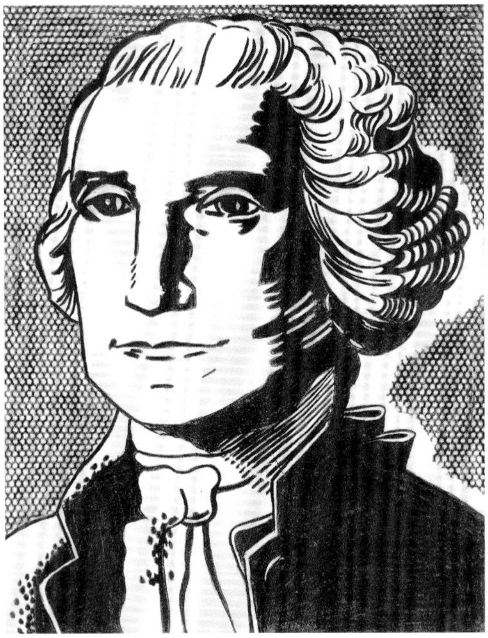

Figure 37. *George Washington,* 1962. Pencil and frottage on paper, 14⁹⁄₁₆ × 11¼ in. (37 × 28.6 cm). Private collection

pictorial models, with the pictorial tending to win out. Certain of his images (like *Mail-Order Foot* and *Keds*) reference the possibility of automatic marking, and his formal devices mimic the stamped quality of mechanical printing techniques, yet his work never completely embraces the mechanical function of the index, which Krauss sees as emerging fully only in art of the 1970s.[43] In his work the painter's hand would not be given over fully to the automatic stamp of the machine. Or, in Lichtenstein's own words: "I am not against industrialization, but it must leave me something to do."[44]

At least one contemporary critic seems to have picked up on Lichtenstein's engagement with the index and its relation to mechanical reproduction. Max Kozloff began a 1963 article critical of Lichtenstein—and Pop in general—with the following anecdote:

> In 1926 Roger Fry . . . conducted a famous experiment. Placing his tracing of a Paul Klee line drawing next to a reproduction of the original, Fry nicely demonstrated that the "art" of Klee, even in something so elementary as a few pen marks, consisted of their scratchy, wiry testimony to the nervous pressure of the artist's hand—a fact clearly shown by Fry's exact but lifeless copy. Quite recently, in 1963, a New York artist, Roy Lichtenstein, exhibited a canvas which magnifies a linear diagram of a Cézanne. Because he has changed merely the scale and context of his motif, rather than its linear quality, Lichtenstein performs a

> *volte-face* on the Fry incident, and subverts its meaning. Mechanical reproduction, so culpable for Fry, and overtly utilitarian for the author of the Cézanne diagram, Erle Loran, is—we are obliged to think—"artistic" for Lichtenstein.[45]

In the course of roundly criticizing the artist, Kozloff seems to have recognized on some level that the status of the index was being contested in Lichtenstein's work, caught—as he precisely lays out the tension—between the aesthetic and the mechanical. Yet his description of the Fry incident contains a striking aporia that gets to the heart of the problem around which Lichtenstein's project circulates. Kozloff's account is strangely ambiguous: when he writes of "Fry's exact but lifeless copy" is he referring to the tracing or the printed reproduction? We are unsure which copy comes closer to purveying the magical presence of the artist's hand: the one traced by Fry or that produced by the machine?

It is tempting to see the embrace of mechanical facture and effacement of the signature in Lichtenstein's work as merely reflecting a broader historical shift in modes of authorship. Cultural historians have tracked the evolution of models of authorship in the twentieth century, from more traditional notions of the creative act arising primarily from the author's originality, to a model more closely aligned with the trademark, in which the author or artist is treated more like a corporate brand name than an originating subject.[46] Yet the evidence demonstrates that Lichtenstein's practice cannot be considered as merely reflecting broader cultural developments. Rather, it draws attention to and flags the very tensions that accrue between divergent models of authorial identity. In this way his work does not embody the postmodern "death of the author" in any clear-cut way. His Pop paintings express a great deal more ambivalence: they represent the artist's clinging to notions of originality and creativity in the face of his incorporation of the mechanical into his practice. Lichtenstein's work explores the possibility of opening up some space for the artist, and the creative act, within mechanical repetition. It also addresses a corollary concern: whether the artist—and more broadly the subject—can ever be thought unique, or is merely the product of repetition. His grappling with that problem is no less in evidence than in the fate of a proposed series of portraits he began to execute in 1962. As it was planned, each painting in the series was to have utilized the same stenciled image—a young man in jacket and bow tie—yet was to have borne the name of a different one of the artist's friends and associates. Diane Waldman reports that Lichtenstein "produced two identical portraits, one entitled *Portrait of Ivan Karp* and the other *Portrait of Allan Kaprow* and wearied of the idea before completing the projected ten other versions" (figs. 38 and 39).[47] It seems that even the suggestion of a duplication of the individual—a possibility that his colleague Andy Warhol embraced with the utmost enthusi-

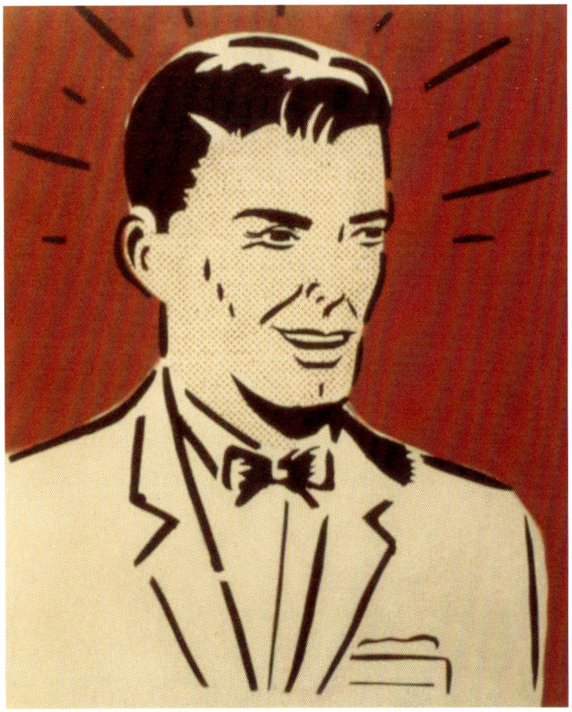

Figure 38. *Portrait of Ivan Karp,* 1961.
24 × 20 in. (61 × 50.8 cm). Private collection

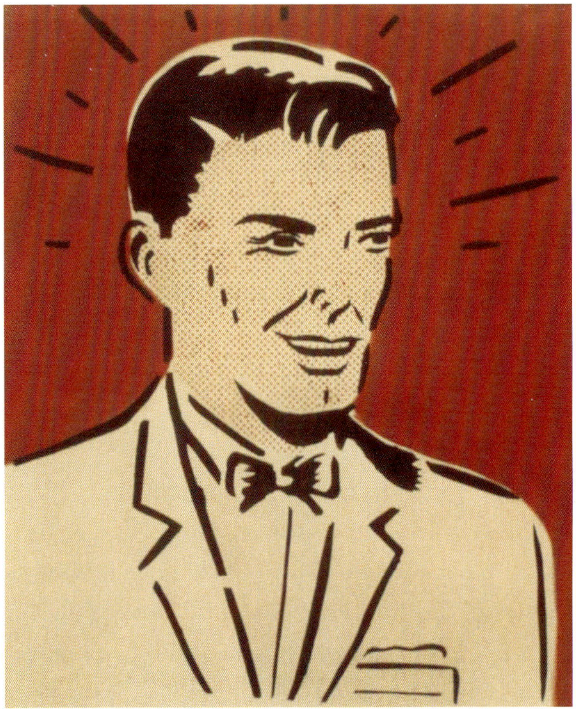

Figure 39. *Portrait of Allan Kaprow,* 1961.
24 × 20 in. (61 × 50.8 cm). Private collection

asm—was something Lichtenstein would not abide. And in this case that repetition would have only been emphasized by the similarity of the men's surnames (*Karp* and *Kaprow*). Writing on Pop, Roland Barthes summarized the problem that seems to have prevented Lichtenstein from completing the projected series: "Repetition of the portrait induces an adulteration of the person (a notion simultaneously civic, moral, psychological, and of course historical)."[48] It was precisely Lichtenstein's continued commitment to the notion of the "person"—of the unique and creative individual—that was at issue in his work.

Lichtenstein's ambivalent approach to the issue of authorship—especially as it relates to his representation of consumer objects—is particularly apparent in a self-portrait he executed in 1978 (fig. 40). By the time he produced this painting his style had changed somewhat from that of the early 1960s: he had adopted a slightly more diverse palette, had begun to employ patterns utilizing dots of varying sizes, and was using diagonal lines (in addition to dots) as a formal motif in his canvases. In this self-portrait a T-shirt substitutes for his torso, and his head is replaced by a rectangular mirror—a reference to his *Mirror* paintings from the early 1970s. The painting seems to signify an almost total self-effacement, not only in

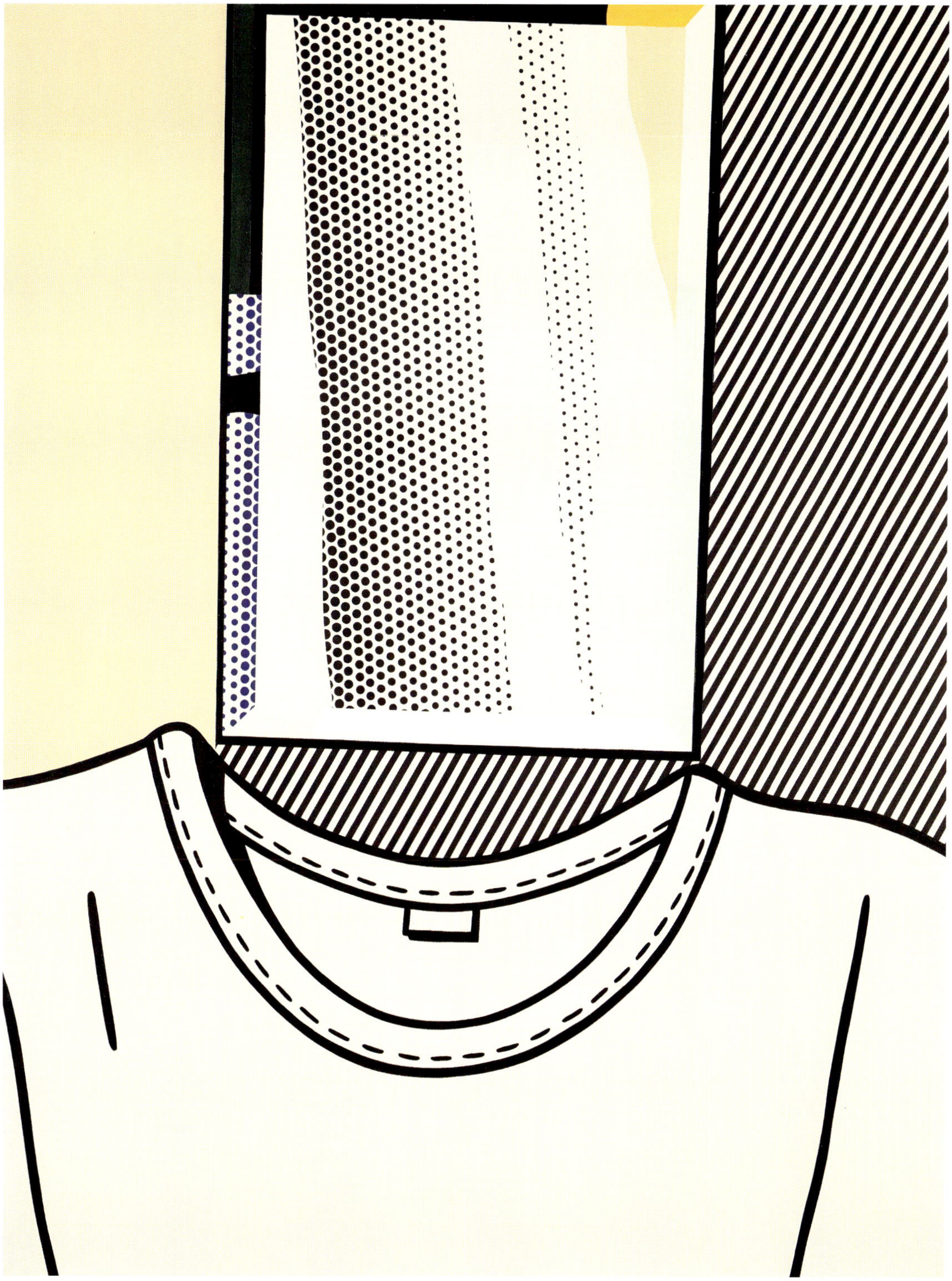

Figure 40. *Self-Portrait,* 1978. Oil and Magna on canvas, 70 × 54 in. (177.8 × 137.1 cm). Private collection

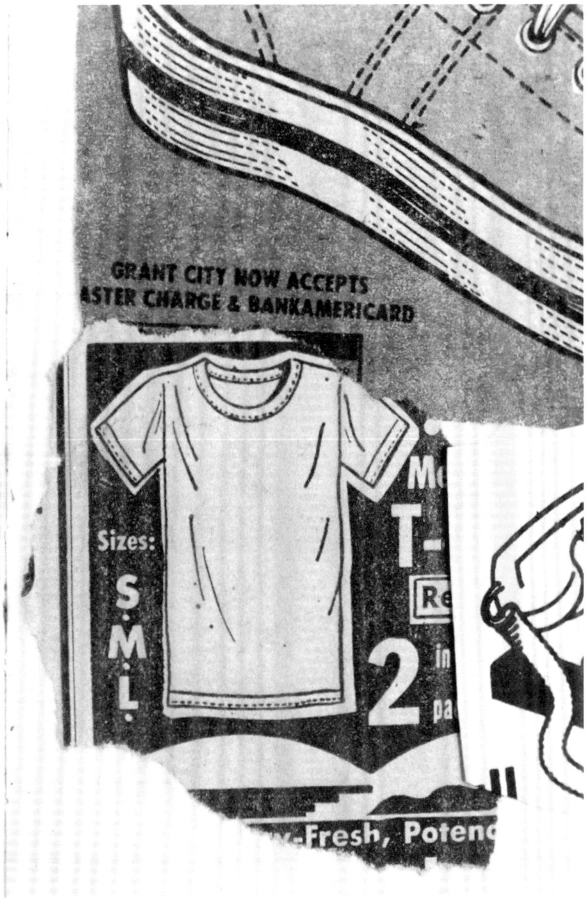

Figure 41.
Detail of page from Roy Lichtenstein's source notebooks

the ostensive blankness of the mirror but in the emptiness of the T-shirt as well. Although this is admittedly a later self-portrait, in it Lichtenstein looked back to his practice of the early 1960s, inasmuch as the painting makes central use of yet another common object. In fact, he pasted what seems to have been the source for that T-shirt into one of his notebooks, alongside other images of consumer objects that served him as inspiration or reference (fig. 41).[49] If we compare that source with the T-shirt motif in *Self-Portrait,* one subtle yet significant difference becomes apparent: in his painting the artist took care to add a small label inside the shirt's collar. Like the blank lines in his *Compositions* paintings that label has been left free of any mark of name, trademark, or logo; in other words, Lichtenstein has inscribed a signifying absence into the work. Yet if *Self-Portrait* seems to constitute a clear-cut effacement of the author, it contains another element that prevents such a straightforward reading. If the artist's substitution of a mirror for his head and face suggests that he saw himself as a smooth, reflective surface—a literal image duplicator—we must remember that this is a mirror only within the fiction of the painting. In fact, it is nothing more than a rectangular form framing a group of pictorial codes (regularized dot screens, thick outlines, and flat expanses of color) that by that time had come to signify none other than "Roy Lichtenstein." In this way, like the rest of the artist's work, the painting oscillates between an erasure of the self and an attempt—however conflicted or provisional—to reconstitute a semblance of authorial presence.

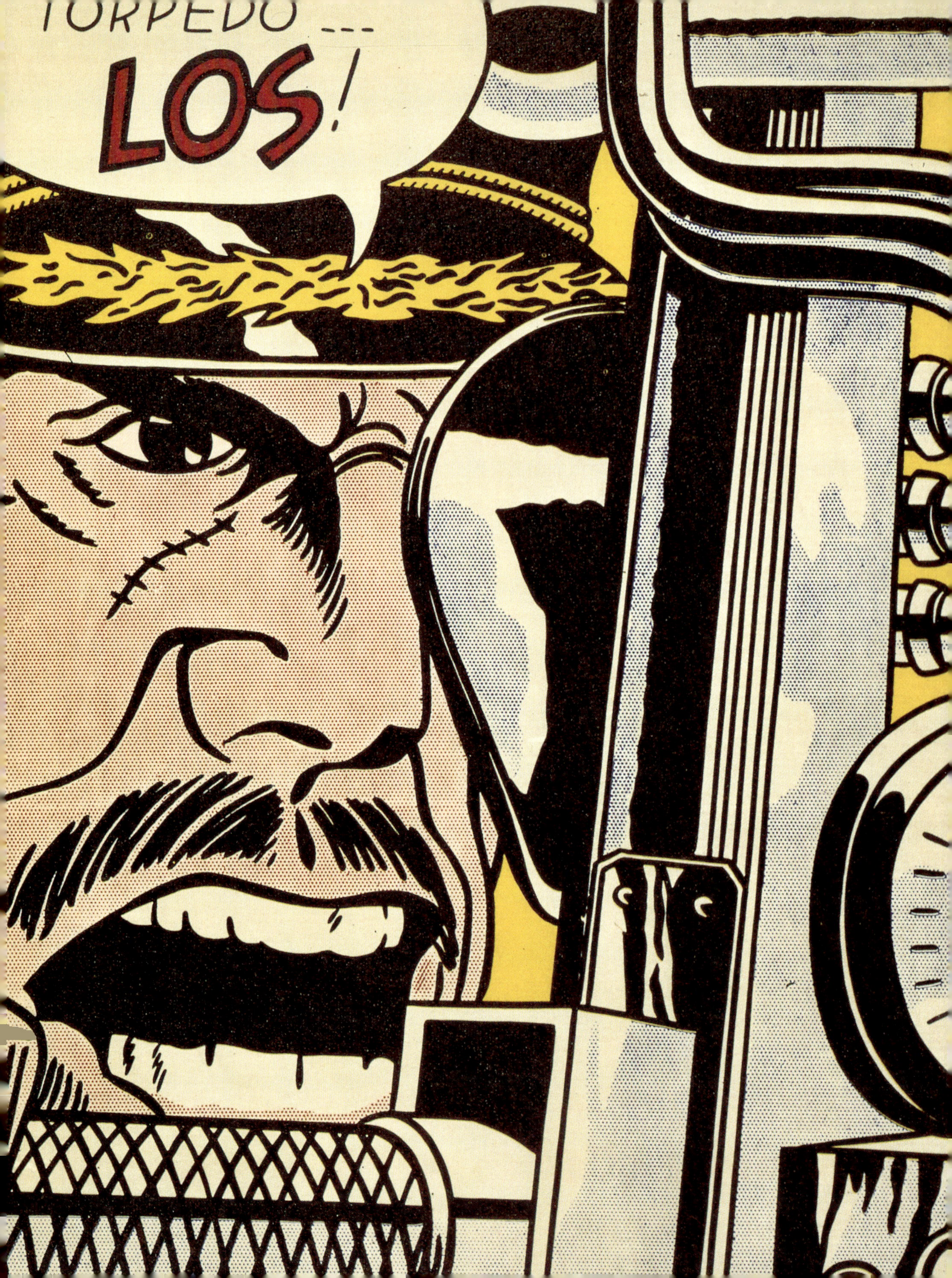
TORPEDO ...
LOS!

Technology Envisioned: Lichtenstein's Monocularity

In the summer of 1961, soon after beginning his experimentation with Pop, Lichtenstein executed a large canvas entitled *I Can See the Whole Room! . . . And There's Nobody In It!* (fig. 42). In the painting an outstretched finger pushes aside the cover of a circular peephole, revealing the face of a male figure; a word balloon above displays the lines of text that make up the painting's title. Lichtenstein appropriated the image from the final panel of a *Steve Roper* Sunday newspaper comic strip that had shown the character Mike Nomad inspecting a locked room through a peephole (fig. 43). The move from comic strip panel to canvas has a significant effect on the meaning of the image: removed from its narrative context and presented as an easel painting it reads as a visual pun on abstraction, for if one imagines that peephole swinging closed the painting is read projectively as a monochrome canvas. A black canvas, that is, which recalls the roughly contemporaneous work of abstract painters Ad Reinhardt and Frank Stella.[1] In this way Lichtenstein offers a scene in which the monochrome has been quite literally punctured by both figuration and language: a fitting image for an artist who had recently discarded an abstract mode for a figurative one. Moreover, a slight change in the text has altered the image's relation to the viewer as well. The exclamatory text in the original panel had been addressed to Trooper, another character in the comic strip narrative. With the name removed from the word balloon, the text now makes a direct address to the viewer: it effectively erases the painting's implied viewing position, at least in terms of the observation that "THERE'S NOBODY IN IT!" The figure looks directly out from the canvas, but sees no one.

I Can See the Whole Room is, fundamentally, a painting about vision. It foregrounds the act of looking on various levels: in the figure that stares out from the very center of the painting; in the title (displayed in the word balloon above), with its reference to seeing; and in its engagement with—and strange erasure of—us as viewers. In fact, we will see how the work points not merely to visuality as a central

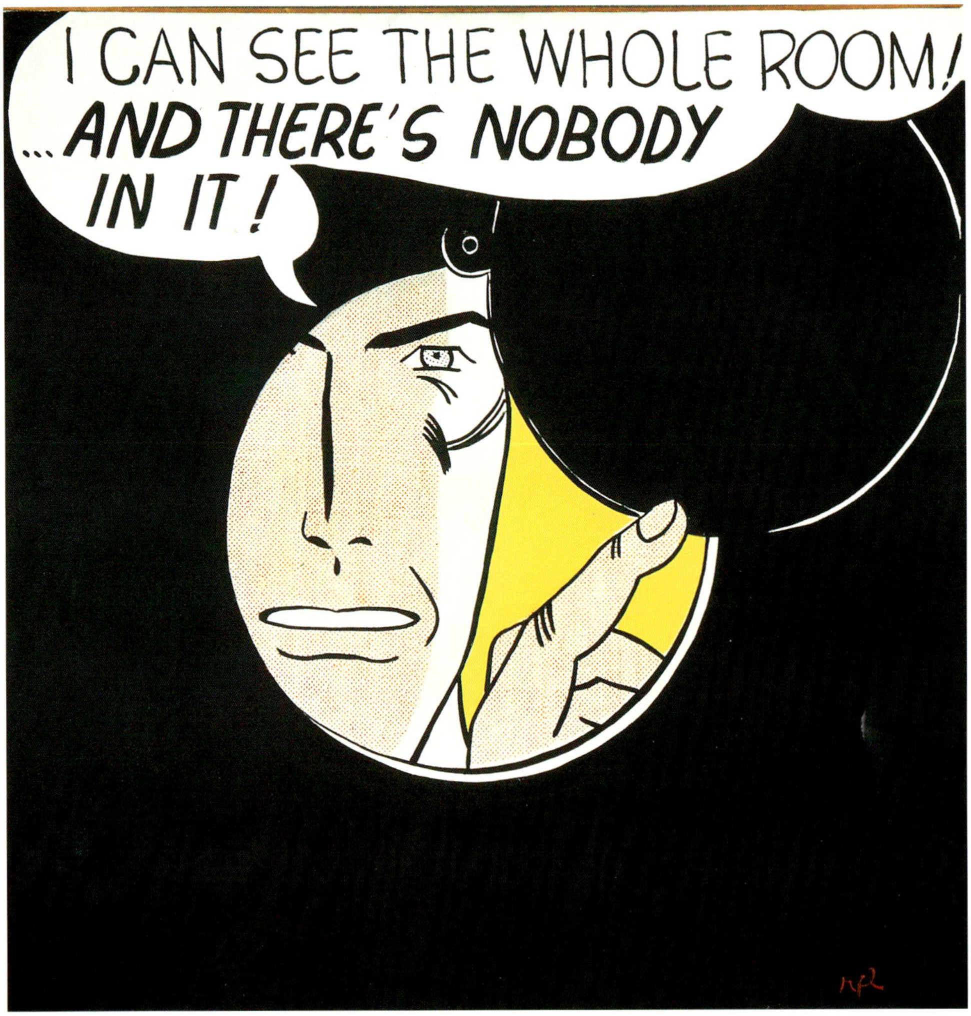

Figure 42. *I Can See the Whole Room! . . . And There's Nobody In It!*, 1961.
Oil and graphite on canvas, 48⅜ × 48 in. (122.7 × 121.8 cm). Private collection

thematic of the artist's work, but more specifically to the relation between embodied vision and machines. If Lichtenstein was concerned in the early 1960s with the problem of imaging the consumer object, at the same time he also undertook a sustained consideration of the possibilities offered and problems posed by visual technologies. A close examination of his work from this period demonstrates the conflicted nature of his investigation into these issues. To better understand the basis of such concerns in his practice, we need to consider his early studies with Professor Hoyt Sherman, who had developed a unique program of art instruction through training in vision.

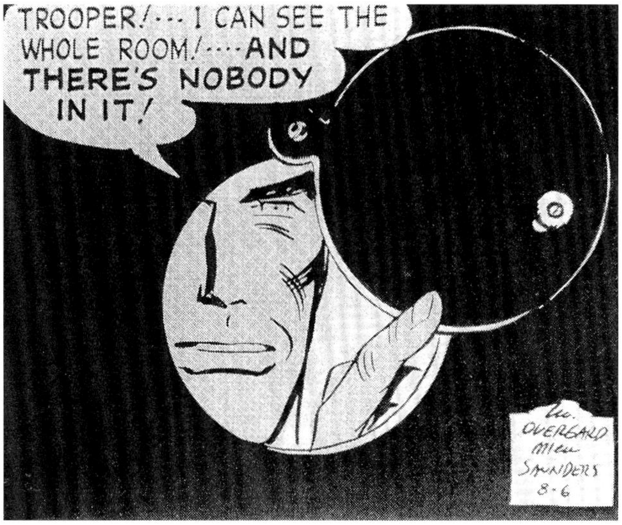

Figure 43.
Saunders and Overgard, panel from *Steve Roper* (August 6, 1961)

MONOCULARITY: BODY AS MACHINE

According to Lichtenstein, his first prolonged, intensive training in art came when he began his undergraduate studies at Ohio State University and came under Sherman's tutelage.[2] By all accounts Sherman seems to have cut a striking figure of authority, one who was engaged in developing a sweeping program for testing and training visual acuity. What his project lacked in theoretical rigor it made up for in sheer spectacle; in addition to various published texts Sherman instituted his program in two veritable laboratories for testing and training visual perception. His Visual Demonstration Center was a room-size collection of fifteen models and displays that demonstrated various principles of visual perception, particularly optical illusions.[3] Its format had been appropriated from a similar set of demonstrations built by Adelbert Ames Jr. at Princeton University and at the Hanover Eye Institute in New Hampshire. One representative display was the "Distorted Room," which was built in forced perspective so that the room appeared square even though its back wall stood at a marked angle. An illustration from Sherman's handbook for the Visual Demonstration Center showed the effect of that illusion when people were posed behind the windows on that angled wall; the room and back wall looked square, yet one of the figures appeared inexplicably smaller than the other (fig. 44).

In other words, the display was meant to show how past experience (in this case, that rooms are square) infringed on the viewer's ability to perceive the true nature of this particular room. While its name would seem to indicate that the Visual

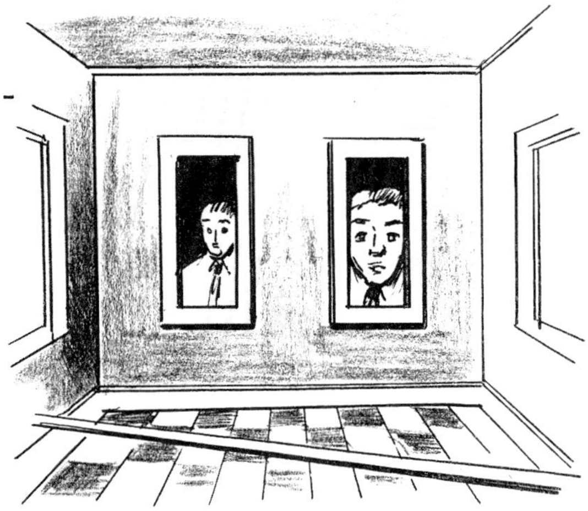

Figure 44. Illustration from Hoyt Sherman, *The Visual Demonstration Center* (1951)

Demonstration Center was a series of mechanisms for demonstrating essential properties of visual perception, it would be more accurate to describe it as a series of tests that demonstrated the failures or deficiencies of vision. Sherman intended to show the viewer how various components of the perceptual process (such as binocular vision or the individual's prior knowledge of objects in the world) infringed on the possibility of an ostensibly pure—that is to say, unmediated—perception of the visual field.

In contrast, the dream of access to an idealized mode of aesthetic vision was embodied in another segment of Sherman's grand project, in which he used the tachistoscope to create a unique program of instruction in drawing. That program took place in a specially constructed seventy-foot-long studio (converted from a former artillery shed on OSU's campus) from which all exterior light sources had been sealed off. Inside, students sat in front of drawing tables on four terraces facing a series of projection screens (figs. 45, 46):

> Above and slightly behind the terraced section of the space was a "bridge" containing a massive slide projector. Sherman had fitted this device with a "tachistoscope," a mechanical shutter, first devised by late-nineteenth-century psychologists, that made it possible for him to control the duration of a slide projection within a fraction of a second. . . . After ten minutes of relaxation and preparation [at the beginning of class] had passed, Sherman would show the first of the twenty slides he would use in each class; or rather he would "flash" it, since it appeared on screen for a tenth of a second or less. Cast again in darkness for the remainder of a minute, the students would draw the configuration they had barely glimpsed, depending mainly on the afterimage.[4]

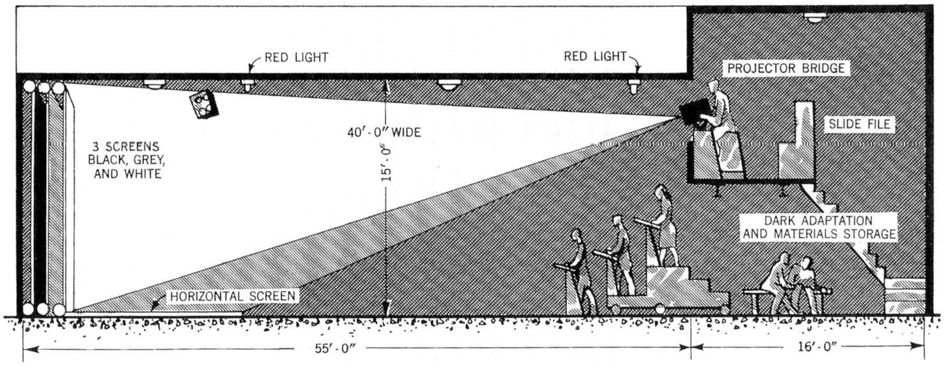

Figure 45. Cross section of the flash lab, from Hoyt Sherman, *Drawing by Seeing* (1947)

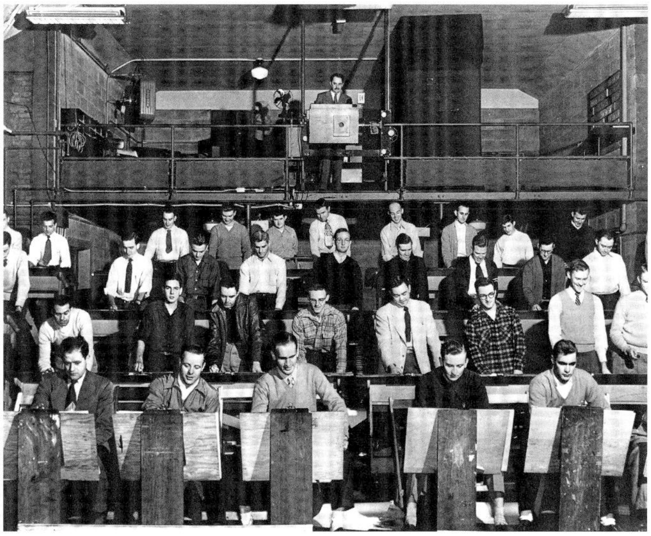

Figure 46. Students in the flash lab, Ohio State University, c. 1949

The course continued over the semester, with the duration of the flash eventually lengthening and the subjects of study moving from Sherman's own two-dimensional abstract configurations (projected onto a screen) to complex three-dimensional still-life groupings. According to Sherman's theoretical program, the speed of the flash prevented the student from exercising any power of composition or intellection; this was intended to help the student see the image instead with "perceptual unity"—that is, as pure form (a concept Sherman derived largely from Gestalt theory). Moreover, he called this process "drawing by seeing" in order to emphasize the automatic nature of the act: the drawing would be a kinaesthetic trace of the afterimage that had been left—in a flash—on the student's retina.[5]

It is clear that Sherman's systematic approach to artistic instruction had a significant impact on Lichtenstein. While the artist never took a full course of instruction in the flash lab, he taught in the lab between 1946 and 1949. After leaving Ohio State, Lichtenstein attempted to reconstruct the flash lab on two separate occasions: during a subsequent teaching stint at the State University of New York at Oswego, and as an assistant professor of art at Douglass College. Bruce Breland, a colleague of Lichtenstein's at Oswego, has recounted: "Roy and I taught the freshman design course. Roy did the two-dimensional part which he called painting and drawing. I did the three-dimensional part which I called sculpture. Roy immediately installed the Hoyt Sherman flashroom technique."[6] Likewise, Allan Kaprow recalls that "Roy continued Sherman's work in his courses at Rutgers. He built a small strobe projector for that purpose."[7] In an interview with the author, Lichtenstein confirmed Kaprow's recollections. When asked "Had you constructed [a flash lab set-up] yourself?" Lichtenstein responded:

> Yes, but I mean it was really primitive, because in the flash room they really got rid of light altogether. It's almost impossible to get rid of light in a room by pulling the shades down or something. . . . I would flash the thing, but of course you can also see what you're doing, which you couldn't do in the flash room. . . . But even though it didn't have the same effect, it was something anyway, and I tried to explain that if you . . . actually, if you show a series of flashes you go kind of blind to the stuff in between because the flash changes the aperture of your retina . . . I mean your eye. So it's a little effective, you know, but I wish that I could build one—they're quite hard to do, because it's rare that you can really cut all the light out.[8]

It is telling that Lichtenstein's aside in that last sentence—"I wish that I could build one"—was formulated in the present tense, despite the span of almost fifty years between his undergraduate training and the time of the interview.

Sherman's influence on Lichtenstein has been cited repeatedly in treatments of the artist's work, in part because of Lichtenstein's own assertion (when interviewed in 1963 by Gene Swenson) that "the ideas of Professor Hoyt Sherman [at Ohio State University] on perception were my earliest important influence and still affect my ideas of visual unity."[9] The literature on the artist has generally taken this statement at face value, as if Sherman's effect on his pupil was somehow direct and unmediated. However, if Lichtenstein's work was "influenced" by his training, that influence was by no means uncomplicated, for it was embedded in a profoundly ambivalent project. David Deitcher has pointed to the tension in Sherman's program:

> At the same time, then, that Sherman followed the transcendentalist impulse familiar from the discourse of Abstract Expressionist and other modernist art, he was also determined to supply his students with the means to function more

efficiently, and with a greater sense of "integration." In short, his course acknowledged the productive imperative that dominated American life more than ever at the dawn of the late-capitalist consumer culture.[10]

Although I might differ with Deitcher's historical conclusions, his account does make clear the aporia at the heart of Sherman's project. While Sherman's goal was to impart the means to an aesthetic way of seeing, the idealist premise of his project was undercut by—or at least in profound tension with—its mechanistic means.

It is Lichtenstein himself who provides further insight into this particular problematic, one located in the flash lab's imbrication of body and machine. Reminiscing in 1987 about his training at Ohio State, Lichtenstein recalled that in the flash lab "you'd get a very strong afterimage, a total impression, and then you'd draw it in the dark—the point being that you'd have to sense where the parts were in relation to the whole. The images became progressively more complex, and eventually you would go out and try to work the same way elsewhere—would try to bring the same kind of sensing to your drawing without the mechanical aid of the flash room."[11] Yet to do so—that is, to "try to work the same way elsewhere"—would imply that the work of the machine had already been incorporated into one's body.

There was a tension in Sherman's project between its humanistic rhetoric about the individual's capacities for aesthetic vision and its attempt to ground those capacities in mechanical processes. Sherman had developed his drawing-by-seeing program in order to provide students access to the perceptual abilities presumably possessed by "great masters" like Cézanne. Yet the means to that end was for the student to become—through the shock of a flash of light—a machine that recorded the visual field without the intrusion of cognition or intellection. As Lichtenstein points out, the flash lab was intended to increase the individual's visual acuity. It was designed to help the student repress the prior knowledge that prods us to differentiate elements in the perceptual field and read them as things, objects, or bodies in space; in other words, it was intended to transform the subject into a machine that might record nothing but pure visual form. There is, of course, a name for a machine like this, one that presumably records the play of forms in the visual field "perfectly," without the intrusion of a human subjectivity that might muddy that visual record: the camera.

For all its rhetoric of imparting "aesthetic vision," Sherman's instructional program in the flash lab more or less placed the student in the position of the photographic apparatus. Students were placed in a completely darkened chamber (*camera obscura*); exposed to a flash of light; led to believe that an afterimage had been left by that flash on their retinas (as if on a photographic plate); and expected to draw that image automatically (in Sherman's own words, "kinaesthetically") on the sheets of paper in front of them. The flash lab even incorporated elements from the photographic developing process, as described in a passage in *Drawing by Seeing* devoted to describing the flash lab's equipment: "For illumination during the dark-adaptation period, a red light is set in the ceiling over the drawing stands. This light is the regular darkroom lamp used in photography. It proves to be a convenience when students drop their chalk, run out of paper, or otherwise need to locate an object during the blackout period."[12] Did Lichtenstein recognize the extent to which Sherman's program pushed the student's body toward the condition of the photographic apparatus? An answer to that question may be found, in part, by looking back to *I Can See the Whole Room.* Note that the work presents a scenario in which the viewing subject is located in a darkened room with a hole in one wall—in other words, a camera obscura.[13] Yet on reflection this description is not entirely accurate. For one, the camera obscura generally uses a smaller hole—even at times a pinhole—to produce its image, quite unlike the large opening depicted in the painting. More significantly, that opening has been outfitted with a circular cover that swivels back and forth; another name for that device would be a *shutter.* Lichtenstein's painting thus constructs for us a schematic view of a primitive photographic mechanism.[14] In this way it provided the artist a vehicle through which to confront certain problems raised by Sherman's program of training in modernist aesthetic vision. Sherman certainly recognized that the drawings of each student would have a personal or individual style (in *Drawing by Seeing* he expressed his belief that these differences should in fact be encouraged).[15] Nevertheless, Lichtenstein seems to have responded most strongly to the extreme mechanization of vision presented in his teacher's project. Its instrumentalization of the body suggested not that individuality was being prized, but rather that in the shock of the flash the student's subjectivity was effectively erased as he or she became a machine for recording visual stimuli. This may give further meaning to the figure's declaration in Lichtenstein's painting, which suggests not only that there is "nobody," but also more pointedly no body, within the confines of that darkened chamber.

In *I Can See the Whole Room* the relation between machine and embodied vision is condensed into one particularly charged element: the motif of monocularity.[16] For one, monocular vision stands for the photographic apparatus itself: this much is clear in the artist's depiction of the central peephole, which pierces the darkened chamber of that primitive photographic mechanism. The single exposed eye of the figure peering through that hole rhymes with the monocular format of the camera lens. This was not the first time a monocular presentation of the human body had been used to imply a rhyming (or competition) with the lens of the camera; in fact, an earlier example provides a useful model for understanding

Sherman's project. In an essay on Jean-Martin Charcot's late-nineteenth-century photographs of hysterics, Ulrich Baer has called our attention to an image of Hortense J., one of Charcot's patients (fig. 47). As Baer points out, "Hortense's symptom imitates the photographic apparatus: her light sensitivity, the squinted eye, catalepsy—the hysteric's face mimics the camera and the cameraman."[17] Charcot's project is of use to us as a precedent for Sherman's scientistic attempt to align the human body with the photographic apparatus. Baer outlines what he calls a "poetics of the flash" through an analysis of Charcot's 1880s photographs of hysterics at the Salpêtrière hospital in Paris. Charcot had attempted to use photography, in conjunction with the mechanism of the flash, as an aid to the diagnosis of hysteria. Placed in a darkened room, his patients were exposed to a flash of light that froze them in a pose (to be later categorized as "hysterical") that could be photographed by one of his assistants. Although there are marked differences (historical, cultural, theoretical) between Charcot's and Sherman's projects, the two are linked inasmuch as both employed the flash to forge a conjunction between the camera and the body. On Charcot's cataleptic patients, Baer writes:

> Catalepsy retains by way of the body what photography retains by way of the camera: it freeze-frames and *retains* the body in an isolated position that can be viewed and theorized outside of a sequence of motion. . . . The "dark chamber" into which [Charcot's patients] were led, and where their bodies froze into immobile statues, may thus be said to allegorize the photographic process itself. The technical process suddenly becomes visible as a human body that has been frozen by a flash in a *cabinet noir* that translates, as if by accident, into the "chambre obscure" of photography—the *camera obscura*.[18]

If, as Baer argues, the frozen positions of Charcot's patients mimicked the photographic process, Sherman's students were, in a sense, prodded to imitate the apparatus even more closely. The flash was meant to provoke in them not paralysis but rather motion: an automatic movement through which their hands were to trace the afterimages ostensibly imprinted on their perceptual systems.

This automatism—in which the movement of the hand is taken as a direct response to the reception of a visual stimulus in the eye—is expressed in Sherman's project on a number of levels. While the use of the flash was intended to heighten the intensity of the image's reception, it also prevented the students from seeing their drawings while working on them. Sherman even includes in *Drawing by Seeing* an illustration of a shield to be placed below the student's chin in those teaching situations in which a totally darkened room is not available (fig. 48; I will return shortly to the issue of gender raised by this image and the preceding one). Sherman explained:

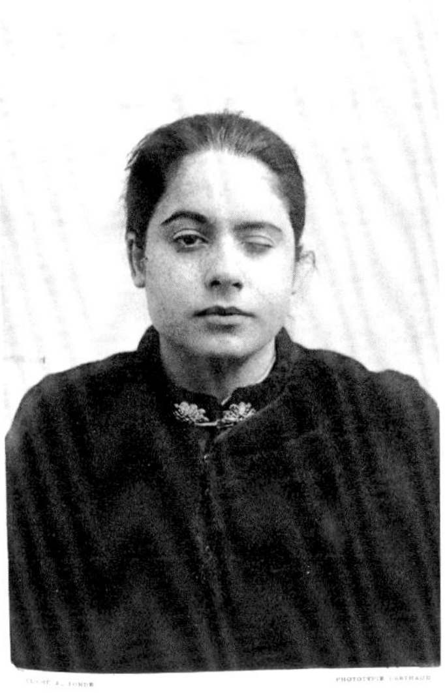

Figure 47.
"Blépharospasme Hystérique,"
from *Nouvelle Iconographie de la Salpêtrière* (1889)

> As a matter of emphasis, one does not try to *draw* with unity; rather one tries to *see* with unity and to let the image thus seen become the dominating force in organizing the drawing. If the student consciously works at getting unity in his drawing, the effect will be stilted. . . . The discipline of creative work in the visual arts, in other words, consists more in ruling out extraneous stimulations to muscular action than in aggressively forcing the charcoal or paintbrush here and there on the paper. The body "knows how" to draw, so to speak, if it is but permitted to draw in accordance with the full dictates of the creating image. This means taking the emphasis off the manual manipulations so that the act of drawing can be instrumental rather than primary.[19]

This passage points out the extent to which Sherman's rhetoric tends to repress any cognitive activity in the act of drawing and concurrently emphasizes a strange kind of automatism (as embodied in his reference to the act of drawing as "instrumental"). In the initial stages of instruction the student is prohibited from seeing the drawing in process and thus prevented from making any visual corrections; rather, she or he is expected to depend on a "kinaesthetic" (in this context perhaps a more accurate term would be "mechanical") response in rendering the image. This is why Sherman referred to it as the "seeing-and-drawing" act, in that the work of the eye and that of the hand are linked by one unified action: an automatic one much like that of a machine. Sherman's project, then, embeds the modernist practice of automatism (such as that pioneered by the Surrealists) in a thoroughly mechanical paradigm.[20] Hence we might suggest that for Lichtenstein it was no longer tenable to link such automatism to the unconscious or the primi-

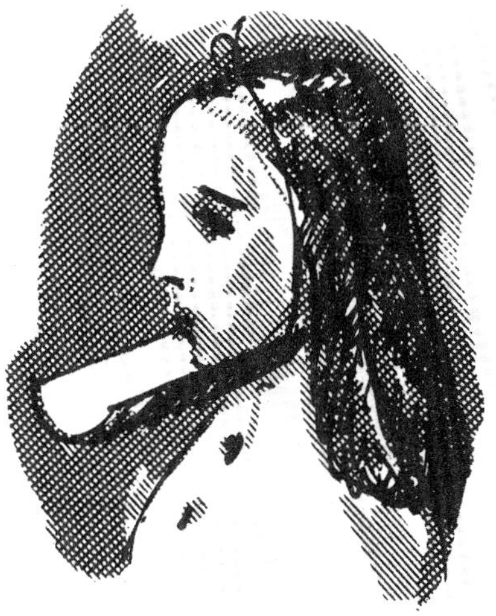

Figure 48. Illustration from Hoyt Sherman, *Drawing by Seeing* (1947)

tive (as had been done so readily by the preceding generation of Abstract Expressionist painters), since for him it had become so fully aligned with the machine.

Sherman also makes mention of the body reacting automatically if "permitted to draw in accordance with the full dictates of the creating image." This idea of the image or motif determining its reception by the body was another major component of his theoretical project. He asserted that the capacity to draw aesthetically would be achieved by effectively repressing past experience and returning the individual to the state of what John Ruskin called the "innocent eye."[21] In his text on Cézanne, Sherman repeatedly argues that the artist's work was "non-volitional," that Cézanne had to forget his experience with the perceptual world and return to a state of pure perception in which he could recognize the order already imposed on vision: "Paradoxically, Cézanne's struggle was essentially, therefore, to 'unlearn' the customary appearance of objects in order to achieve that which was fundamental to vision."[22] This concept was not new to modernist discourse, yet by inserting the machine into the equation Sherman's program pushed the technological instrumentalization of vision to an extreme.

If monocularity seems to have been linked in Lichtenstein's work to the structure of the photographic camera with its single lens, it would have had even further meaning for him in the context of his teacher's project. Sherman had utilized the adjective *monocular* to refer to that very mode of vision he had located in the work of Cézanne, and which he attempted to impart to his students in the flash lab.[23] Cézanne's importance lay in the artist's consistent use of compositions centered concentrically around a single focal point, which Sherman argued was the key component of aesthetic vision. An illustration from his text on Cézanne shows how he diagrammed the artist's work in order to demonstrate its monocular organization (fig. 49). Cézanne's work thus provided the foundation for Sherman's project; he used the term monocular in part because he believed that seeing with perceptual unity required that the individual relate all points or elements in a field to a single focal point: "Teaching students to draw with satisfactory pictorial organization is to a major degree a process of teaching them to see with perceptual unity—that is, to see all points in a motif with relation to a focal point. The artist needs to be able to see the whole field at which he is looking and to see it in such a way as to place the parts in the whole through referral of the parts to a focal point."[24] In addition, he maintained the assertion—as demonstrated by certain models in his Visual Demonstration Center—that binocular stereopsis was irrelevant to aesthetic perception. He believed that binocular vision impinged on the subject's perception of pure form—in this case, that of tonal or color contrast—because "in binocular viewing, contrast is instrumental to distance, whereas in monocular viewing, contrast tends to be an end in itself."[25]

It is in this dialectic between monocular and binocular modes that we may begin to locate the tension in Sherman's theoretical project, which is then confronted in Lichtenstein's work. The human body is seen as fundamentally deficient or flawed; the very corporeality of vision must be overcome (or perhaps more accurately, repressed) in order to reach the transcendent ideal of aesthetic vision.[26] And if that ideal, as I've argued, is a technological one—that of the photographic apparatus itself—then it is significant that *I Can See the Whole Room* images that apparatus using the very terms of compositional unity set forth by Sherman. While the source for the painting was a rectangular comic panel in which the peephole

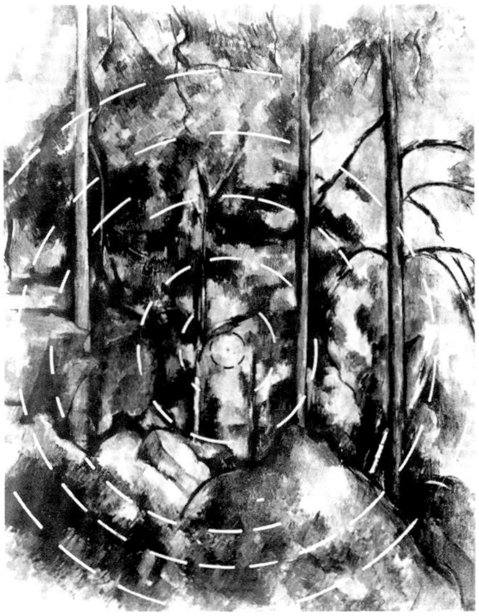

Figure 49.
Illustration from Hoyt Sherman, *Cézanne and Visual Form* (1952)

was placed off-center along the vertical axis (in part to make room for the accompanying word balloon), Lichtenstein gave his painting a square format with the peephole at its very center. In this way the work can be seen as embracing Sherman's artistic principles even as it offers an incipient critique of them.

As Lichtenstein said years later, Sherman's project "was a mixture of science and aesthetics, and it became the center of what I was interested in."[27] Yet the mixture of science and aesthetics resulted in this case in an instrumentalization of the body, in which hand and eye were to be connected automatically, as in a machine. Another index of Lichtenstein's response to that project can be located in his repeated imaging of a disconnection between hand and eye, in such images as *Drowning Girl* (see fig. 89), *The Refrigerator,* and the two-panel war painting *Live Ammo (Take Cover!)* (fig. 50). In each of these paintings a figure's face is juxtaposed with a corresponding hand that, although presumably connected to the figure's body, is cut off from it in some way. In *The Refrigerator* the hand is cut off below the wrist by the lower framing edge of the canvas; in *Drowning Girl* it emerges from the rippled water at lower right; and in *Live Ammo (Take Cover!)* the figure's hand is cleaved by the text below. Certainly by this time Lichtenstein's treatment of figures tended toward a close-up framing that prevented any full imaging of the body.

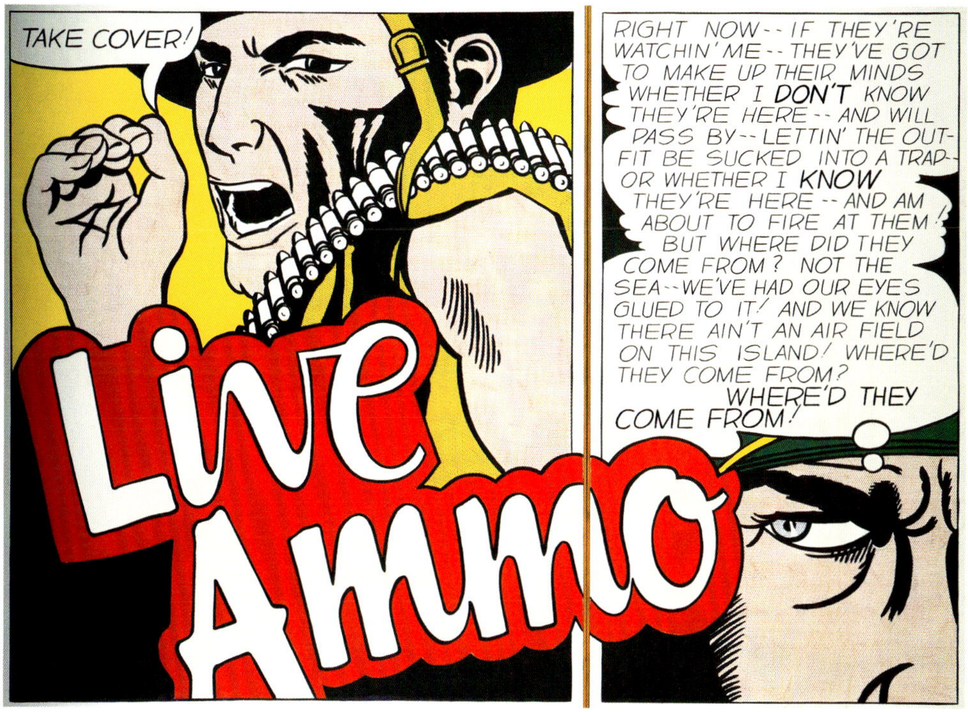

Figure 50. *Live Ammo (Take Cover!),* 1962. Oil and Magna on canvas, two panels 68 × 92 in. (172.7 × 233.6 cm) overall. Private collection

Further, the disconnection between head and hand in these images allowed him to play signs of spatial depth against the flatness of the canvas. Nevertheless, because Lichtenstein's images are derived from preexisting illustrations we tend to overlook the "making-strange" of the body that is often evident in his work. There is something uncanny about the artist's presentation of these hands as corporeal fragments, an effect only emphasized by the flatness at play in his paintings. That such an effect relates to his use of the motif of monocularity becomes evident upon inspection of the right-hand panel of *Live Ammo (Take Cover!)*. Underneath the meandering text in the thought balloon—which takes up over half of the painting's vertical composition—appears the single, staring eye of a soldier. The text above—with its repeated references to watching, eyes, and looking—only emphasizes that vision is a central concern of the work.[28]

The model for the cleaving of hand and eye may very well have come from *I Can See the Whole Room*, in which hand and face are the only elements visible through the peephole. Yet if Lichtenstein's depiction of such fragmentation can be interpreted as a provisional rejection of automatism (which implied a direct circuit between the registration of the impulse in the eye and its nonvolitional recording by the hand), *I Can See the Whole Room* presents that separation in a decidedly ambiguous manner. Here as well there is something strange about his treatment of the hand. The more one examines the extended digit the less certainty there is as to whether it represents an index finger or thumb. No manual configuration seems to square with the representation: is it supposed to represent a left hand or a right hand? Lichtenstein's transcription only increases its ambiguity, for he does away with any indication of shading below the finger, thus making its spatial position even less clear. This making-strange of the hand suggests a corporeal disconnection, yet it is at odds with another detail. In the painting Lichtenstein altered the line of the figure's neck so that it connects with the lower left edge of the hand. That hand has been disconnected from the body only to be reconnected in an uncanny way.

In calling attention to this concern with a veritable circuit between eye and hand I do not mean to suggest that Lichtenstein's working process was photographic, or that he thought—to any extent—that his project involved an automatic transcription of preexisting imagery. However, as I've described, he made consistent reference to his ability to "unify" an image, a skill he ascribed to his training under Sherman. In short, if he maintained the conviction that the artist's aesthetic faculty interposed itself somewhere between eye and hand, his training would only have lent the gnawing suspicion that such a mysterious ability might be attributed as much to a mechanical source as to any creative, human capacity.

Considering the polysemic charge that monocularity held for Lichtenstein (it represented an aesthetic ideal that could be achieved only through the repression of vision's corporeality), it comes as no surprise that he would return to the monocular again and again in his work. For one, there is the 1963 canvas *Magnifying Glass*, which provides the viewer the virtual experience of monocular viewing (fig. 51). The painting plays on our tendency to view the large dots within the circular boundary of the magnifying glass as actual enlargements of the smaller dots in the background: the same type of perceptual illusion that Sherman had employed to such effect in his Visual Demonstration Center. Further, *I Can See the Whole Room* and *Live Ammo (Take Cover!)* are just two among a group of works from this period in which monocularity is represented by a depicted figure. That list would also include *Popeye*, one of the artist's first Pop canvases. Popeye is a character so well known in popular culture that it is easy for us to overlook one of his essential features: he's a *one-eyed* sailor. Yet his significance is not limited to his inherent monocularity; Michael Wassenaar has pointed out the extent to which the figure of Popeye (beginning particularly with the Fleischer Studio animated cartoons of the 1930s) has been linked to metaphors of engineering and the machine.[29] In this way Lichtenstein's painting can be read in part as an image of the body as a veritable machine; according to Wassenaar's analysis, that open, empty can at lower left is a sign that Popeye has ingested his trademark strength-giving spinach, which marks "a moment of increased efficiency of the organism. It is a dynamic change in that the level of energy within the human mechanism is maintained, if not increased, as it is put to work, often times by punching his nemesis, Bluto, repeatedly around the room."[30]

In one of his next canvases Lichtenstein turned to Popeye's hapless sidekick Wimpy, depicting him with a dark, hatchmarked circle—comic book shorthand for a blackened eye—around his left eye (fig. 52). Taken together, *Wimpy (Tweet)* and *Popeye* demonstrate Lichtenstein's conflicted approach to the motif of monocularity. For one, in both of these paintings monocular vision is only referenced, not directly imaged. In the comics, Popeye is conventionally represented with one eye open and the other closed—usually denoted by a single dot (open) contrasted with a short horizontal line or dash (closed)—yet Lichtenstein depicts him with both eyes shut. Likewise, the blacked-out left eye of the title character in *Wimpy (Tweet)* suggests the monocular without a direct representation of that state. Since these two paintings were made at the very beginning of Lichtenstein's move into Pop—they are probably among his earliest canvases in that idiom, executed in the summer of 1961—it could be that at this early stage he was experimenting with possible ways to represent the motif. Or it could be that monocular vision represented something so significant—yet so charged—to him that he would only allude to it rather than represent it directly in these canvases. Further, the figural

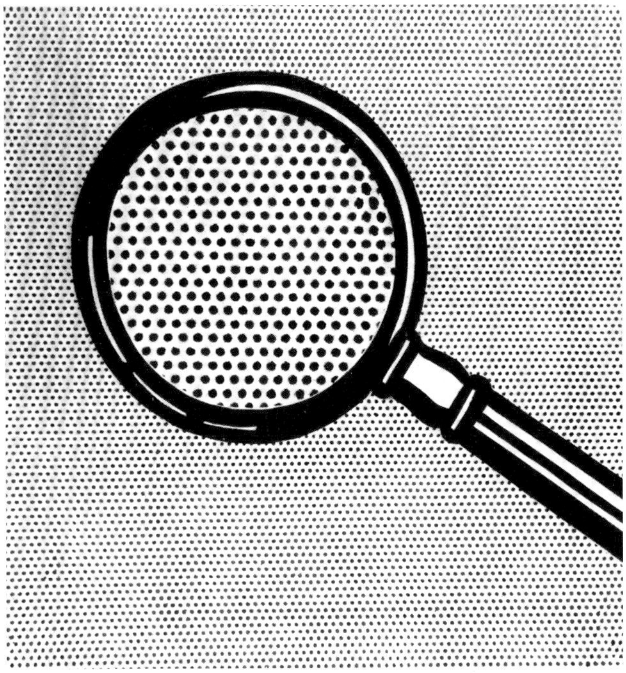

Figure 51.
Magnifying Glass,
1963.
Oil on canvas,
16 × 16 in.
(40.6 × 40.6 cm).
Private collection

representation of monocularity in each of these works is diametrically opposed. Popeye is depicted at the moment he smashes his rival into submission; Wimpy is shown defeated and prostrate, his very name—and the tweeting bird above his head—further evidence of his weakness. The same motif, it seems, could sustain widely divergent meanings.

A monocular figure would again take center stage in one of Lichtenstein's most striking war images, entitled *Torpedo . . . Los!* (1963). The painting depicts a submarine captain peering through a periscope, his exposed eye serving (much like that of *I Can See the Whole Room*) as the focal point of the painting (fig. 53). A comparison of the painting with its comic book source (fig. 54) demonstrates the significant changes Lichtenstein made in producing his image, including the enlargement of the foreground figure's head and the editing of text into the terse command in German that gives the painting its title. Some of the most substantive alterations are to be found in the structure of the periscope viewer. In the comic panel the periscope was a simple, boxy shape; in Lichtenstein's painting it has been transformed into a baroque tangle of wires, tubes and mechanical fittings. With these changes it reads more resolutely as a mechanical device. It also provides a more substantial formal contrast with the face of the foreground figure, thus more effectively emphasizing the visual tension between human figure and machine. But there is another, perhaps less noticeable change that Lichtenstein effected on the image, one that further demonstrates the significance—and com-

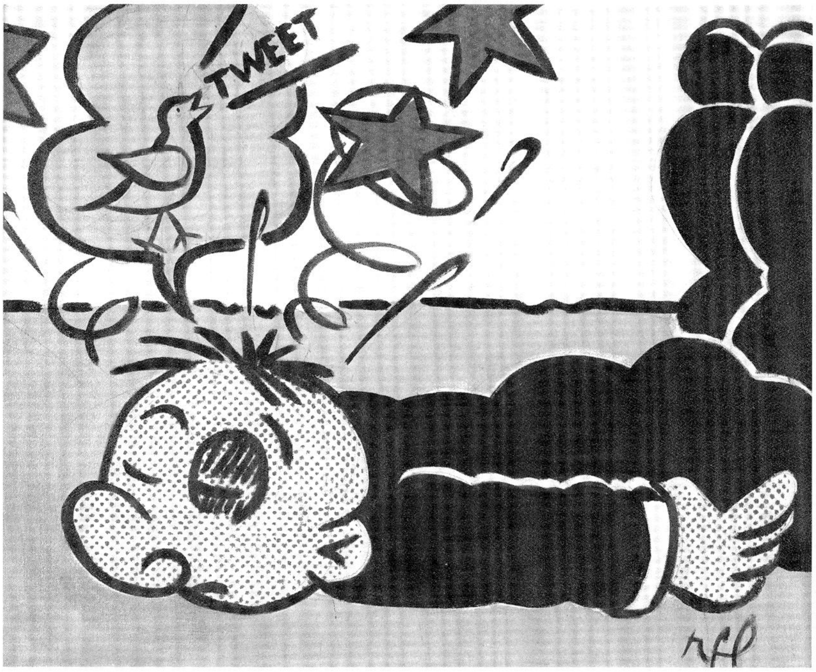

Figure 52.
Wimpy (Tweet),
1961.
Oil on canvas,
16 × 20 in.
(40.6 × 50.8 cm).
Private collection

plexity—of his use of monocularity as a motif for representing the relation between vision and technology. In the comic book panel, the exposed (right) eye of the submarine commander had been depicted as closed (and shaded with diagonal hatchings), suggesting that he was looking through the periscope viewfinder with his unseen (left) eye. Lichtenstein altered the image, removing the diagonal hatchmarks and depicting the exposed eye as open. On the one hand, the painting now presents us with a central monocular figure, the exposed eye serving as a veritable focal point for the composition. On the other hand, as in *I Can See the Whole Room,* the rest of the figure's face—and more specifically, the other eye—is hidden from view. It is almost as if Lichtenstein had settled on a way to maintain a degree of ambiguity in his depiction of monocular vision, in that the image suggests the presence of another, hidden eye, yet leaves its status utterly in question. In the process he added a significant detail. Beneath the figure's exposed eye he added an arcing line crossed by several short strokes, illustrational shorthand for a scar. That scar seems derived from one that appeared on the figure's face in other panels of the comic book story, although Lichtenstein shifted the scar from the bridge of the nose to a spot directly below the figure's now-opened right eye. That scar functions as a red flag, calling attention to the site of a significant transformation he had effected on the image. It calls attention to the open eye but suggests a loss or wounding as well.

These issues would be addressed in another work from this period that depicted

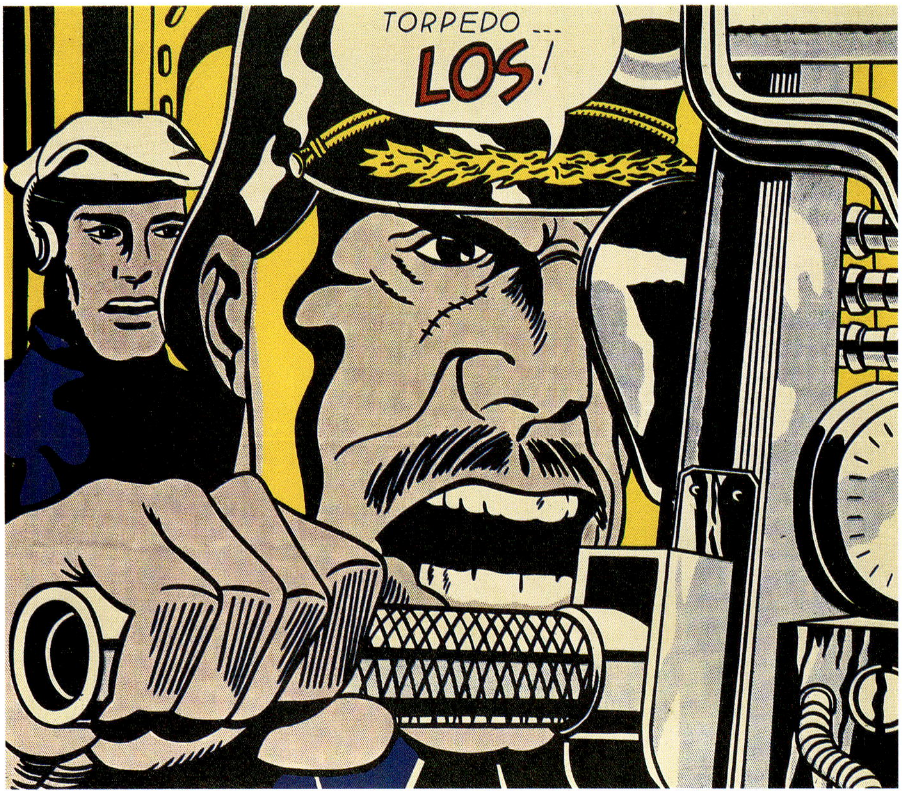

Figure 53.
Torpedo . . . Los!,
1963.
Oil and Magna
on canvas,
68 × 80 in.
(172.7 × 203.2 cm).
Simonyi collection

a monocular figure, an image that also raises the question of sexual difference in relation to the artist's use of the motif.[31] In 1963, to announce his second one-person show at the Castelli Gallery, Lichtenstein executed a print—entitled *CRAK!*—that depicts a beret-clad young woman, her eyes revealed above the barrel of a rifle that fires at an unseen target (fig. 55). The previously unidentified source panel for the work came from a 1962 issue of the *Star Spangled War Stories* comic book (fig. 56). Lichtenstein changed the image, as was his wont by that time: he replaced the earthen mound to the left of the figure with what looks like a pile of sandbags; enlarged and recomposed the letters in that onomatopoetic "CRAK!"; and cropped out the foreground and rearground, thus isolating the figure. In the context of our current analysis, though, one cannot help but notice the eyes above the rifle barrel: one is open, one closed. How are we to understand this image, particularly its difference from Lichtenstein's other representations of the monocular? For one, this is the only image in which we see both eyes, fully exposed, in a monocular configuration. For another, *CRAK!* portrays a female figure, in opposition to those other images we have seen, in which monocular vision is referenced or imaged by a male figure.

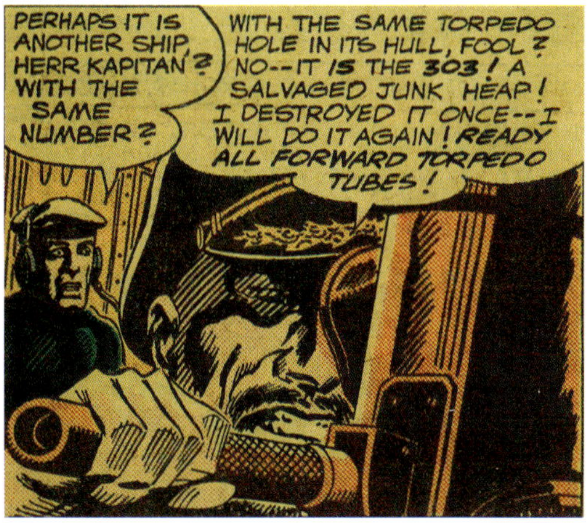

Figure 54. Panel from "Battle of the Ghost Ships!" in *Our Fighting Forces* no. 71 (October 1962)

One way to better understand the meaning of the work—particularly in relation to gender—is to compare it with another image that Lichtenstein produced at the same time for the very same occasion. In fact, the two seem to be pendant images. Like *CRAK!*, *Crying Girl* (fig. 57) is an offset lithograph in red, yellow, and black on a white ground. Both prints are approximately the same size, and both were produced to advertise Lichtenstein's 1963 show at the Castelli Gallery.[32] They also share a similar compositional structure and subject matter, at least in terms of their depictions of the act of looking. In *CRAK!* the figure, positioned toward the left of the image, looks to the right; in *Crying Girl* a female figure, positioned toward the right of the image, looks back toward the left, eyes welling with tears. It is this motif of tears that may help us relate these concerns—specifically with the limits of embodied vision—to Lichtenstein's well-known images of women from this period. Although I will talk about the status of gender in the artist's work at greater length in Chapter Five, we might note here how consistently the artist's romance comic–derived images of the early 1960s have been identified with the act of crying. In fact, writers often refer in shorthand to Lichtenstein's distinctive images of women from this period simply as his "crying girls."[33] There is a long list of such works that portray female figures with tears filling their eyes, a list that would include some of the artist's best-known images of women: *Drowning Girl, Happy Tears, Frightened Girl, Hopeless,* and of course *Crying Girl.* Although these images have often been interpreted as ironic representations of the exaggerated emotionalism found in the romance comics, in the context of our discussion we should also take note of the relation between tears and vision. Tears corporealize the eye; they remind us that our eyes are not ideal, transparent receptors of visual data but rather fully embodied, even capricious organs. Organs, further, at the mercy of our emotional states. And when tears flow they blur our vision, preventing us from seeing

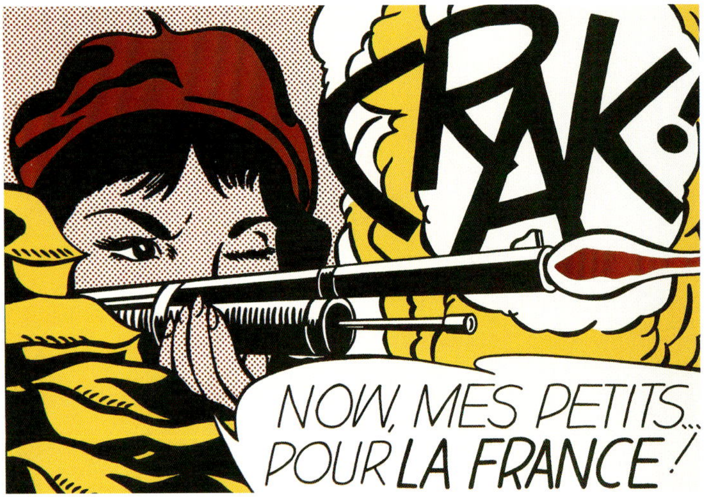

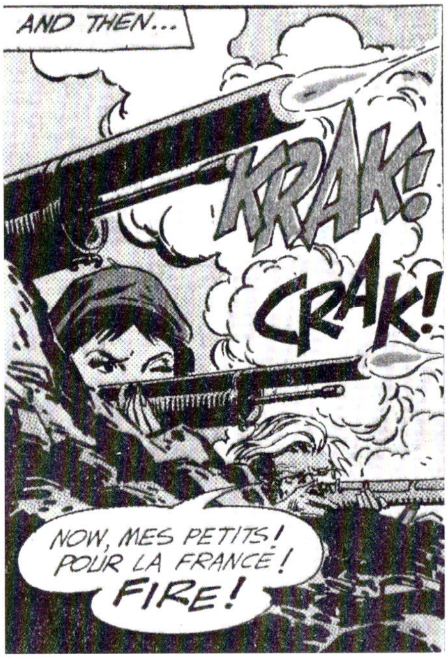

Figure 55. *CRAK!*, 1963–64.
Offset lithograph on paper, 19¼ × 27⅝ in. (48.9 × 70.2 cm)

Figure 56. Panel from "The Town That Wouldn't Die!" in *Star Spangled War Stories* no. 102 (April–May 1962)

clearly. With this in mind, we might consider Lichtenstein's crying figures as standing in part for the recognition of the limits of visual perception.

If Lichtenstein's repeated depiction of women with tears in their eyes is in some ways a recognition of the corporeality of vision—an embodiedness coded as feminine—then we might consider *CRAK!* a work that provisionally bridges the gap between two opposing experiences of visual perception. This image of a monocular female figure, rifle in hand, is positioned somewhere between the emotionally clouded vision of the teary-eyed female figure in *Crying Girl* and the hostile, mechanically augmented vision of the male figure in *Torpedo . . . Los!* Significantly, the figure in *CRAK!* is depicted as choosing the state of monocularity, as opposed to the figures in *I Can See the Whole Room* and *Torpedo . . . Los!* onto which monocularity has been veritably forced by their proximity to machines. The significance of this motif may also help to explain its reappearance in Lichtenstein's work years later. In about 1977 the artist began to experiment with Surrealist imagery, borrowing mainly, as Diane Waldman has pointed out, from the work of René Magritte, Salvador Dalí, and Max Ernst.[34] Yet while these paintings clearly appropriated certain stylistic conceits from those artists—the abrupt juxtaposition of incongruous objects and elements, the notion of the dream landscape—many of them also contained a recurring image: the monocular female figure, often depicted in tears (fig. 58). The persistence of this motif speaks to the problem of vision and its limits as an enduring concern in the artist's work.

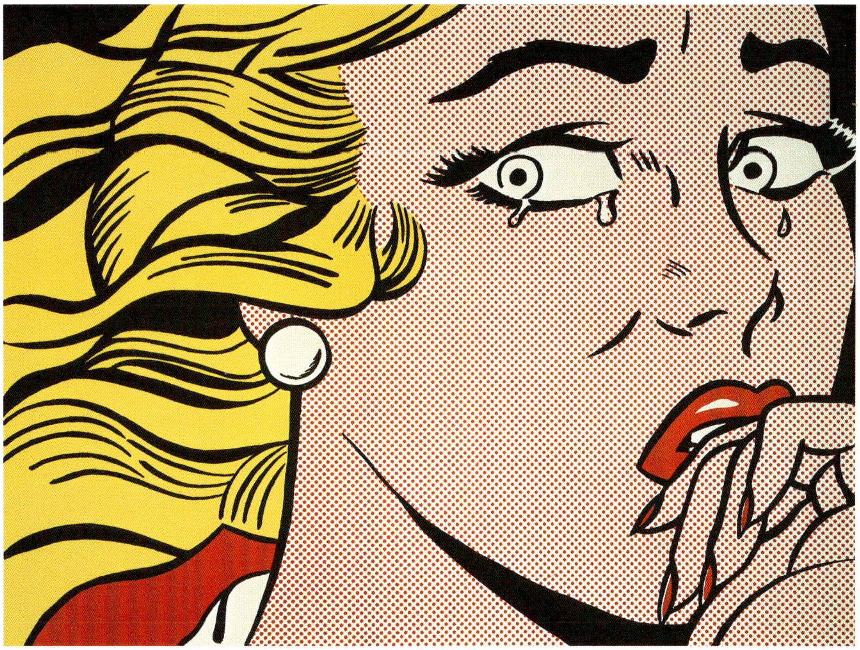

Figure 57. *Crying Girl,* 1963. Offset lithograph on paper, 18 × 24 in. (45.8 × 61 cm). National Gallery of Art, Washington, D.C. Gift of Roy and Dorothy Lichtenstein

MONOCULARITY: BODY AND MACHINE

We have seen how *I Can See the Whole Room* (along with other works from this period) confronts the possibility—impelled by Lichtenstein's immersion in Hoyt Sherman's theoretical program—of subjectivity being threatened through the experience of the human body approaching the automatism of the machine. Yet it also suggests another, parallel reading; if the painting imagines the viewer as erased by (or merged with) the photographic apparatus, then it also depicts a figure interacting with a monocular mechanical device, inasmuch as the male figure peers out at the viewer through a primitive shutter mechanism. This is true as well of *Torpedo . . . Los!* and *CRAK!*: in these paintings vision is directed through some sort of mechanical device which takes a monocular format.

The images Lichtenstein appropriated from the war comics of the time became some of his most widely recognized works in the early 1960s, a group that includes such paintings as *Blam!* (1962), *Okay, Hot-Shot* (1963), and *Whaam!* (1963). All three depict intense moments of aerial warfare, and they show how Lichtenstein manipulated his source materials (especially details like explosions) to render highly abstracted shapes in his canvases, another instance of his alteration of his sources to achieve the greatest formal effect. While these images have been discussed at length in treatments of the artist's work, their significance to our discussion relates to their depiction of interactions between body and machine. For instance, Diane Waldman has suggested that in *Okay, Hot-Shot* (fig. 59) Lichtenstein "updated the headgear of the pilot by substituting an astronaut's helmet for a World War II fighter pilot's helmet at a time when space-flight programs were under way in the U.S. and the U.S.S.R."[35] Waldman is, I believe, incorrect—the element she reads as an astronaut's helmet was meant to depict the canopy of a fighter plane—yet her misreading is understandable because of how Lichtenstein compacted the pilot's physical form into the machine around it, so that the white surface just visible in the lower right seems more like an astronaut's fitted spacesuit than the metal skin of an airplane.

If *Okay, Hot-Shot* contains the figure of a pilot encased within the structure of his fighter plane, both the 1962 drawing *Jet Pilot* (fig. 60) and the 1962 painting *Bratatat!* (fig. 61) depict a seemingly half-human, half-mechanical figure: a fighter pilot inside the close confines of a cockpit, his eyes the only visible features of a body otherwise hidden by the helmet and oxygen mask. The 1962 canvas *Brattata* (see fig. 77—not to be confused with the aforementioned *Bratatat!*) depicts a similar scene—a close-up view of the profile of a fighter pilot engaged in aerial combat—although here the unbuckled mask does reveal the lower portion of the pilot's face. There are intimations in these images of the cyborgian interconnection of human body and machine. Significantly, the first uses of the term cyborg are roughly contemporaneous with Lichtenstein's practice, and with the emergence of Pop art in the United States.[36] However, I am concerned here specifically with visual technologies, evidenced by the presence of a particular element in each of the three images cited above. Like *Torpedo . . . Los!* and *CRAK!* each of these works contains the image of a mechanical aid to vision. A reexamination of

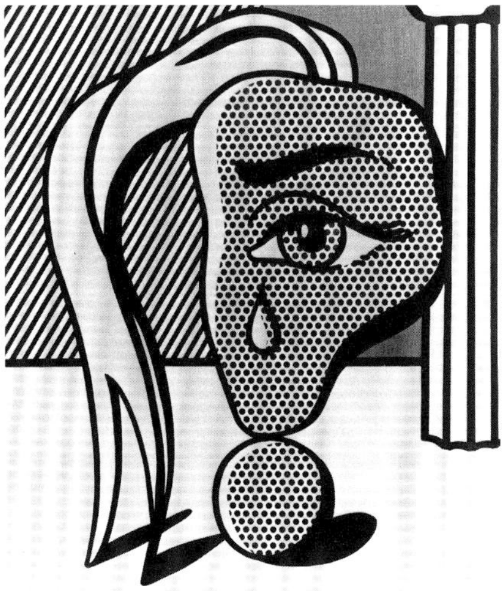

Figure 58.
Girl with Tear III, 1977.
Oil and Magna on canvas,
46 × 40 in. (116.8 × 101.6 cm).
Private collection

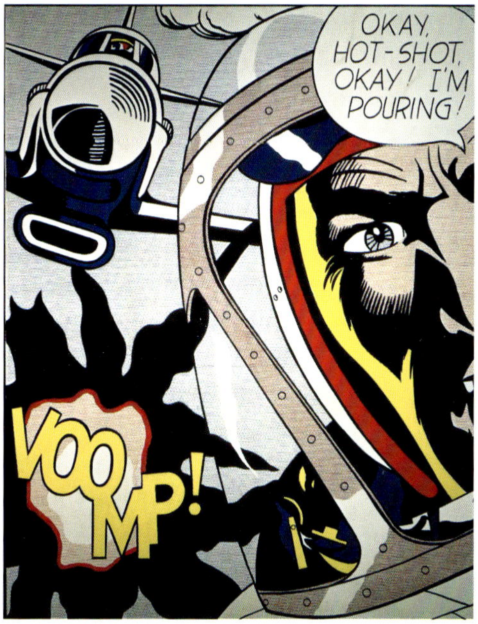

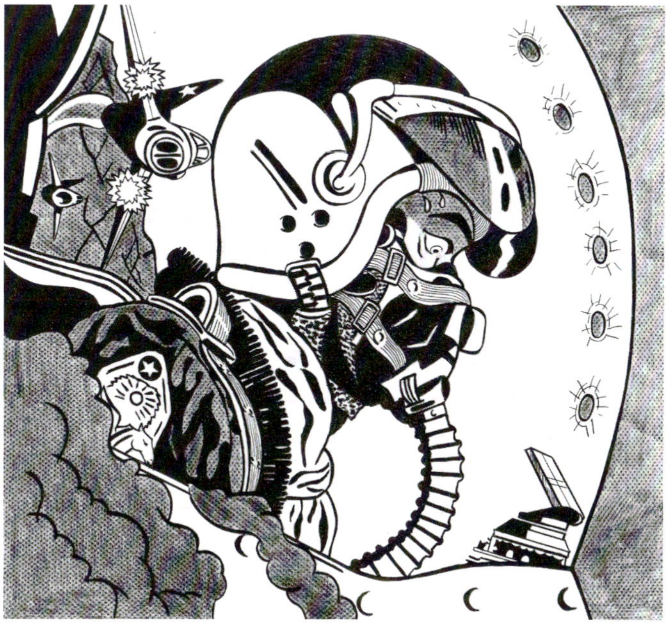

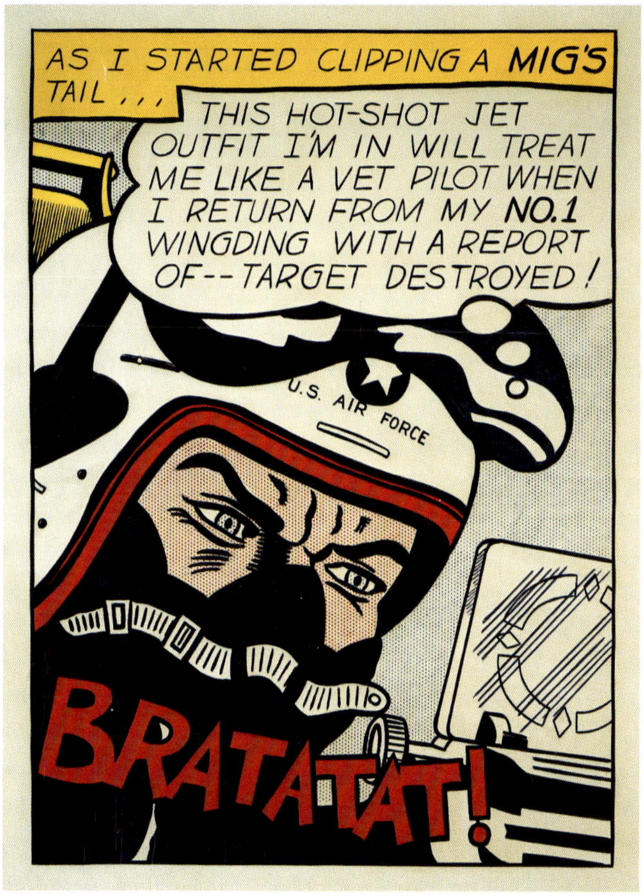

Figure 59.
Okay, Hot-Shot, 1963.
Oil and Magna on canvas,
80 × 68 in. (203.2 × 172.7 cm).
Private collection

Figure 60.
Jet Pilot, 1962.
Pencil and frottage on paper,
15 × 17 in. (38.1 × 43.2 cm).
Yale University Art Gallery,
New Haven.
Richard Brown Baker Collection

Figure 61.
Bratatat!, 1963.
Magna on canvas,
46 × 34 in. (116.8 × 86.4 cm).
Simonyi collection

CRAK! shows that Lichtenstein took care to add a small sighting element at the end of the gun barrel (a detail absent from the comic book source). If he added a rather rudimentary aiming mechanism to the gun in that image, the aforementioned fighter-pilot works depict a more sophisticated device used for much the same purpose: a type of gun sight that was developed during World War II to help pilots achieve better firing accuracy. A variation on this kind of sight appears in each of these three images: in the lower right of *Bratatat!;* in the cockpit's lower right corner in *Jet Pilot;* and in the mid- to lower left of *Brattata,* right at the tip of the pilot's nose.

A major problem in aerial gunnery involves the difficulty in accounting for how the combination of various factors—including range, aircraft speed, and angle of deflection—will affect the trajectory of the pilot's gunfire. Additionally, the gun sight must be placed in the cockpit so as to minimize its interference with the pilot's line of vision. A certain type of sight developed during World War II—and depicted in the works by Lichtenstein cited above—provided solutions to those problems. Both Britain and the United States developed technology whereby the pilot or gunner could adjust an aiming mechanism according to a series of variables (speed, size of enemy aircraft, and so forth) that would then be corrected for in the gun sight lens itself. It seems that one of the most common forms of these computing sights, especially for fighter pilots, was the reflector sight, in large part because it minimized intrusion into the pilot's visual field. The reflector gun sight is composed of a small glass panel tilted down at about a 45-degree angle that is fixed above the other cockpit instrumentation directly in front of the pilot's field of vision (fig. 62). An adjustable lamp and lens assembly inside the gun sight projects the image of a reticle or aiming schema—a combination of circles, dots, or lines—onto the glass panel above. It is through this projected image of the reticle that the pilot targets the enemy aircraft (fig. 63).[37]

The works by Lichtenstein cited above image those very reticular schema on the glass panels of their depicted gun sights. In *Jet Pilot* two thin horizontal lines cross a longer vertical one; in *Brattata* the reticular schema is composed of short bars that mark off twelve positions much like those on a clock face; and in *Bratatat!* a set of diamonds and semi-circular bars mark off the aiming ring. A comparison of the artist's works and their source images indicates that Lichtenstein made alterations that gave increased visual attention to these devices. For instance, in *Whaam!* he took care to delineate—in the cockpit close to the pilot's profile—a raised rectangular silhouette that signifies the interruption of the control panel's upper edge by a gun sight like the ones described here (in the painting's source that interruption is indicated barely, if at all) (fig. 64). His adjustments to the image in *Jet Pilot*—including his ninety-degree reorientation of the composition—

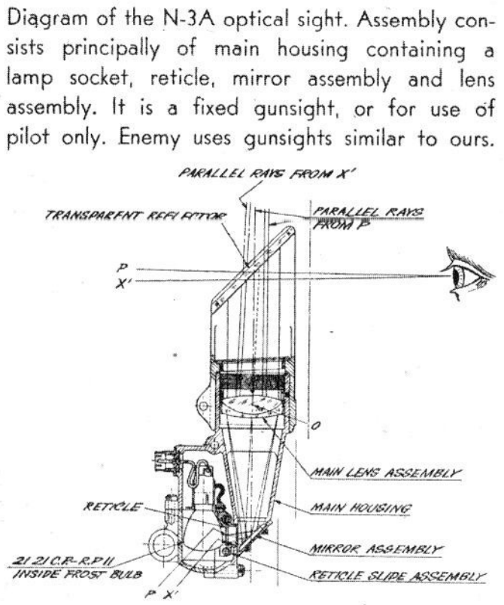

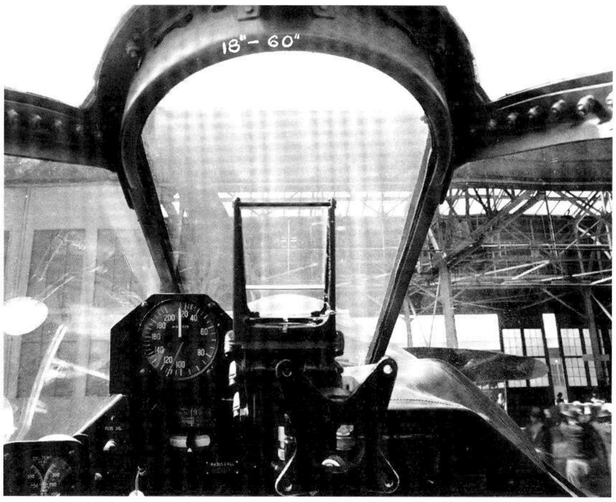

Figure 62. Diagram of the N-3A Optical Sight

Figure 63. Military aircraft cockpit interior with reflector gun sight at center

direct visual attention to the depicted gun sight in a similar way. Even though he tended to simplify his images in the process of transcription, the gun sight in *Jet Pilot* is more carefully delineated than that in the source (a panel on the cover of *All American Men of War* no. 89, January–February 1962) (fig. 65). His redrawing also allows more of it to show above the lower framing edge of the cockpit. In the comic book panel the line of bullet holes in the cockpit canopy was directed toward the pilot's broken air hose, providing a narrative intensity. A bullet had clipped the hose: would the pilot survive without his oxygen supply? Lichtenstein's editing out of this narrative detail provides further insight into his approach to the comic book stories he used as sources for his imagery. His removal of this detail indicates that he may have wanted to suggest some, but not too much, narrative: while *Jet Pilot*—like so many of the artist's other war paintings—depicts a figure engaged in a moment of intense affect, the broken air hose seems a detail that might have required too much narrative closure.[38] Lichtenstein not only depicted the air hose unbroken, but he also redirected the line of bullet holes around the arc of the plane's canopy. That line of holes now points directly toward the reflector gun sight that seems almost to face off against the wide-eyed pilot.

That facing-off is key to my discussion, because Lichtenstein's repeated treatment of this motif, and the visual attention his images draw to these gun sights, brings us back to the issue of monocularity. In the context of the analysis developed so far, a work like *Bratatat!* can be viewed as an image of the body's binocular vision played off against a seemingly monocular machine. And not just any machine: the computing reflector sight was a machine used to correct the shortcomings of human perception. As an early account reported, "The gunsight automatically computes factors which previously the pilot had to estimate, such as the time lag between the bullets leaving the attacking plane and reaching their fleeting

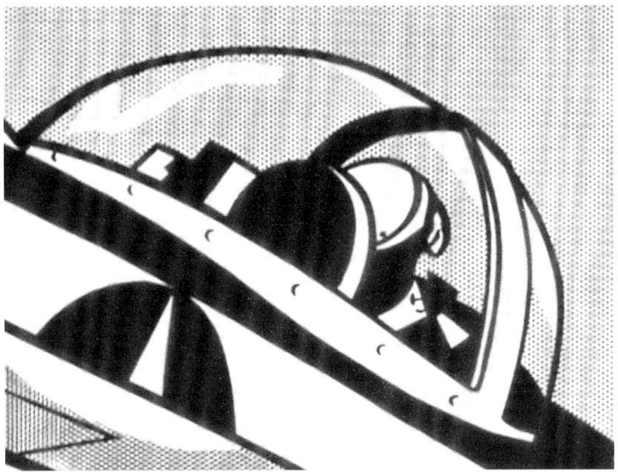

Figure 64.
Detail, *Whaam!*, 1963.
Oil and Magna on canvas,
two panels 68 × 166 in.
(172.7 × 421. 6 cm) overall.
Tate Gallery, London

quarry, the effects of gravity and air density on the bullet, relative motion of the target and other factors."[39] In short, it was a machine that served as a corrective to the pilot's inability to effectively sight his target when faced with the speed and intensity of modern aerial warfare. According to Allan Kaprow it was that very problem of adapting vision to aerial combat that provided the impetus for Sherman's development of the flash lab:

> Sherman had been instrumental in the military effort during World War II because of his experiments with perception. He found that most of us tend to see details of situations rather than overall configurations. This proved a rather serious problem when it came to aerial gunnery because gunners couldn't perceive modern enemy aircraft in motion. They moved too fast. Then men had been trained to identify insignia, tail and wing shapes, etc., in still pictures. Sherman's program proved effective.[40]

In this way Sherman's program was engineered toward solving the same problem as the computing gun sight: to augment the individual's visual perception by mechanical means. The machine is understood here as testing or training the subject's responses to the increased visual stimuli of modern life, just as it was used by product and logo designers to test the individual's responses to the increased stimuli of a burgeoning consumer culture. Kaprow's account provides insight into comments made by Lichtenstein when I asked him about his first experience with the flash lab:

> Well, Sherman was developing it before I went to the army. In fact the Renshaw Recognition System, which had to do with the Navy, sort of happened through Hoyt [Sherman], who I guess was in the hospital, and Renshaw took this to the Navy or something, I don't know, there was some story, they didn't get along

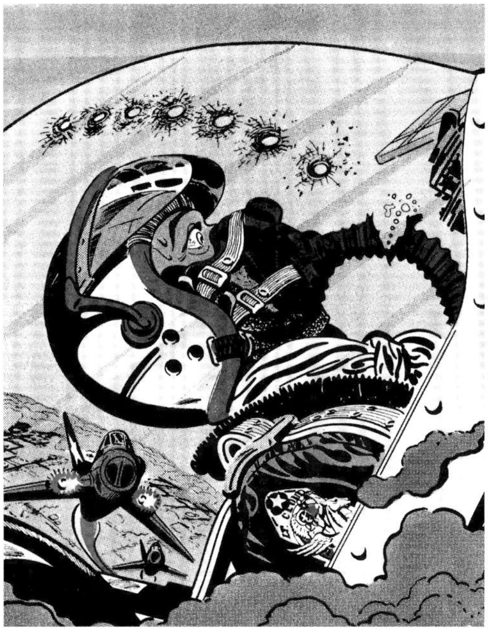

Figure 65. Panel from the cover of *All American Men of War* no. 89 (January–February 1962)

very well after that. But anyway Hoyt didn't care about recognition, that wasn't the point, unifying was, and so forth. So he started working on it, and I knew what he was going to come up with, but then he had built the flash room—I believe, if I've got this straight, while I was away—and then when I came back I was teaching.[41]

Taken alongside Kaprow's account, Lichtenstein's version of events tells us this: that he understood Sherman's project to have originated in the problem of heightening visual perception through mechanical means in response to the demands of modern aerial warfare. Lichtenstein had his own brush with the possibilities of aerial combat; as he mentions in the above account, his undergraduate training was interrupted by his induction into the Army in 1943. After time spent in basic training and several semesters in an engineering training program at De Paul University in Chicago, in 1944 Lichtenstein arrived at Keesler Air Force Base in Biloxi, Mississippi, for a pilot training program. But he received no training; soon after his arrival, the Army canceled that program because more ground troops were needed in Europe after the Battle of the Bulge. In February 1945 he was sent overseas as a member of the engineer battalion of the 69th Infantry Division of the Ninth Army.[42]

Because Lichtenstein did not receive any formal training as a pilot, it cannot be determined how much he knew about the reflector gun sights that were used by fighter pilots in World War II and which he repeatedly depicted in works from the early 1960s.[43] We do know, however, that during his basic training at Fort Hulen, Texas, Lichtenstein trained with anti-aircraft guns that could be adjusted in much the same way as those of fighter plane computing gun sights. He recounted that those anti-aircraft guns "were 40 millimeter I think at the time. I think they were guns of a type that got replaced after that by a higher caliber, and more automatic or something. But they had a separate range-finder box in which you would track the plane and it would automatically set the gun."[44] Regardless of Lichtenstein's specific knowledge of gun sight technology, these instruments—and his imaging of them—provided another opportunity to consider the triangulation of body, vision, and machine, which would again be condensed into the motif of the monocular.

The details of Lichtenstein's military service in World War II offer further insight into why he turned to a consideration of these issues after years of working through other problems of form and subject matter in his paintings. For his move into Pop represented a return of sorts, to a moment when body, vision, and mechanical transcription had been brought together in an uneasy mix. In the midst of the war that had interrupted his studies with Sherman, and through which he would come into contact with other mechanical aids to vision, Lichtenstein was called on to perform an unlikely task. Although his duties in the army while stationed in Europe—from working on a garbage truck to cleaning the commanding officer's quarters—seem to have been decidedly mundane, at one point the colonel in charge discovered that Lichtenstein was an artist. That colonel, a fan of the military cartoonist Bill Mauldin, assigned him a repetitive—albeit artistic—task. As Lichtenstein described years earlier: "Here we are in the Battle of the Bulge and I was in the headquarters office and my job at that time was to take the Bill Mauldin cartoons as they came out in the army newspaper *Stars and Stripes* and enlarge them and frame them so that each time the issue came out I would copy the cartoon, which is my present occupation too."[45] "My present occupation" indeed: the rote, mechanical transcription of a cartoon writ large. In light of this we might see Lichtenstein's development of a Pop idiom as a veritable reduplication of his army experience: in both cases the use of the appropriated comic image offered him new possibilities for working as an artist at the same time it meant giving himself up to the repetition and industrial facture of the machine.

In closing, I return to the painting with which I began the chapter to suggest that, considering its confrontation of issues so central to Lichtenstein's project, it be taken as a kind of self-portrait. *I Can See the Whole Room* is, after all, an image of a male figure pushing an extended digit through a circular opening—one much like the perforations in the dot-screen stencils the artist had just begun to use in his work. After experimenting in *Look Mickey* and *Popeye* with various methods of applying regular patterns of dots to the canvas, Lichtenstein had manufactured his own rudimentary dot-patterned stencil by drilling holes in a piece of aluminum.[46] At the time he produced the painting, sometime in the summer of 1961, he had recently begun to apply paint in this distinctive way; the work can thus be read as well as an attempt at self-imaging, with that finger standing in for the brush the artist used to push pigment through the holes in his dot-stencil. The awkward, almost instrumental quality of the hand supports this interpretation.

If we consider *I Can See the Whole Room* as a kind of self-portrait, then the tension between monocular and binocular modes in the artist's work can best be brought out by comparing it with another image central to his project, namely *Image Duplicator*. In fact, such a comparison suggests that the latter canvas represents a veritable correction of the former. In each a figure peers out at the viewer through an intervening surface plane, although the earlier representation of monocular vision gives way in the later work to the aggressive binocularity of those two glaring eyes. There is a formal element that lends further support to this reading; the arcing lines under the exposed eye of *I Can See the Whole Room,* used to denote the shading of a cheekbone, are almost exactly repeated in the thick black outline of the mask in the lower right corner of *Image Duplicator*. We might even consider the aggression depicted in the later work as compensating for its rejection of monocularity, in that a refusal of the terms of technologized vision was less than secure in Lichtenstein's practice. Monocularity was a fitting—albeit conflicted—vehicle for representing the relation between body, vision, and machine. Conflicted because it suggests both an intensification of vision (think of the common experience of closing one eye in order to fix an object in the gaze) and a cutting-off or loss of the ordinary experience of embodied vision. Nevertheless, the artist's experiences with visual technologies had shown him that something had to be sacrificed if the machine was to augment human perception. His paintings from this period bear the marks of a struggle between two irreconcilable positions: on the one side sits the idealism of Sherman's dream of pure, unmediated vision, couched in the technological language of the machine. On the other sits the belief in a perceiving subject whose imperfect corporeality denies access to such transcendence, yet may provide an imaginary space of safety set away from the machine's erasure of subjectivity. In the end, it was the irresolvable tension between these two positions that drove Lichtenstein's work at this time, as he began to experiment with the possibilities—and problems—inherent in his chosen approach to painting.

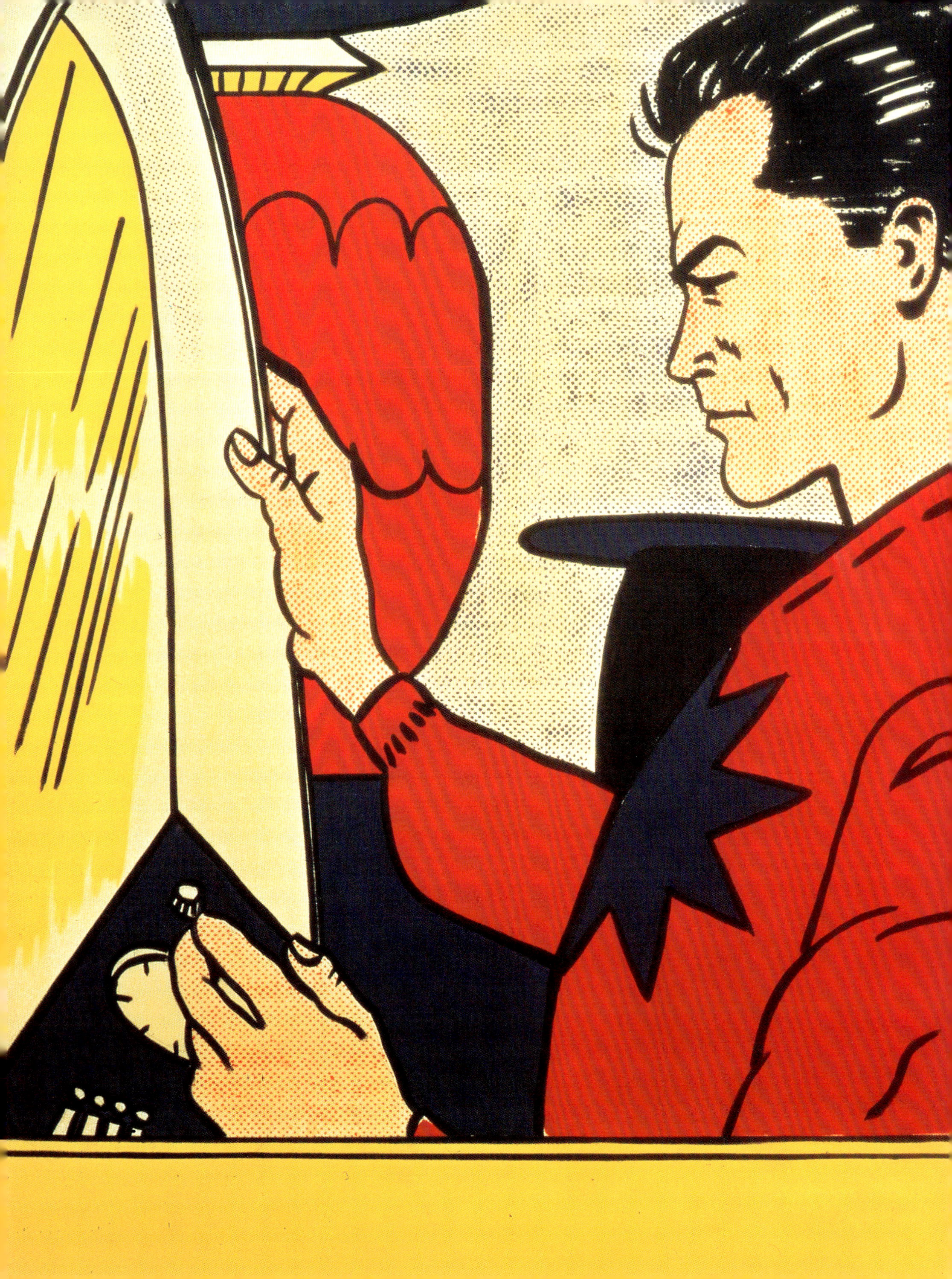

The Image Duplicators

The significance of monocularity to Lichtenstein's project was not limited to its engagement with theoretical problems relating to the mechanical augmentation of vision. In fact, its imaging by the artist was not even limited to its embodiment by human figures. This becomes evident when we examine *Like New* (fig. 66), a painting likely based on an advertisement for a screen door repair service. The right panel contains a field of regular dots, its jagged edges roughly repeating the rectangular enclosure of the canvas. In the left panel an almost identical field is interrupted at its center by an irregular hole. Lichtenstein emphasized the edges of the hole by enlarging and skewing some of the dots in an otherwise regularized field, demonstrating that he was not averse to disrupting mechanical regularity for formal effect. In the first year or so of his Pop practice Lichtenstein produced three such works, each composed of two identically sized panels hinged together; the others are *Bread in Bag* (fig. 67) and *Step-On Can with Leg*. How then does the motif of monocular vision relate to these object-diptychs? Look closely. The conjunction of the two panels in each of these works describes the simplest form of binary opposition: open versus closed. This is the selfsame opposition inscribed on the face of the female figure in *CRAK!*, with one eye open and the other closed. In other words, the configuration of the figure's eyes in that work exemplifies the simplest form of structural difference.

In order to better understand this aspect of the object-diptychs, it is useful to compare Lichtenstein's work with that of his colleague Warhol. It has been a conventional strategy, in treatments of Pop art, to group Lichtenstein's *Like New* (or one of the other object-diptychs) with a group of similar images by Warhol, the *Before and After* canvases of monumentalized nose jobs (fig. 68).[1] Such a comparison can be used to show Pop's indebtedness to commercial modes of illustration. Or it may be used to demonstrate how these artists shared an interest in narrative, particularly the simple narratives (such as fixing a broken screen door or reshaping a

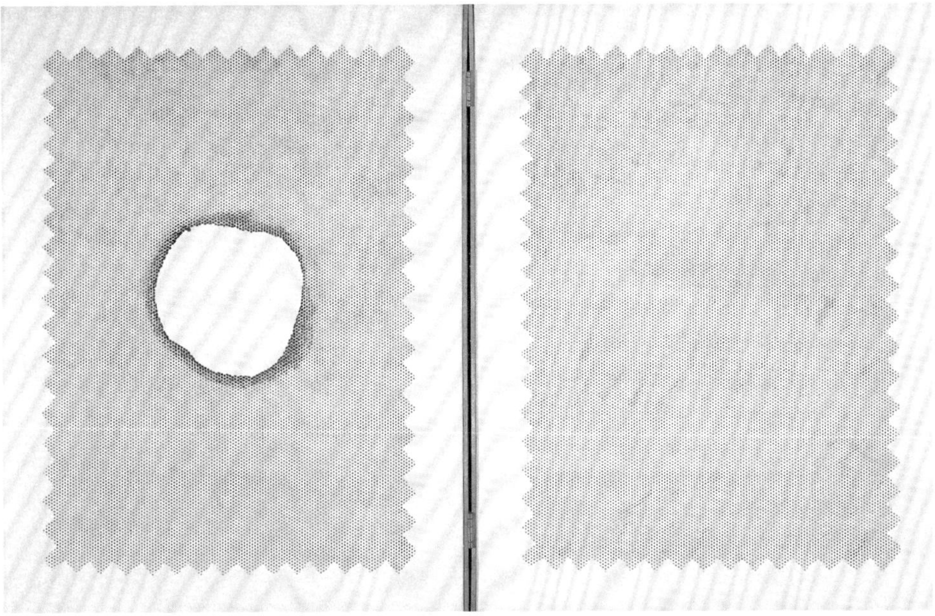

Figure 66.
Like New,
1962.
Oil on canvas,
two panels
36 × 56 in.
(91.4 × 142.2 cm)
overall.
Private collection

nose), at which advertising images excel. Yet there are crucial differences between their treatments of a similar subject. While Warhol pairs his "before" and "after" images on a single canvas, Lichtenstein's paintings are all diptychs, indexing his general resistance to incorporating even minimal repetition within the frame of a canvas. Moreover, in Warhol's work the paired images are distinguished by an alteration in the shape of the woman's profile—a morphological distinction—while, as I've noted, Lichtenstein's paintings all depict what would be described as a fundamentally structural difference. In the next chapter we will more fully explore the semiological—and gendered—implications of the artist's treatment of such difference in his work. Yet Lichtenstein's use of the simplest form of binary opposition points to another set of concerns addressed in his practice during this period, relating to the mechanical transmission of images.

A contemporaneous text, itself steeped in many of the same discourses as Lichtenstein's project, makes clear the correlation between the binary form and mechanical reproduction. In 1960 the art historian E. H. Gombrich published *Art and Illusion,* which collected in print a series of lectures he had delivered in 1956 at the National Gallery of Art in Washington, D.C. In his text Gombrich extended the psychology of perception to the analysis of art objects, treating such problems as the nature of optical illusion and the historical evolution of modes of naturalistic representation. In his first chapter Gombrich recounts an anecdote about painting and the post office to frame a discussion of art as the transmission of codes:

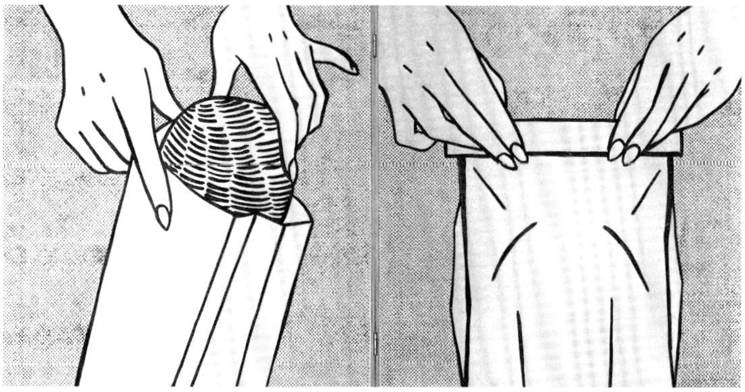

Figure 67.
Bread in Bag, 1961.
Oil on canvas, two panels
28½ × 57 in. (72.4 × 144.8 cm) overall.
Private collection

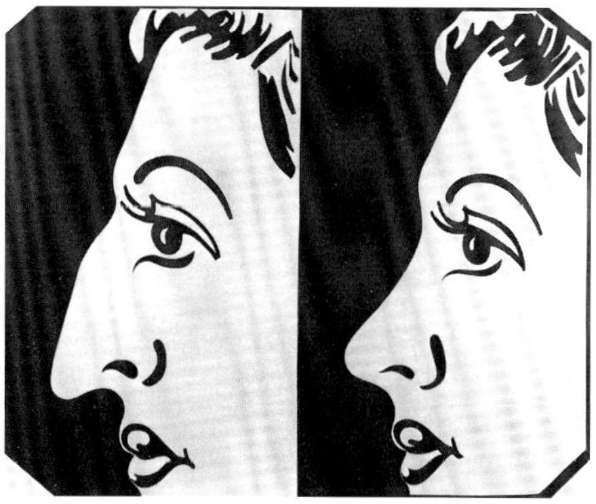

Figure 68.
Andy Warhol, *Before and After 3,* 1962.
Synthetic polymer paint on canvas,
72 × 99⅝ in. (182.9 × 253 cm).
Whitney Museum of American Art,
New York. Purchase, with funds from
Charles Simon

> Post offices (in England, at least) do transmit such visual information as weather charts and photographs by means of telegraph and radio, and to do so they must in fact "code" them into simple signaling systems. The technicalities of this process need not concern us, suffice it to show that a simple but serviceable image can be translated into equal units which are either filled or empty. Any large street sign composed of electric bulbs will demonstrate this principle—a notation of which are to be "off" or "on" will create the required configuration of light. The telegraphed picture and indeed the television screen, produced as they are by the varying intensities of one beam scanning the field, illustrate the principle involved.[2]

The binary oppositions—filled and empty, on and off—cited by Gombrich as necessary for image transmission are the very same described in the three object-diptychs by Lichtenstein (and embodied by the monocular figure). And Gombrich's point that this binary coding is present in most forms of mechanical image transmission—telegraph, radio, electric street sign, and so forth—impels a rereading of certain aspects of Lichtenstein's work. Even though the regularized dots that the artist began to employ during this period are routinely referred to by critics as Ben Day dots—thereby reducing their range of reference to one specific type of half-tone printing technology—they may be interpreted as standing more broadly for any number of methods by which visual information is encoded in order to be transmitted by mechanical means. In a 1974 interview, the artist himself referred his use of dots to a broader context of information transmission: "The dotted areas seem to say 50% red or 50% black or whatever color, making reference to mechanical and insensitive relationships; and they have a meaning relating to the new ways data can be transmitted."[3] In an unpublished 1981 interview he made a similar observation in response to a question about whether his work (specifically those paintings in which he quoted earlier artists like Matisse and Picasso) constituted a response to the ubiquitous color reproduction of artworks: "Yes, [they are] a comment on the fact that we see everything second or third hand and the way information is disseminated through television: reading dots or newspapers' printed pictures of little dots. It's not visible that way, but you know that this is how it's been done. We're getting a sort of yes/no, black/white pattern and that's fairly simple still, but it's fairly complex information."[4]

Although the facture of Lichtenstein's imagery might seem to make reference only to techniques of mechanical printing, his comments suggest that his work was also concerned with the broader implications of image transmission, whether mechanical or electronic. In this way his project addresses concerns that were central to art historical inquiry in the same moment. In this chapter I consider the connections between the artist's work and three roughly contemporaneous projects in art history and criticism. If such a comparison helps us better understand Lichtenstein's engagement with these issues, our analysis will not be limited to examining how textual approaches—that is, those of history, theory, and criticism—shed light on works of art. Rather, such a comparison will be mutually enlightening. We will also see how the artist's practice can, in turn, illuminate the critical approaches taken by scholars who considered how mechanical reproduction had changed the artist's—and viewer's—relationship to the work of art.

LORAN AND REPETITION

Art history is, of course, not the history of works of art; it's the history of slides of works of art.
—Craig Owens, *Beyond Recognition*

The art historian Erle Loran was probably Lichtenstein's most vocal critic in the early 1960s. In concurrent articles in the September 1963 issues of *Art News* and *Artforum* Loran set forth his argument that Pop (as represented by Lichtenstein's work) was not art because it did not embody the principle of "transformation." Loran's critique included—or perhaps more accurately, was based on—reproductions that compared diagrams from his text *Cézanne's Composition* with Lichtenstein's paintings. For example, his *Art News* article "Pop Artists or Copy Cats?" juxtaposed Lichtenstein's *Portrait of Madame Cézanne* with its source image from the author's book (fig. 69). Loran commented: "When it comes to the 6-foot canvas titled *Portrait of Mme. Cézanne* and sold by the Ferus Gallery, Los Angeles, I need not be too worried about whether it is art or not. What I know is what anybody should be able to tell: it was copied from my drawing titled *Diagram.* It appears on page 85 of my book *Cézanne's Composition.* Very well copied too, I must admit. In fact I can see no objection to substituting Lichtenstein's diagram for my own, in the next edition."[5] It seems that Loran just couldn't resist adding that last dig at the artist. For one, he felt that Lichtenstein had effectively stolen what was properly his; note how he refers to his diagram as a drawing with its own title, effectively describing it as a work of art. He also couldn't resist including those reproductions (one of a Loran diagram, the other of a Lichtenstein painting) nestled alongside the text of the article, for they provided the evidence to support his claim.

Such evidence, labeled in the art historical vernacular as "compare-and-contrast," has been used to produce meaning time and again in the discourse of art history.[6] And produce meaning it does, for it depends on the simple Saussurean principle that meaning is produced through difference; any two images placed side by side can be used to construct a story of historical progress, stylistic variation, or the like.[7] In his 1963 article Loran showed his skill with this model, although here it was the implied lack of difference that produced the meaning he was after. With that simple juxtaposition Loran was able to make his case, arguing: "Copies are not transformations. A glance at the two reproductions, Plates I and II, make it clear that the one by Roy Lichtenstein has been copied from my own Diagram on p. 85 of 'Cézanne's Composition.' "[8] This quote is taken not from *Art News* but from the same month's issue of *Artforum:* a strange critical repetition indeed. Was the threat that Lichtenstein's work posed so great that Loran had to present his challenge in two magazines simultaneously? Or did the repetition embodied by the artist's work force the critic to duplicate his own efforts, as if the only way to launch an assault was to use the enemy's tactics against him?

Lichtenstein's and Loran's respective projects were not as diametrically opposed as the critic would have liked to believe. The very form of Loran's critique mimicked the practice he was attacking; in other words, his argument depended on a skillful use of photomechanical reproduction and the attendant eclipse of the original work of art. For it is only in a context in which the original no longer has any authority that a small, printed diagram taken from a book and a large—six-foot-tall, Loran himself tells us—painted canvas can be reproduced side by side, their material differences utterly negated. To make his case, Loran must force the authenticity of the original to wither. Taken this way, we see not that there is a fundamental opposition between critic and artist but rather that both are caught in the same bind: each of their projects required an embrace of techniques of me-

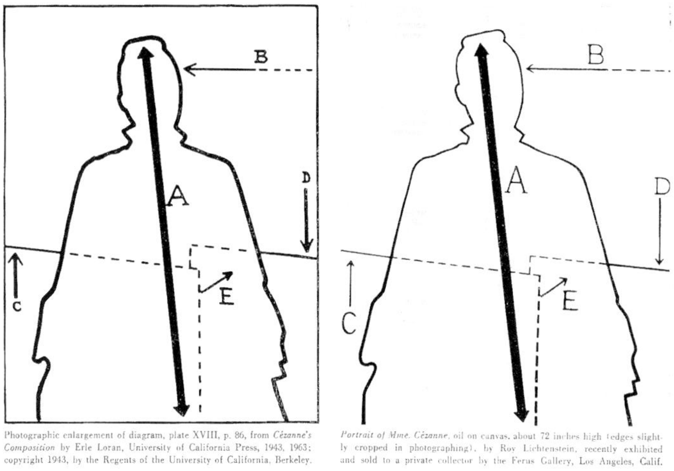

Figure 69. Illustration from Erle Loran, "Pop Artists or Copy Cats?" in *Art News* 62, no. 5 (September 1963)

chanical reproduction yet included a valorization of the original (i.e., the work of art) as a special thing, bracketed off from the realm of reproductions. Despite Lichtenstein's treatment of images appropriated from mechanically reproduced contexts (comic books, print advertisements, and art reproductions), he continued to rely on the illusory uniqueness of the work of art to distinguish himself from commercial artists. Ironically, Loran found himself in much the same bind; his project was founded on access to reproductions of works of art (his book *Cézanne's Composition,* after all, juxtaposes the author's own diagrams with reproductions of Cézanne's paintings).[9] Yet the fundamentally reproductive nature of his project is joined to a concurrent fetishization of the original, which appears ever more completely lost.

This inescapable logic of the lost original (as an intrinsic component of Loran's project, and perhaps of art historical discourse more generally) is no more evident than in *Cézanne's Composition* itself. Loran's attempt to get at the truth of the artist's work did not consist merely in his creation of those rather odd little diagrams of Cézanne's paintings; he also went back to the landscape in order to gain a fuller understanding of the artist's work.[10] As Loran wrote, "The photographic material for this study was collected when, for more than two years, I lived in Cézanne's studio in Aix-en-Provence, painting in the Cézanne country and taking snapshots whenever I came upon motifs of Cézanne's paintings."[11] His book thus juxtaposes photographic reproductions of Cézanne's paintings, diagrams of their compositional structure, and photographs of the actual sites in the landscape from which the artist ostensibly drew his paintings (fig. 70). It is as if, lost in the welter of reproductions that are his stock-in-trade—the photographs, the slides, the diagrams—Loran had to search back even farther, to the natural landscape itself, to

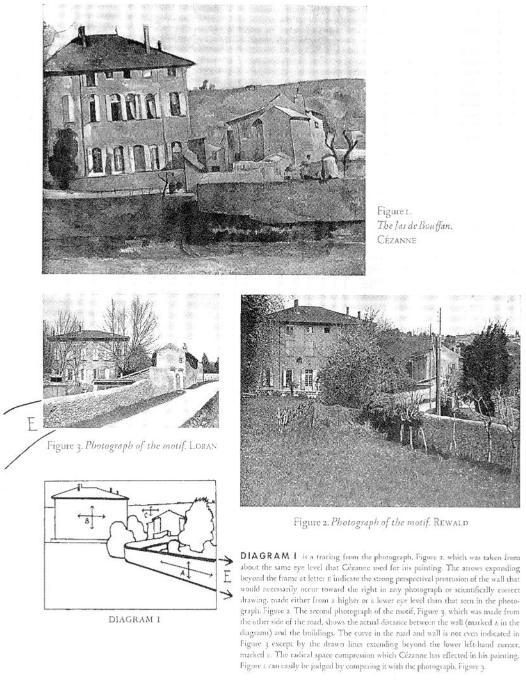

Figure 70. Page from Erle Loran, *Cézanne's Composition* (1943)

attempt to locate the true origins of Cézanne's art. Ironically, his search for a lost original results only in the dissemination of more reproductions, namely the photographs of the landscape that fill his book. In the context of his project, art history comes to appear as a veritably melancholic discipline; the art historian may fixate on the lost original as a balm against the discipline's submersion in reproduced imagery of every sort.[12] Lichtenstein was in a similar position. His continued allegiance to the practice of painting—which allowed him to mark off his work as radically different from the "reproductions" that preceded and followed his images—demonstrated his investment in the authenticity of the original.

Even as a student Lichtenstein would have recognized the enormous impact of mechanical reproduction on what Walter Benjamin called the aura of the work of art.[13] He noted in an early interview that he rarely had access to art objects in school: "Almost everything was slides. I doubt that we even visited [the museum]. . . . It was all done in the classroom."[14] Significantly, that widely used method of art history—the simple juxtaposition of two images, side-by-side—would later make an appearance in his work in object-diptychs like *Bread in Bag* and *Like New*. In these works the artist seems to be flagging, even parodying, the Saussurean truism noted earlier: the differences between each pendant image act as a kind of visual pun, demonstrating the simplest means by which narrative (bread is put in a bag, a garbage can lid is opened) can be constructed.[15] This is especially true of *Step-On*

Can with Leg (fig. 71). What is striking is the relative lack of difference between the two panels: there is only the slightest indication of a thinning of the leg in the right panel (which would indicate a flexion of the foot), and of a shifting of the skirt. Even so, these almost imperceptible modulations, taken along with the contrast between the closed and open lids, suggest a particular reading: between the left and right panels the feminine foot pushed down on the pedal, opening the lid.[16] In this way *Step-On Can with Leg* expresses not so much that there is always difference within repetition but that even the slightest amount of difference introduced into repetition may allow for narrative, for a story to be told. Lichtenstein referred to this possibility in 1963 when he discussed the distance between his work and his comic book sources:

> I think my work is different from comic strips—but I wouldn't call it transformation; I don't think that whatever is meant by it is important to art. What I do is form, whereas the comic strip is not formed in the sense I'm using the word; the comics have shapes but there has been no effort to make them intensely unified. The purpose is different, one intends to depict and I intend to unify. And my work is actually different from comic strips in that every mark is really in a different place, however slight the difference seems to some. The difference is often not great, but it is crucial.[17]

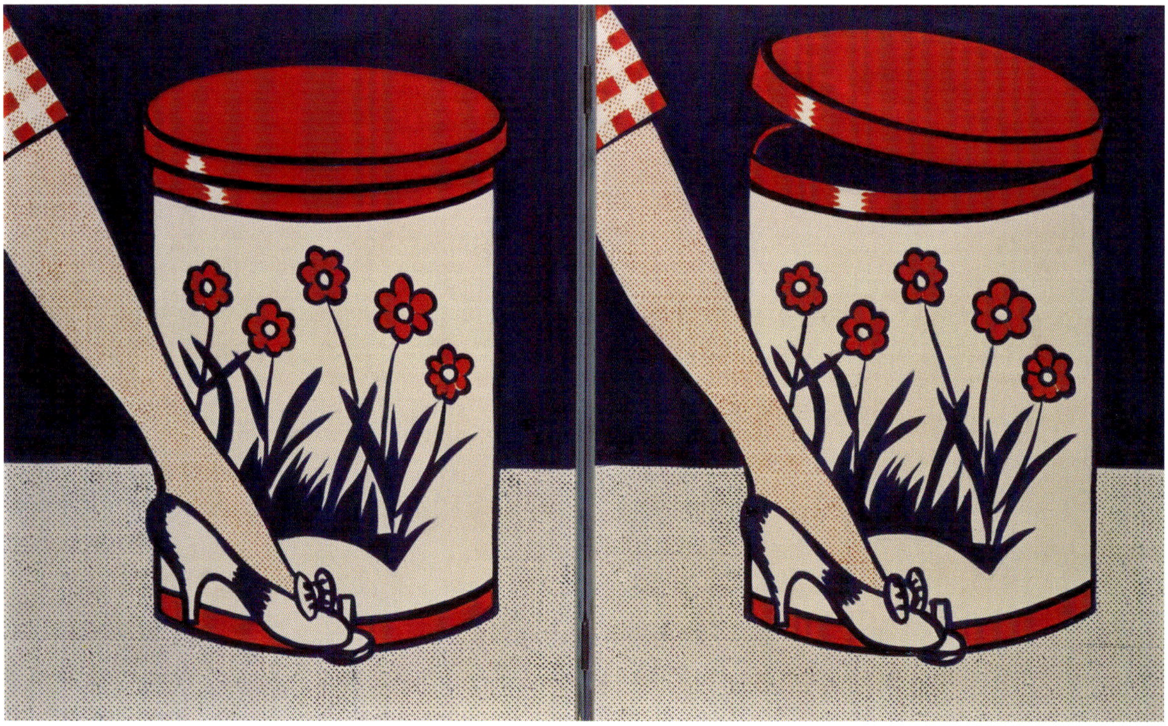

Figure 71.
Step-On Can with Leg, 1961.
Oil on canvas, two panels 31⅞ × 52 in. (81 × 132 cm) overall.
Kaiser Wilhelm Museum, Krefeld. Lauffs Collection

Listen to the artist's conviction: he asserts here that within repetition, even slight differences are crucial, for they provide a space for the artist to work. That is his hope against all hopes. However, the strength of his assertion is evidence enough that he recognized yet another, more threatening possibility: that within repetition there may be nothing but repetition—and thus no space for articulating subjectivity, artistic or otherwise.

GOMBRICH AND REPRODUCTION

If Loran's attacks provide us substantial insight into problems of originality and repetition embedded in Lichtenstein's project, the work of E. H. Gombrich serves to connect the artist's practice with another set of issues central to art historical analysis. Earlier in the chapter an excerpt from Gombrich's 1960 text *Art and Illusion* helped point out the relation between binary coding and mechanical image transmission. There is some evidence to suggest that Lichtenstein read *Art and Illusion* just before or soon after his initial experimentation with Pop imagery; the issues raised in the book correspond with the artist's concerns in a number of ways.[18]

Gombrich's text was a significant addition to the literature on art and perceptual psychology—a literature, we will remember, central to Hoyt Sherman's project. For this reason it is unsurprising that *Art and Illusion* contains a number of images that are found as well in Sherman's published texts.[19] Gombrich's book includes an extended discussion of the Ames demonstrations, those peep show–like demonstrations of optical illusion that Sherman had appropriated and expanded on in his own Visual Demonstration Center. If Gombrich's interests in visual perception and illusion intersected with those of Lichtenstein's teacher (and of the artist himself), there is even more in his text that may have struck a chord with an artist beginning to experiment with cartoon imagery. Gombrich devotes an entire chapter of *Art and Illusion* to what he calls the Experiment of Caricature, in which he analyzes caricature's foundation in the artist's ability to grasp a series of conventional notations. His discussion of the difficulty of notating emotional expression parallels Lichtenstein's own experimentation—in his military- and romance-comic images—with simplified, conventional techniques for depicting emotion. Moreover, in its claim that the development of caricature had a great deal in common with developments in modern art, the form of Gombrich's argument resonates with Lichtenstein's own approach to art making.[20] For his text is studded with reproductions, not only of works of art (by Rembrandt, Dürer, Giotto, and others) but also of a variety of images from popular culture: *New Yorker* cartoons, advertising posters, Al Capp's Shmoo and Walt Disney's Dumbo. This in-

Figure 72.
Joseph Bieder, *Poster,* 1953, from E. H. Gombrich, *Art and Illusion* (1960)

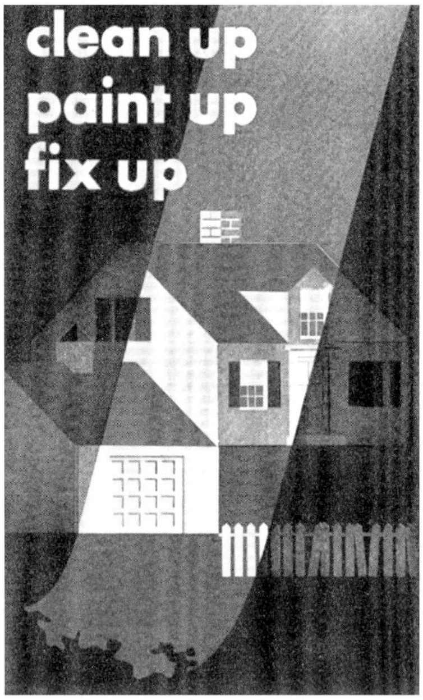

terest in what might be termed visual culture—in which the work of art maintains some equivalence with the broader category of the image in general—puts Gombrich in the role that Lichtenstein would soon assume: appropriator of images from popular culture.

One of those images, in fact, would seem to be the final evidence needed to demonstrate that Lichtenstein read—or at least made use of—Gombrich's text at some point during this period. On page 56 of *Art and Illusion* Gombrich reproduced a 1953 poster for the National Clean-Up Paint-Up Fix-Up Bureau (fig. 72). Although that governmental agency has long since faded into history, we can still understand Gombrich's use of the image: it quite effectively demonstrates how in an otherwise low-contrast image an abrupt tonal variation can provide startling illusionistic effect. As Gombrich noted, "It is particularly the impression of light, as we know, that rests exclusively on gradients and not, as one might expect, on the objective brightness of colors. Wherever we observe a sudden steep rise in the brightness of a tone we accept it as a token of light" (55). In two paintings from 1962—*Sponge* and *Sponge II*—Lichtenstein exploited this illusion for an effect nearly identical to that in the poster from Gombrich's text (fig. 73). If he derived the woman's hand from elsewhere, it is likely that he appropriated from Gombrich's book this playful visual shorthand for cleaning.[21] From this point on it is utterly tempting to see *Art and Illusion* as a kind of primer or code book for much of Lichtenstein's work at this time, from the treatment of visual illusion to the recuperation of the art of caricature and cartoon. This is particularly true when we

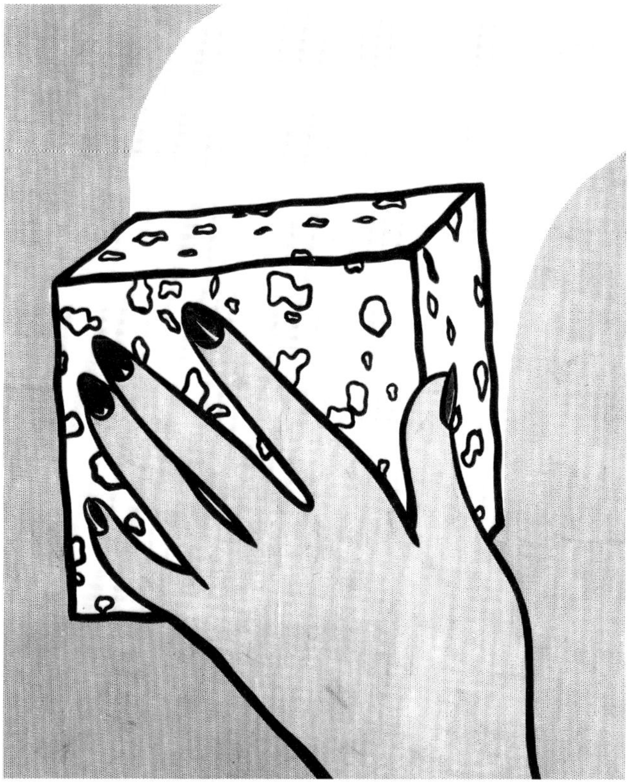

Figure 73.
Sponge, 1962.
Oil on canvas,
68 × 56 in.
(172.7 × 142.2 cm).
Private collection

read the conclusion of the fifth chapter of Gombrich's text, in which he refers to the "moving testimony" of a group of drawings by the painter John Constable:

> It is a series of copies by Constable from a drawing book by Alexander Cozens, the eighteenth-century landscape painter who published for the use of his pupils a series of schemata for clouds. Constable, the bold critic of tradition, sat down and carefully copied these plates, which teach the student a variety of typical skies. . . . We know by now what Cozens teaches Constable. Not, indeed, what clouds look like, but a series of possibilities, of schemata, which should increase his awareness through visual classification (176–178).

This heartfelt narrative of nature, artistic schema, and copying echoes Lichtenstein's own landscape works of 1964–69, which use a conventional system of notation to depict vistas of land, sea, and sky (fig. 74). Nevertheless, the artist's output cannot be reduced to an illustration of Gombrich's theoretical observations, just as we cannot explain his work as a direct outgrowth of—or in David Deitcher's words, "complement" to—Hoyt Sherman's instructional principles.[22] When asked at length about Sherman's flash lab and Visual Demonstration Center, Lichtenstein asserted that his experience with those experiments in visual perception had

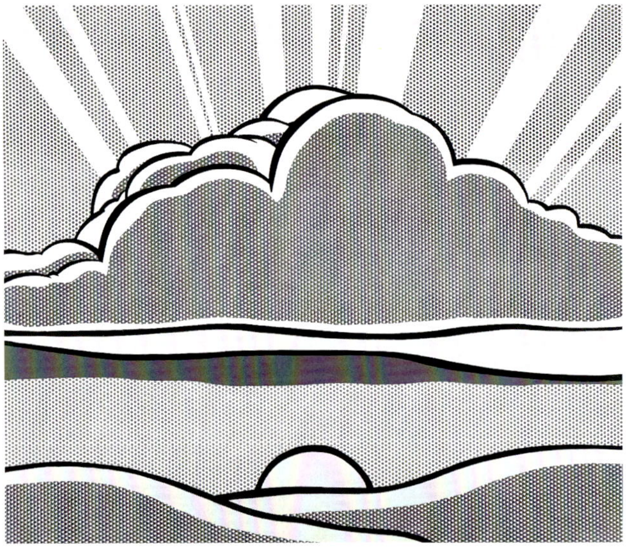

Figure 74.
Sinking Sun, 1964.
Oil and Magna on canvas,
68 × 80 in. (172.7 × 203.2 cm).
Private collection

"always influenced [my] painting, but only in that it drove home certain things clearly . . . I don't think that the painting is a visual demonstration."[23]

Gombrich's work was significant because it marked a historical shift in the discourse on art and visual perception. As his discussion of Cozens and Constable indicates, Gombrich wanted to challenge the received method by which perceptual psychology accounted for the historical evolution of artistic styles. His challenge in *Art and Illusion* was in part to the modernist conceit of the "innocent eye," the notion that the evolution of naturalistic representation had consisted of a gradual stripping away of the artist's knowledge of the world and an attendant embrace of pure perception: "To Ruskin, as to Roger Fry, it is our knowledge of the visual world that lies at the root of all the difficulties of art. If we could only manage to forget it all, the problem of painting would become easy—the problem, that is, of rendering a three-dimensional world on a flat canvas. In reality, Ruskin thought, we do not even see the third dimension. What we really see is only a medley of colored patches such as Turner paints" (296). Gombrich rightfully saw as naive this view of an unmediated relation between the painter's vision and the perceptual world, and he attempted to correct it by inserting into the equation a third term: the accumulated history of prior representational schema, in other words *pictures*. Gombrich argues that it is a "memory of pictures seen" that mediates between the visible world and the painter's canvas (314). Discussing this archive of images in the painter's mind, he remarks on a particular aspect of a landscape study made by Constable at the age of twenty-two: "On the reverse he wrote the following note to aid his memory: 'Fine, blowing day, tone very mellow, like the mildest of Gaspar Poussin and Sir George Beaumont, on the whole deeper toned than this drawing' "

(315). Further on in his discussion, after musing on Constable's dependence on Gainsborough, Gombrich considers the implications of the artist's reference to preexisting conventions of representation:

> If Constable saw the English landscape in terms of Gainsborough's paintings, what about Gainsborough himself? We can answer this. Gainsborough saw the lowland scenery of East Anglia in terms of Dutch paintings, which he arduously studied and copied. We have his drawing after Ruisdael, and we know that it was this vocabulary which he applied to the rendering of his own idyllic woodland scenes. And where did the Dutch get their vocabulary? The answer to this type of question is precisely what is known as the "history of art." All paintings, as Wölfflin said, owe more to other paintings than they owe to direct observation (316–317).

There are limits to applying this analysis to Lichtenstein, in large part because Gombrich is mostly concerned with the history of naturalistic representation. Nevertheless, the quote indicates what might be termed the provisionally postmodern turn expressed by Gombrich's theory, in that it places importance on a preexisting storehouse of images on which the artist's work is understood to depend. In short, a notion of what might rightly be called "image duplication"—a dependence on a set of cultural codes—plays a central role in Gombrich's theory of art and visual perception. Even if one rejects Gombrich as a direct influence on Lichtenstein—for the artist had been using appropriated (albeit significantly altered) imagery in his paintings since at least the early 1950s—then at the very least the two seem to have come at the same historical moment to remarkably similar positions vis-à-vis the conventionality of the image.

Norman Bryson has categorized Gombrich's theoretical position in much the way I've described the tension underlying Lichtenstein's artistic project. Bryson considers Gombrich's analysis as transitional in that he discarded the received reading of direct interaction between artist and world (by recognizing the mediating effect of preexisting representational schema) yet retained a fairly conventional model of perception.[24] We may view Lichtenstein's work in much the same way: he developed certain strategies that were in many ways antithetical to the mainstream modernist discourse of the time (including his wholesale appropriation of preexisting images and his use of formal devices borrowed from commercial illustration and mechanical printing), yet in the end he used those strategies in the service of aesthetics as such.

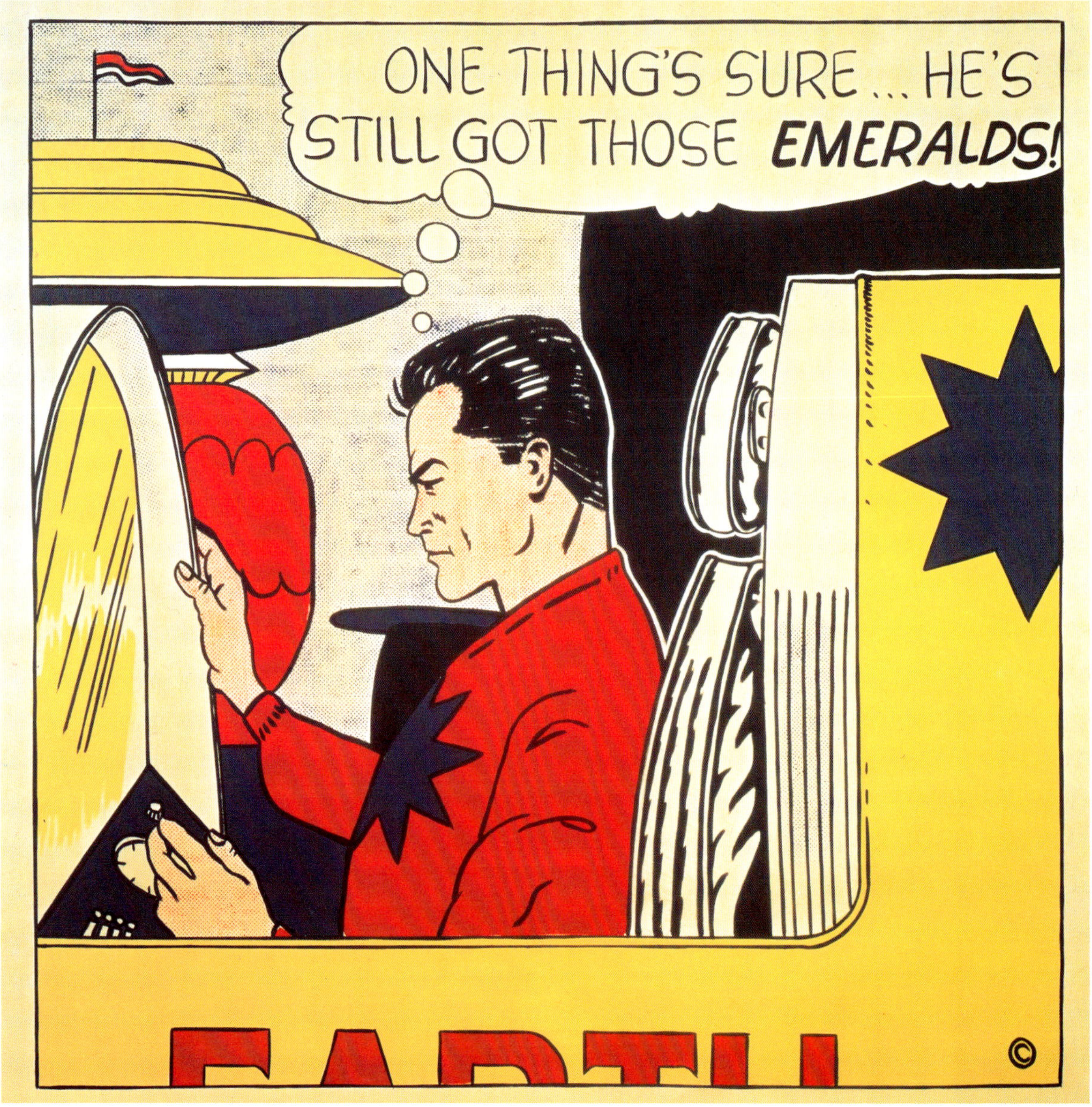

Figure 75. *Emeralds,* 1961. Oil on canvas, 68½ × 68½ in. (174 × 174 cm). Private collection

STEINBERG AND REPRESENTATION

If, as we have seen, developments in image technologies have an impact on the work of the artist, they affect the role of the viewer as well. In fact, Lichtenstein's work bears evidence of his concern with historically changed modes of viewership, in that certain paintings from this period compare or correlate the surface of the

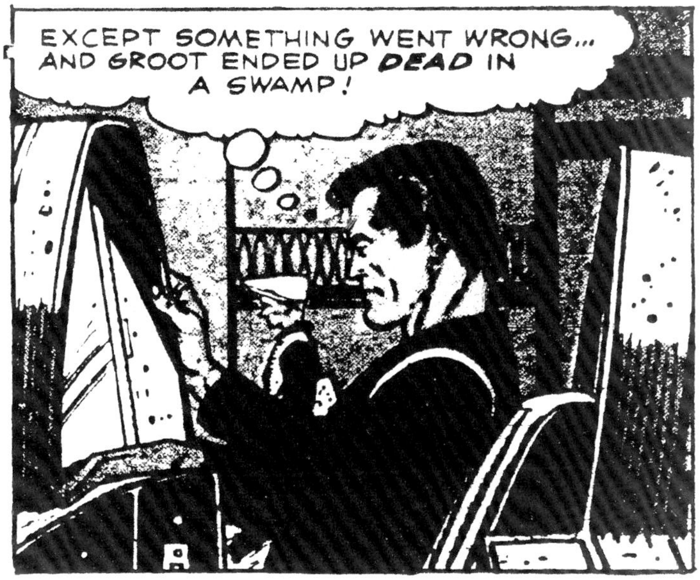

Figure 76.
George Tuska,
panel from *Buck Rogers*
(July 23, 1961)

canvas with electronic viewing screens. His concern with such issues again connects his work with art historical interest in the changing status of visual representation in the face of technological developments.

Close to the time he painted *I Can See the Whole Room* in the summer of 1961, Lichtenstein produced another work that depicted the interaction between a human figure and a machine. In that painting, entitled *Emeralds,* a male figure is shown seated—in profile—at the controls of a futuristic vehicle (fig. 75). Lichtenstein appropriated the image from elements in the *Buck Rogers* Sunday comic strip, making significant changes to the image in the process of executing his painting (fig. 76).[25] For one, he borrowed the overall image from the second panel of the strip but substituted a line of text ("ONE THING'S SURE . . . HE'S STILL GOT THOSE *EMERALDS!*") from a subsequent panel. That dialogue is more in keeping with the elliptical texts that Lichtenstein seems to have favored in this early moment of experimentation with Pop (as in works like *The Engagement Ring* and *Mr. Bellamy*).[26] He vertically lengthened the composition to turn a rectangular panel into a square. He changed the background in various ways: he erased a passing figure, removed a decorative motif from directly behind the seated figure's profile and incorporated a vaguely futuristic architectural structure in the left background. He also added the top segments of letters (that look to spell out "EARTH") and a starburst design to the exterior of the vehicle in which the figure is seated, and he applied a similar starburst to the figure's clothing. It is unclear why those last several changes were made. At this early stage Lichtenstein may have envisioned himself experimenting with various genres of comic-strip narrative (which would include the military theme of *Mr. Bellamy,* the feminine romance of *The Engagement Ring,* and the action-suspense of *I Can See the Whole Room*). In this way he might have intended *Emeralds,* appropriated as it was from the *Buck Rogers* comic strip, to stand for the science fiction genre, yet the panel in its original format—particularly when separated from its larger narrative context—might not have sufficiently signified the futurism of that genre. His alterations to the image may have been intended to address that problem: the barely legible inscription on the side of the vehicle allows the viewer to place the scene on Earth, while the structure in the background and the futuristic vehicle signify that this could be a scene taking place only in the future.

The control panel facing the figure in *Emeralds* is in keeping with the seeming futurism of the image. Lichtenstein completely added this motif, both the viewing screen and the instrument panel below. We have already seen how he consistently incorporated signs of technology into his work, particularly in the war-comic images that present an interaction between a human figure and a machine; note then the structural correlations between *Emeralds* and the 1962 fighter pilot image *Brattata* (fig. 77). In each of these images a figure in profile is depicted sitting at an electronic console. The paintings are linked, then, both in their compositional approaches and in their related depictions of acts of viewing with mechanical devices. In the later painting the figure is much larger in relation to the overall composition, his helmeted head taking up almost half the canvas. This trend toward ever-greater magnification of the figure—toward the state of the cinematic close-up—characterizes Lichtenstein work as it developed during the early 1960s. Yet aside from this difference, each of these paintings depicts a human figure facing a flat screen, one that the artist seems to be correlating with the surface of the canvas itself.

Lichtenstein's alteration of his sources demonstrates the extent to which he was making connections between the picture plane and these electronic viewing screens. In *Emeralds* the connections are made on several levels at once. In artist George Tuska's *Buck Rogers* comic strip we are afforded other views of the title character's futuristic vehicle, which seem to indicate that the depicted glass at left is not a vertical screen at all but rather a portion of the vehicle's canopy. Lichtenstein reconstructed the vehicle, depicting a flat screen—like that of a television set or other viewing-device—in front of the figure. He added a diagonal line to indicate where its lower edge meets the control console below; applied more extensive diagonal hatchings than Tuska had used to signify reflections off the screen; and added a field of uneven yellow marks—running roughly parallel to and beneath the black hatchings—that further suggest a reflective surface. Moreover, Lichtenstein's wholesale addition of the control console (that panel studded with knobs and dials directly below the screen) involved the alteration of yet another element. In Tuska's comic strip Buck Rogers is shown with his hand on the foreshortened, open door of his craft, a sign that he has just entered the vehicle and is in the process of closing the door. In the context of the strip this served as a narrative element, providing a bridge between the prior panel—which shows him walking toward the vehicle—and the subsequent one, in which his craft is shown flying away. Lichtenstein's removal of this motif (that is, the hand closing the door) does more than merely discard a now-unneeded narrative element. In his painting there is no trace of a door at all. A wide, unbroken yellow band runs along the bottom edge of the image, turns up at the right corner, and extends about three-quarters up the side, creating an L-shaped band that frames the bottom and right edges of the painting.

A frame, most certainly. In his comic strip panel Tuska had taken pains to treat the rightmost canopy element volumetrically; he had carefully applied shading to it, tilted it diagonally backward, and shown its curved edge receding back. In contrast Lichtenstein only retains a minimal (one might even say vestigial) area of shading, while he does away with those other elements completely. The resulting L-shaped band appears utterly flat, even more like a frame because its sides run parallel to the framing edge of the canvas. That band is pushed up to the surface of the canvas with the figure appearing behind it, much like the flat plane (with its peephole) through which the figure appears in *I Can See the Whole Room.* Lichtenstein even inscribed elements onto that band—those upper portions of lettering that seem to indicate the word "EARTH," and the starburst motif—that emphasize not only its virtual flatness but also its function as a surface for inscription.[27] If the image suggests a correlation between the depicted figure's orientation toward an electronic screen and the viewer's orientation toward the painting, this is only emphasized by the innermost corner of that yellow framing band. Lichtenstein gave the corner a slight curve that recalls the distinctive inner corners of a television screen.

The artist continued to work through this connection between depicted viewing screen and canvas in *Brattata.* A comparison of his painting with the comic book panel on which it was based again shows how subtle changes affected the meaning of image, particularly in terms of the viewer's relation to the depicted scene. In the source image for *Brattata*—a panel from the *All American Men of War* comic book (fig. 78)—artist Russ Heath had not only (correctly) depicted the reflector gun sight panel tilted down, but he also slightly angled the cockpit's con-

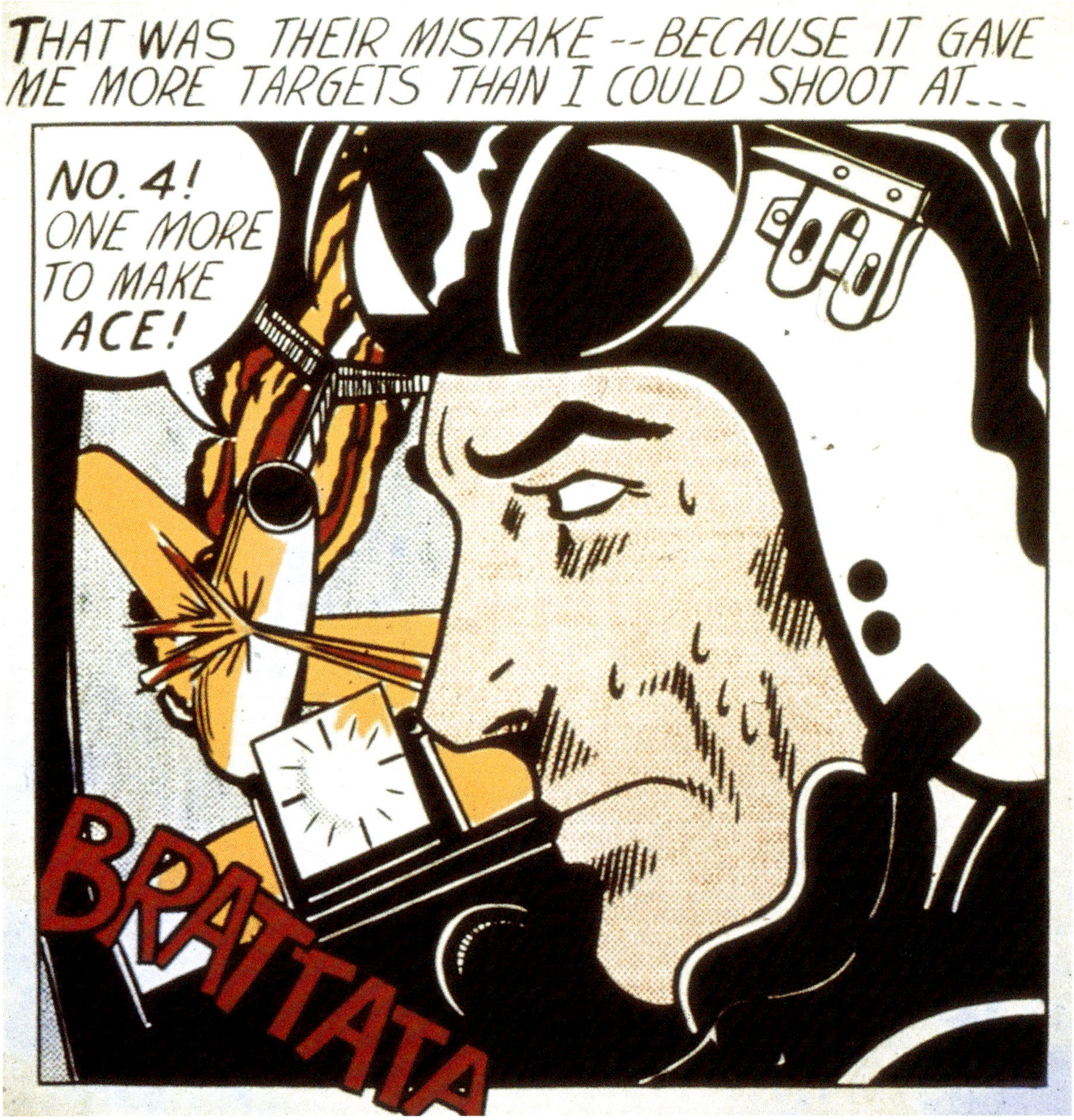

Figure 77. *Brattata,* 1962. Oil on canvas, 42 × 42 in. (106.7 × 106.7 cm). Private collection

trol panel so that it reads as spatially receding to the right. In contrast, in Lichtenstein's painting the glass reflector and control panel are depicted straight on—that is, parallel to the plane of the canvas. The image thus more readily implicates the viewer, rather than the depicted pilot, in the activity of targeting and firing at the enemy plane. This reading is given further force when we notice the artist's

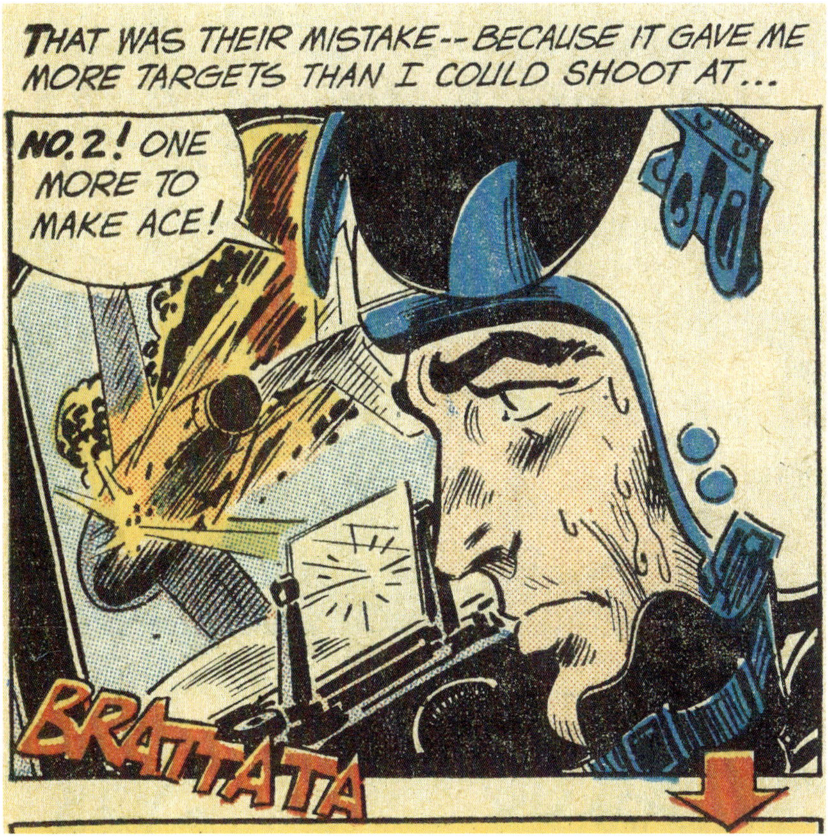

Figure 78. Russ Heath, panel from "Aces Wild!" in *All American Men of War* no. 89 (January–February 1962)

treatment of the control knob directly below the gun sight's reflector panel. Heath had given it only the barest indication (a small arc, less than a half-circle), while Lichtenstein depicts the knob whole, in part by lowering the image's bottom framing edge. Finally, we view a portion of the represented image—the enemy plane being shot down—through yet another screen: the windshield of the depicted fighter plane. In this detail the artist again departed from his source; he changed the orientation of the leftmost band so that, while curved (in keeping with the curvature of a plane's cockpit), it more closely parallels the left edge of the canvas. In other words, here—as in *Emeralds*—he provided visual cues for a correlation between the depicted viewing screen and the material surface of his painting.

In these works, then, Lichtenstein correlates the flat surface of the canvas with that of the viewing screen, not only in the depicted scenarios but in formal devices that call our attention to the picture plane as a kind of screen for viewing. In this way his work confronts issues similar to those addressed by the art historian Leo Steinberg in an important essay—entitled "Other Criteria"—on art of this period.[28] Dissatisfied with the orthodoxies of mainstream modernist criticism, Steinberg desired to find a set of "other criteria" by which to judge artistic practices, criteria at a remove from what he saw as the unyielding, teleological formulations of such modernist critics as Clement Greenberg. As such, he proposed replacing criteria such as the notion of "pictorial flatness" advocated by Greenberg with a consideration of "how the artist's pictorial surface tilts into the space of the viewer's imagination" (82). According to Steinberg, even such twentieth-century movements as cubism and Abstract Expressionism held in common with the work of the Old Masters "the conception of the picture as representing a world, some sort of worldspace which reads on the picture plane in correspondence with the erect human posture. The top of the picture corresponds to where we hold our heads aloft; while its lower edge gravitates to where we place our feet" (82). However, beginning in the 1950s—particularly in the art of Robert Rauschenberg—this "psychic address" of the image changes. The art of the 1960s instantiates a horizontal address to the viewer, representing a shift from nature to culture in the guise of what Steinberg labels the "flatbed picture plane": "The pictures of the last fifteen to twenty years insist on a radically new orientation, in which the painted surface is no longer the analogue of a visual experience of nature but of operational processes" (84). Rauschenberg's world, according to Steinberg, is "not the world of the Renaissance man who looked for his weather clues out of the window; but the world of men who turn knobs to hear a taped message, 'precipitation probability ten percent tonight,' electronically transmitted from some windowless booth" (90).

A world of information, transmitted electronically and received at the turn of a knob: this is the type of experience imaged repeatedly in Lichtenstein's work. In fact, in his essay Steinberg recognized the relation between the artist's work and the issues he was addressing: "When Roy Lichtenstein in the early sixties painted an Air Force officer kissing his girl good-bye, the actual subject matter was the mass-produced comic-book image; ben-day dots and stereotyped drawing ensured that the image was understood as a representation of printed matter" (90). Steinberg's assessment is accurate to a certain extent: as we have discussed throughout, the facture of Lichtenstein's work calls our attention to its relation to modes of mechanical reproduction. Yet there are limits to his account (which, we should remember, was formulated in the context of Rauschenberg's quite different project), particularly in regard to Steinberg's estimation of the "actual subject matter" of the artist's work. This has been a longstanding approach: to reduce the meaning of Lichtenstein's images to their status as representations of "printed matter." However, this approach has only served to draw our attention away from the scenes depicted in his paintings. Our careful examination of his imagery has repeatedly shown that those scenes are key to understanding the significance of his work: they foreground acts of viewing, technologies of vision and display, and the relations between work of art, artist, and viewer. In so doing they raised concerns that were central to the theorization of art at the same moment and formed the basis of his project in the early 1960s.

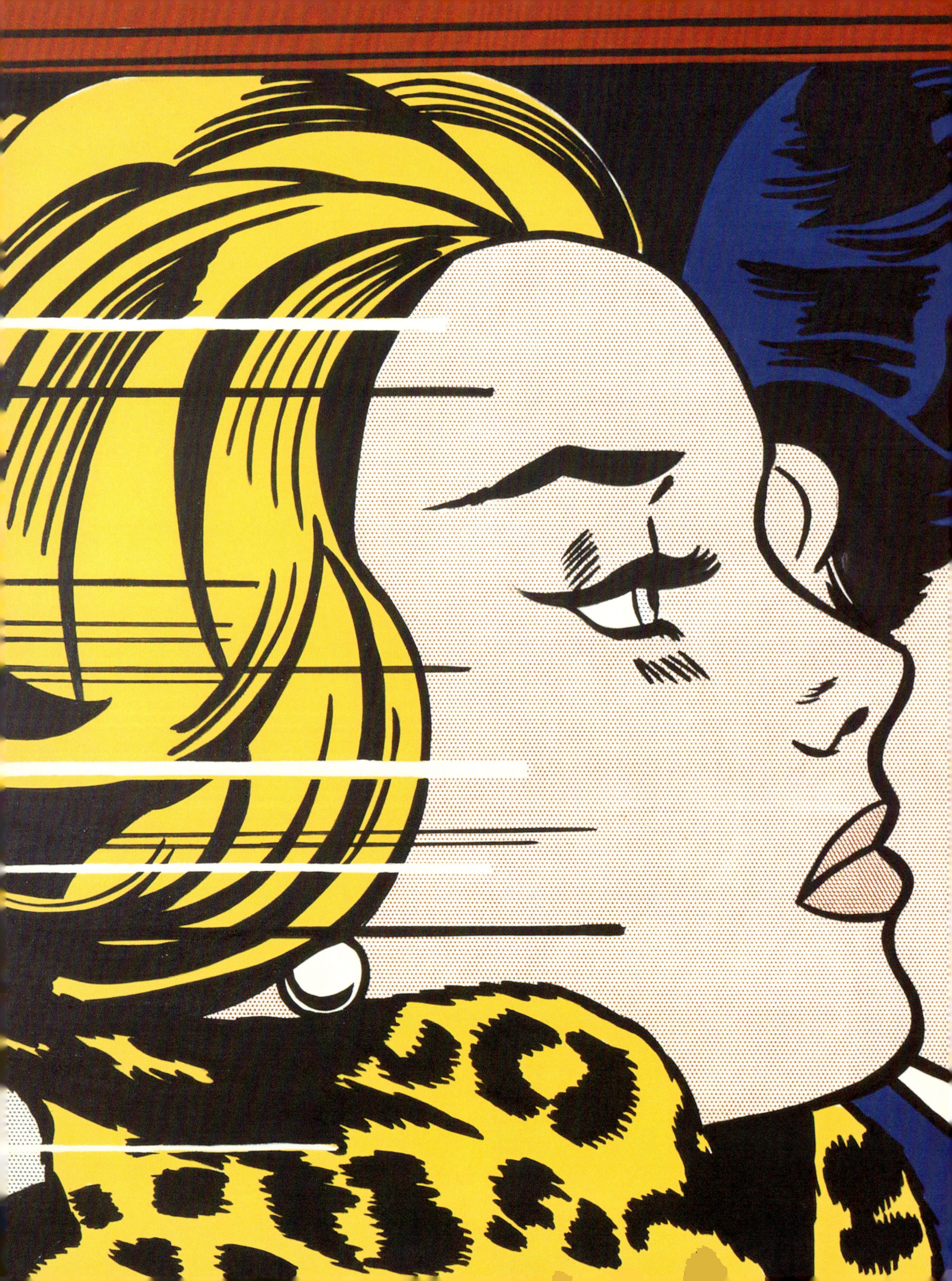

Engendering Difference

Lichtenstein's 1962 canvas *Masterpiece* (fig. 79) is set in the interior of a painter's studio. To the right, a male figure—presumably an artist, garbed in black turtleneck—is shown in rigid profile, looking in the direction of a painting at left. Or rather, at left we see an element that stands synecdochically for a painting: the depicted back corner of a canvas of the kind Lichtenstein would expand on several years later in a series of *Stretcher Bar* paintings. Between the two—male figure and work of art—stands a blonde female figure, who offers a glowing review: "WHY, BRAD DARLING, THIS PAINTING IS A **MASTERPIECE**! MY, SOON YOU'LL HAVE ALL OF **NEW YORK** CLAMORING FOR YOUR WORK!" The image seems an ironic joke on the work of the painter. It proffers the impassive, inscrutable countenance of the male artist; the overblown declaration of a female figure who takes on the traditional role of the artist's muse; and a painting (a presumed masterpiece), albeit one we cannot view. The textual reference to New York, and the diagonal grid partially visible in the left background—visual shorthand for the pitched attic window of the artist's garret or loft—only add to the sense that this is a parodic treatment of the clichéd theme of the artist's studio. However, this is not an isolated image: it relates—structurally and thematically—to other paintings produced by Lichtenstein at about the same time. In the previous chapter, I discussed two paintings, *Emeralds* and *Brattata,* which showed figures positioned before electronic viewing screens. A comparison of these two with *Masterpiece* demonstrates that all three are similarly structured: in each of these works a male figure, shown in profile, looks toward an element or elements at left that represent flat surfaces for viewing, whether electronic screen, windshield and gun sight, or painter's canvas. The connection is also made apparent by the similarity of the male figures in *Emeralds* and *Masterpiece,* right down to the depicted sheens on their jet-black hair. The substitution, in *Masterpiece,* of the painter's canvas for a mechanical device

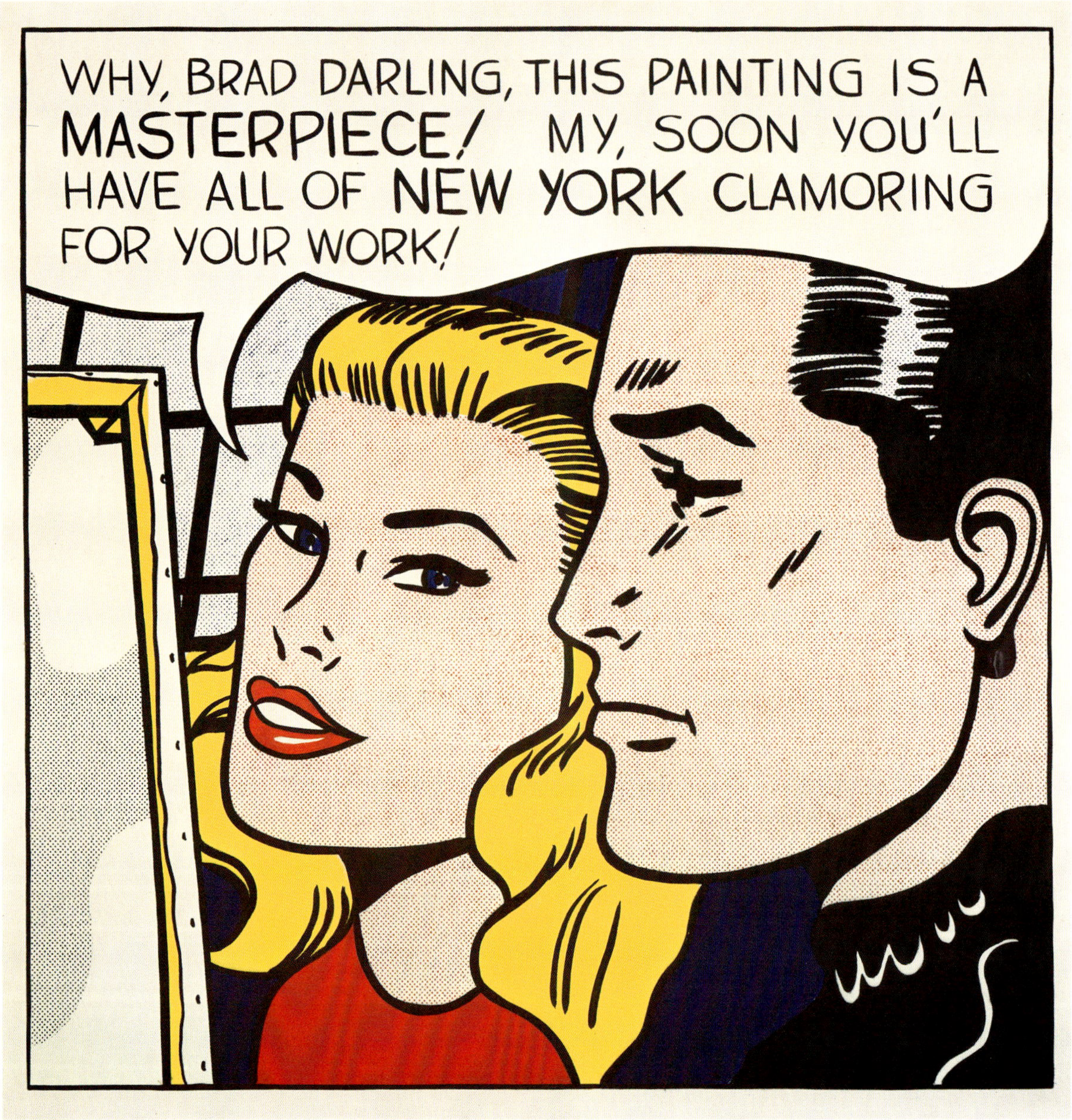

Figure 79. *Masterpiece,* 1962. Oil on canvas, 54 × 54 in. (137.2 × 137.2 cm). Private collection

only reinforces our sense that Lichtenstein's imagery articulates a connection between mechanically augmented seeing and viewing works of art.

However, we have seen that the artist's work consistently attempts to maintain a distinction between those two modes. How, then, might that difference be articulated in these images, if not in his practice, more generally? It is not only that in *Masterpiece* the depicted scene has shifted from the cockpit of a fighter plane or futuristic vehicle to the interior of an artist's studio, for a female figure has been added as well. This is not an incidental change. In this chapter we will see how Lichtenstein used sexual difference to map the imagined distinction between work of art and mechanically reproduced image. The representation of gendered difference provided a way for the artist to work through the conventionalized language of graphic form he had incorporated into his practice at this time.

PAIRING THE GENDERED IMAGE

Lichtenstein's imagery—particularly the comic-derived works of the early 1960s—lends itself to classification along gender lines. Cécile Whiting, for one, has called our attention to the ways in which the artist's images emphasize gender distinctions and thus polarize the opposition between masculinity and femininity.[1] However, in contrasting masculine scenes of war with images of feminine romance Whiting's analysis only takes account of the most generalized groupings of Lichtenstein's work. A closer look at his paintings from this period demonstrates that he was considering gender difference in very specific terms, through the pairing of works that at the same time made reference to the act of image making. This is the case with two related works from 1963: *Mad Scientist* (fig. 80) and *Cold Shoulder* (fig. 81). Each depicts a figure turned obliquely into the space of the canvas. The figure in *Mad Scientist*—clad in the garb of a comic-book villain—is shown in slightly fuller profile, with eye, nose, and mouth fully visible to the viewer, while the female figure of *Cold Shoulder* has been rotated more thoroughly into the space of the painting, her facial features indicated only by the line of chin, cheekbone, and forehead barely interrupted by eyelid and eyelash.

Lichtenstein constructed *Cold Shoulder* from two separate images. He derived the word balloon from a panel in which a woman receives a frosty reception from a jealous rival, who offers a greeting with her back completely turned (fig. 82).[2] Lichtenstein may have recognized that while this image was comprehensible within the narrative context of the comic book story, the depicted bodily motion (or lack thereof) would have seemed ambiguous if isolated as a singular image—that is, as a painting. Instead, he selected a figure from a completely different story, in which the protagonist decides to leave her beloved after learning of his deceitfulness.[3] The panel from which Lichtenstein derived the pose in *Cold Shoulder* depicts her at the very moment in which she turns to leave, and thus more clearly produces the desired reading: this is a figure caught in the action of turning away. As such, the painting constitutes a wonderful visual (or perhaps more accurately, semiotic) pun, in that image and text are in profound disagreement.

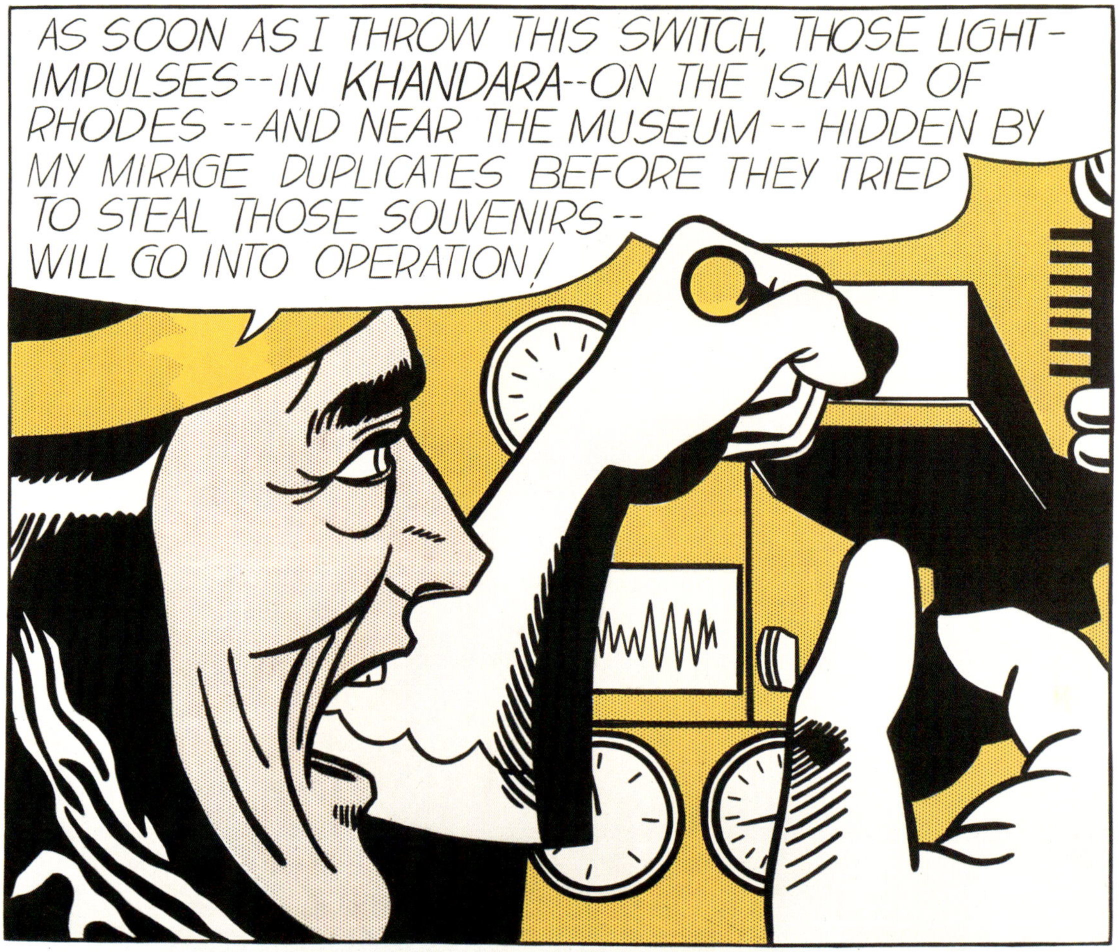

Figure 80.
Mad Scientist,
1963.
Oil on canvas,
50 × 60 in.
(127 ×
152.4 cm).
Wallraf-Richartz
Museum,
Cologne.
Ludwig
Collection

While the text in the word balloon signifies a greeting, the figure's depicted action indicates just the opposite. Those forms that dangle—icicle-like—from the word balloon denote the coldness of the greeting, thus suturing the opposing meanings generated by figure and text.

As noted, the figure in *Mad Scientist* is turned obliquely into the depicted scene much like that in *Cold Shoulder,* although the similarities between the two seem to end there. In many ways such a comparison only emphasizes the differences between the two: *Mad Scientist*'s horizontal composition contrasts with the resolute vertical of *Cold Shoulder;* the former's depicted activity (both hands visible, one grasping a switch) is opposed to the lack of activity (in fact, the very limblessness) in the latter; and the meandering text of the former contrasts with the latter's utterly terse greeting. Wendy Steiner, writing about "the ludicrous deferral of syn-

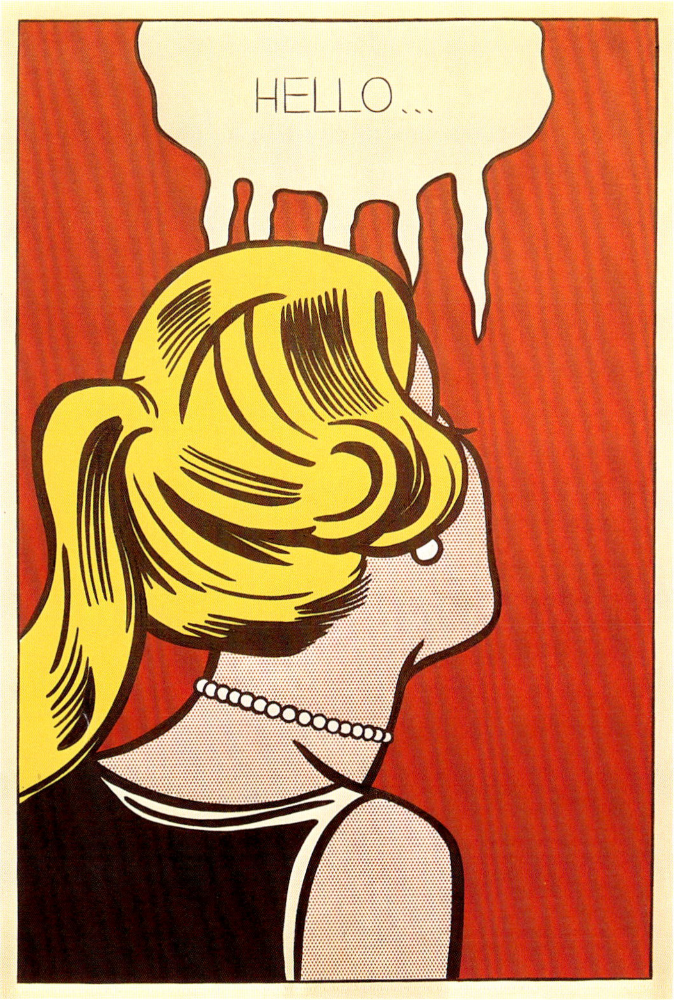

Figure 81.
Cold Shoulder, 1963.
Magna on canvas,
68 × 48 in.
(172.7 × 121.9 cm).
Private collection

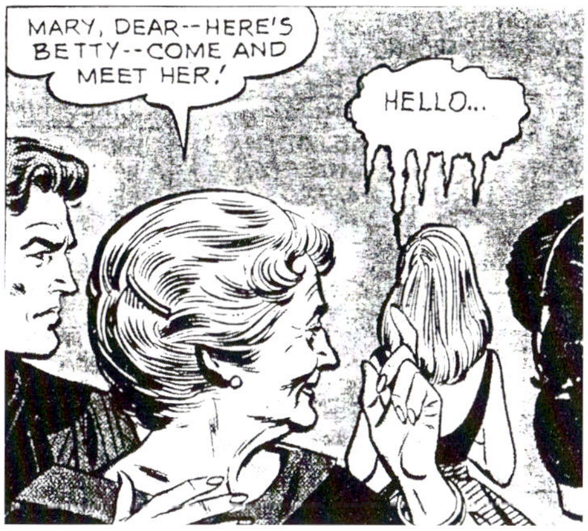

Figure 82.
Panel from "Web of Heartbreak" in *Girls' Love Stories* no. 92 (January 1963)

tactic closure" of the text in *Mad Scientist,* has identified the depicted figure as a stand-in for the artist himself.[4] Whether or not we accept her reading, the image does reference the act of image making, particularly in the figure's bodily positioning. Not only does the figure's orientation into the depicted space of the painting more or less mimic that of the artist in front of the work of art, but the treatment of the hand grasping the electrical switch appears like nothing else than a hand holding the projecting handle of a paintbrush. A comparison of the painting with its source suggests that Lichtenstein made changes to the image to emphasize such a reading.[5] He extended the right-hand side of the composition and added the foreshortened right edge of the switch. Grasped in the figure's left hand, that switch now closely resembles a paintbrush poised in mid-stroke. The figure's other hand—which juts into the composition at lower right—recalls another type of artistic activity. Lichtenstein modified its size and position, enlarging it and pushing it further into the lower right corner of the composition. He also changed its articulation, pressing the thumb and forefinger more closely together—almost as if something were being grasped between them. The resulting manual configuration resembles a hand poised in the act of drawing.[6] In short, whether or not there is any particular referent for the figure in *Mad Scientist*—such as Roy Lichtenstein or even Hoyt Sherman (the image may very well evoke Sherman's flash lab)—the depicted bodily positioning invokes the artistic act of image making. There is a similar effect at work in *Cold Shoulder.* Look closely at the distinctive shape of the word balloon: the elements projecting beneath it—meant in the comic panel to resemble a series of dangling icicles—bear more than a passing resemblance to drips of viscous paint. As we have seen with so much of Lichtenstein's work, the transfer of the image from comic book to canvas is crucial here: whatever the motif signified in the original panel, it produces different meanings when deployed within the frame of a painting.

We may not want to pursue the figural invocation of artistic activity in these paintings too far. It is a commonplace, after all, that works of art are self-reflexive, and we have already seen numerous instances of such self-reflexiveness in Lichtenstein's imagery. However, these two paintings—and it is precisely their pairing that I want to emphasize here—highlight a significant element at work in the artist's practice. They set up a relation between the image—or image making—and sexual difference. He again took up this problematic a year later, in 1964, in another pair of works, *Vicki* and *Girl in Mirror* (figs. 83, 84). These works are not painted, but rather executed in enamel and steel in the manner of street or advertising signs; Lichtenstein designed the images and had them produced in a limited edition by a commercial fabricator. They are identically sized and utilize the same color scheme of red, yellow, black and white. They also display a clearer structural relation than the pairing of *Mad Scientist* and *Cold Shoulder.* In *Vicki* the head, neck, and shoulder of a male figure are seen from behind, left hand grasping the edge of a door or door frame. The face of a female figure appears in the center of the image, framed between the male figure's hand and head. The composition of *Girl in Mirror* basically repeats this figural positioning through a veritable mirror reversal: more than a third of the left side of the image is taken up by a field of yellow interspersed with long, swirling black strokes, presumably the blonde hair of a female figure. As in *Vicki,* a fragment of a hand emerges from the edge of the picture, although here it is a feminine hand that grasps the handle of a mirror. The mirror contains the depicted reflection of the face of a young, smiling woman.

This pairing extends many of the same issues confronted in that of *Cold Shoul-*

der and *Mad Scientist,* although here the relation between the two is even more direct (both formally and thematically). We are again presented with two figures—one male, one female—turned into depicted scenes. Each image suggests the activity of art making, in that a hand is shown grasping an element—a door, a mirror handle—that invokes the artist's handling of a paintbrush or mark-making implement. In *Girl in Mirror* this reading is only emphasized by the positioning of the hand in relation to the streak of blonde hair reflected in the mirror. Note how the curve described by the hair follows the side of the figure's face and continues through the thumb and finger, as if the hand was completing the motion of laying down a stroke. It is as if the figures in those earlier works (*Cold Shoulder* and *Mad Scientist*), which were turned obliquely into the depicted spaces, have here been turned completely away from the viewer. In mimicking the position of the artist—as well as that of the viewer—posed in front of the work of art, such figures have precedents in the work of earlier painters. For instance, they resemble the distinctive *Rückenfigur* (literally, "back-figure") that appears in many of painter Caspar David Friedrich's Romantic landscapes, as well as the "painter-beholder" that Michael Fried has identified as a recurring feature of the work of Gustave Courbet.[7] In both of those earlier instances, as here, the appearance of that figure constitutes a doubling effect, in that the viewer's—and artist's—placement in front of the canvas is duplicated in the painted scene. But we must also take into account that in Lichtenstein's work the representation of such figures is fundamentally connected to the issue of sexual difference. That difference is expressed in these scenes through the staging of our visual access to the depicted figures. In *Vicki* a woman's face is offered up to the viewer's gaze, veritably framed by the configuration of head, shoulder, and hand that reiterates the enclosure of the picture's framing edges. In contrast, the face of the male figure is completely turned away from us. The sense that we are prevented from seeing something in the image is only emphasized by the fact that the female figure looks directly at that unseen face. In contrast, although the depicted figure in *Girl in Mirror* is likewise turned away from us, her visage is reflected back, precisely as an image, in the oval of the mirror at right. The curved white bands that sweep across the oval's right edge signify that this is a reflective surface.

However, we have to step back a moment from the suggestion that the face of the figure in *Girl in Mirror* is reflected back at us. The flattening of space in Lichtenstein's work makes any such spatial reading highly ambiguous. That flattening is only emphasized by the distinctive medium in use; the enameling of the image onto a steel ground gives the work a hard reflectivity that emphasizes its surface qualities. Because of the spatial compression effected by the image's utter flatness, the blonde tresses at left appear to sit almost on the same plane as the reflected face. There is a small passage in which the thick black outline of the hair overlaps the oval frame of the mirror, but this detail creates at most a minimal illusion of depth. In contrast to an illusionistic interpretation of the scene (a blonde woman, seen from behind, looks into a mirror), the work supports quite a different reading: on the right a feminine visage appears as an image on a surface, while at left—in close if not immediate spatial proximity—sits a tangled mass of yellow and black

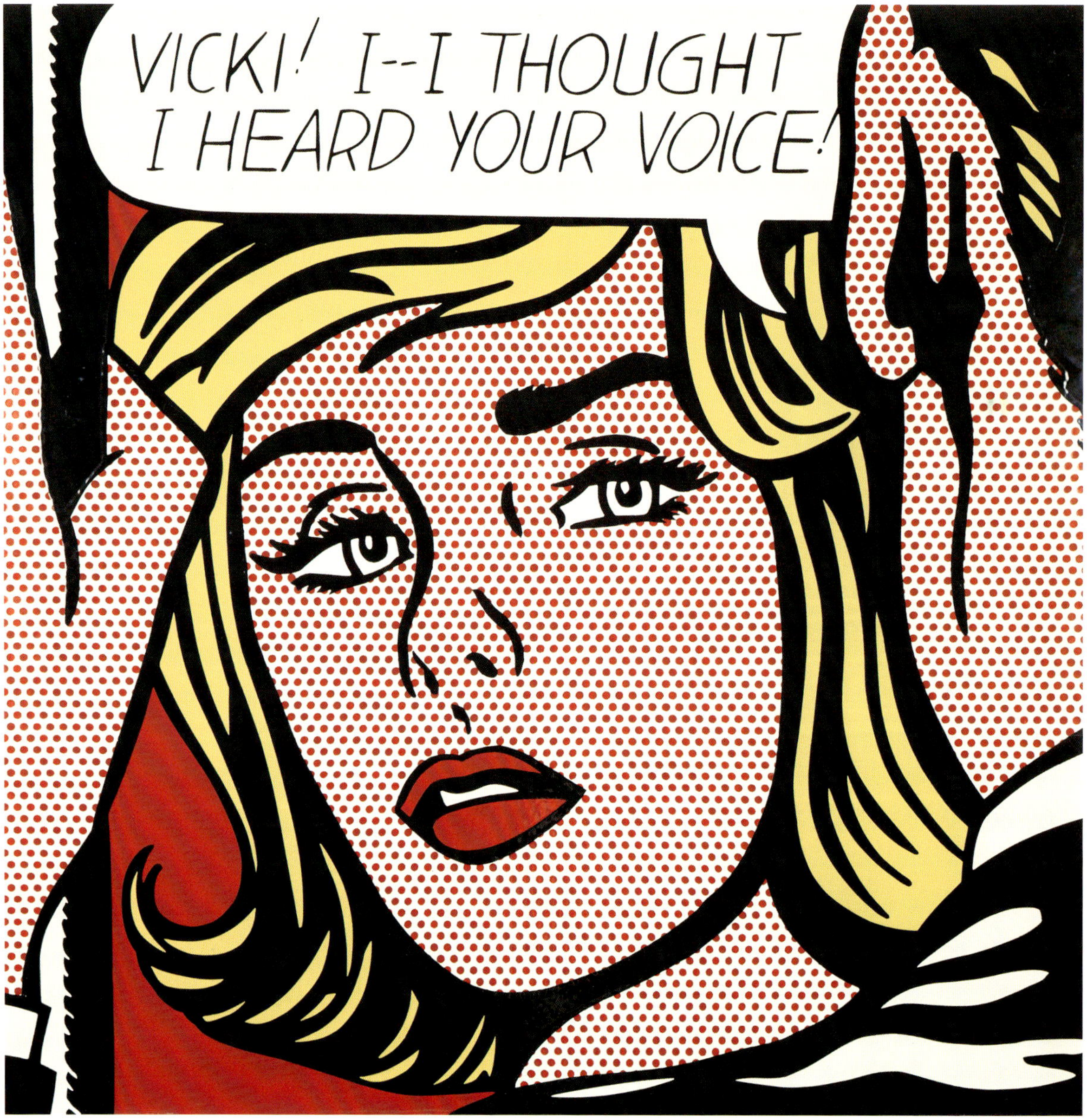

Figure 83. *Vicki,* 1964. Enamel on steel, 42 × 42 in. (106.7 × 106.7 cm). (Edition of 8)

strokes. Perhaps they are a woman's tresses, but they also resemble a swirling mass of painted brush strokes. In fact, within a year Lichtenstein would use forms just like these to depict gestural brushstrokes in his famed series of *Brushstroke* canvases (I will discuss these in the book's concluding chapter). It is as if the feminine figure has been completely dissolved into a tangle of forms arrayed across the surface of the work. Whether or not we identify these leftmost elements in *Girl in*

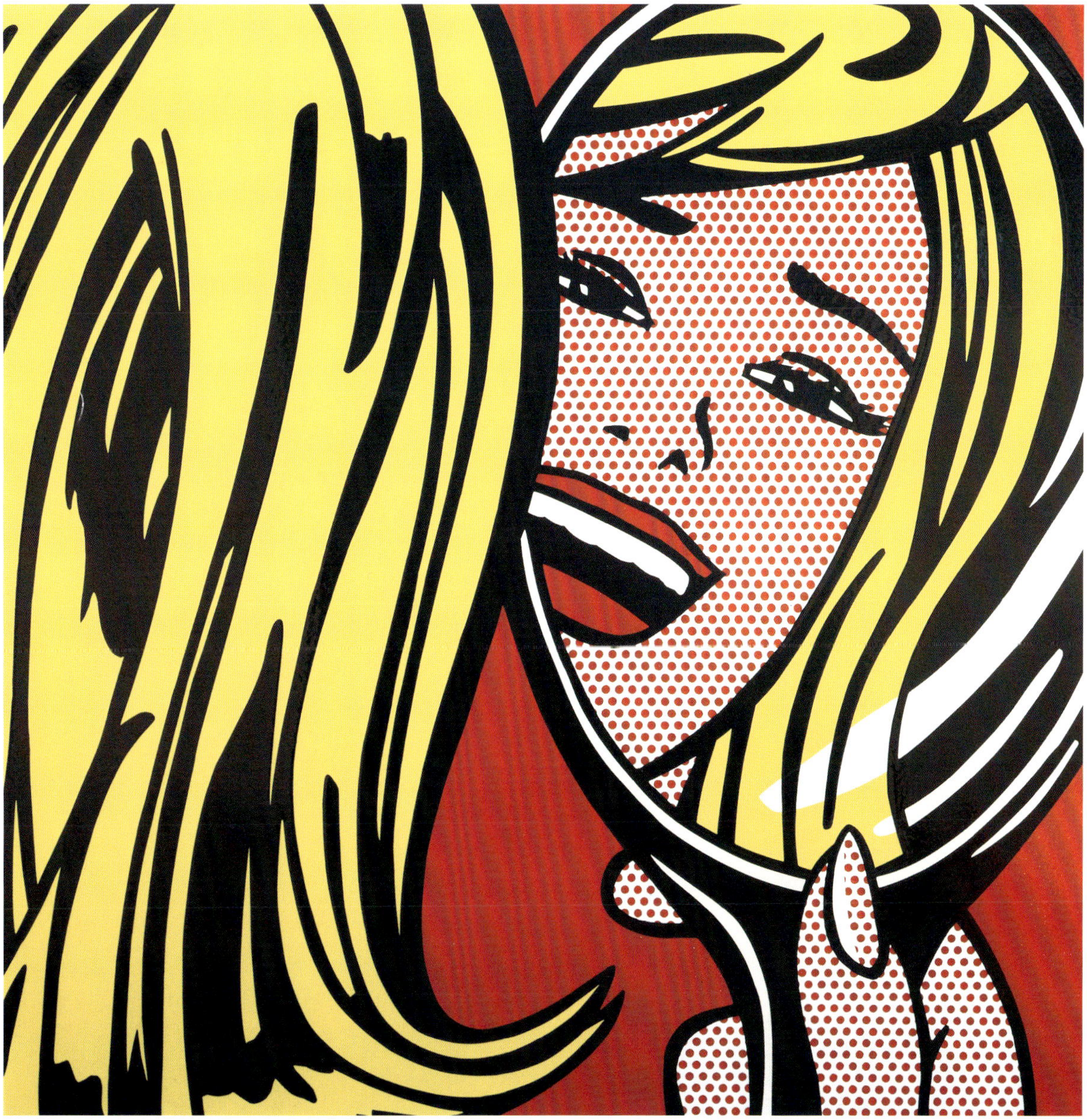

Figure 84. *Girl in Mirror,* 1964. Enamel on steel, 42 × 42 in. (106.7 × 106.7 cm). (Edition of 6)

Mirror as brushstrokes per se, something is being articulated in the work—particularly in relation to the pendant image in *Vicki*—that we need to consider further. A relation between image making, gender, and surface is being worked out here, one that hinges on our visual access to elements within the depicted scene.

ON THE SURFACE OF MELODRAMA

This issue of visual access—of elements either hidden from or offered up to the viewer's gaze—is at work in other, contemporaneous images by the artist. In each of two paintings from 1964, *Good Morning . . . Darling!* and *Blonde Waiting*, a female figure is depicted in bed, caught in the act of looking at an object in the painting's foreground (figs. 85, 86). Yet those objects are turned into the space of the canvas, their faces hidden from us. In each case, the depicted object represents—at least in the comic book narrative from which Lichtenstein appropriated the scene—the absent presence of a male lover, whether in the form of a framed photograph or in the clock by which a woman contemplates her beloved's expected arrival.

A comparison with the work of an earlier artist—one to whom Lichtenstein's practice would refer repeatedly over the years—is useful here. In *Woman Before an Aquarium* (1921), Henri Matisse had painted a scene much like the one in Lichtenstein's *Blonde Waiting:* a female figure, head resting on her crossed arms, is immersed in a state of silent visual contemplation (fig. 87). In both cases (as in *Good Morning . . . Darling!*) the object of her contemplative gaze is poised on a tablelike surface interposed between the figure and the viewer. It is likely that Lichtenstein knew of Matisse's painting, to which these works in part constituted a response.[8] If that is the case, wherein lies the distinction between Matisse's painting and Lichtenstein's approach? Although Matisse's canvas contains signs of nature, those elements are conspicuously absent from Lichtenstein's depictions. *Woman Before an Aquarium* contains the bowl of goldfish and the tabletop element Charles Harrison has identified as a sprig of cedar: these are signs of a natural world cultivated by humanity, but signs of nature nonetheless.[9] In contrast Lichtenstein presents us with objects—a picture frame and an alarm clock—that are fully cultural. Further, each of these proffers information on a flat surface, much like a painting. The closed venetian blinds of *Blonde Waiting* are another sign of the work's closing-off from nature: they signify the presence of window—one that would presumably provide access to a landscape, to some exterior scene—that has been utterly blocked from view.

Harrison provides us with a useful set of terms through which to consider the

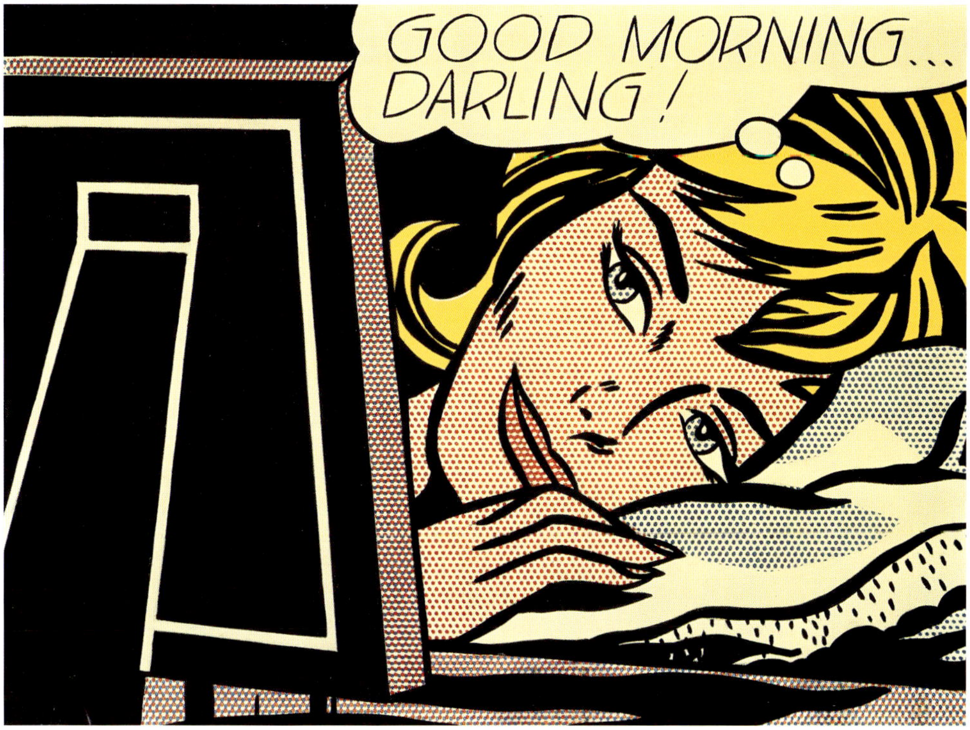

Figure 85.
Good Morning . . . Darling!, 1964.
Magna on canvas,
27 × 36 in.
(68.6 × 91.4 cm)
Private collection

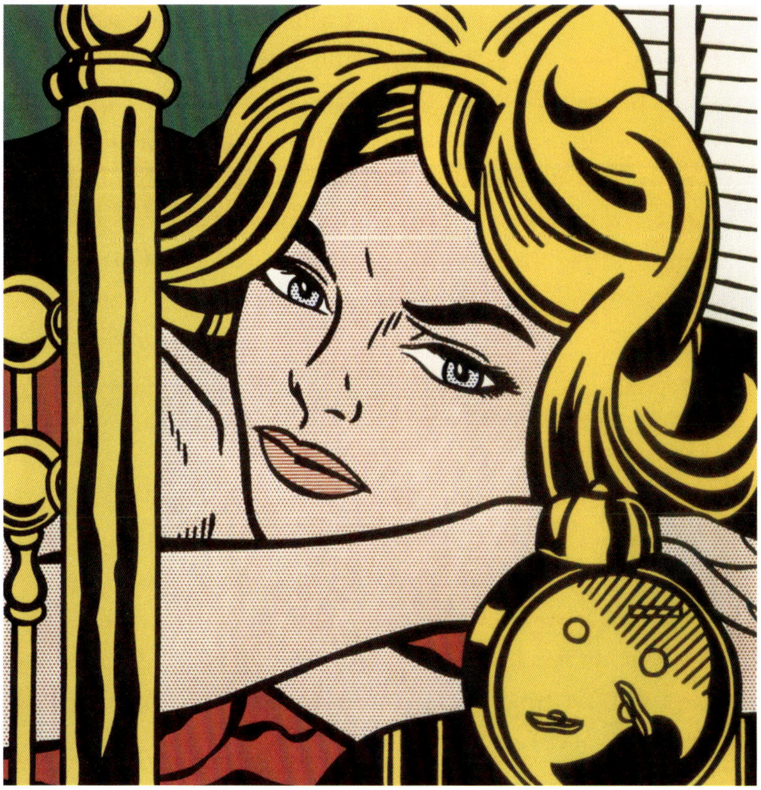

Figure 86.
Blonde Waiting, 1964.
Oil and Magna on canvas,
48 × 48 in. (121.9 × 121.9 cm).
Private collection

Figure 87.
Henri Matisse,
Woman Before an Aquarium, 1921.
Oil on canvas,
31¾ × 39⅜ in. (80.7 × 100 cm).
Art Institute of Chicago.
Helen Birch Bartlett Memorial Collection

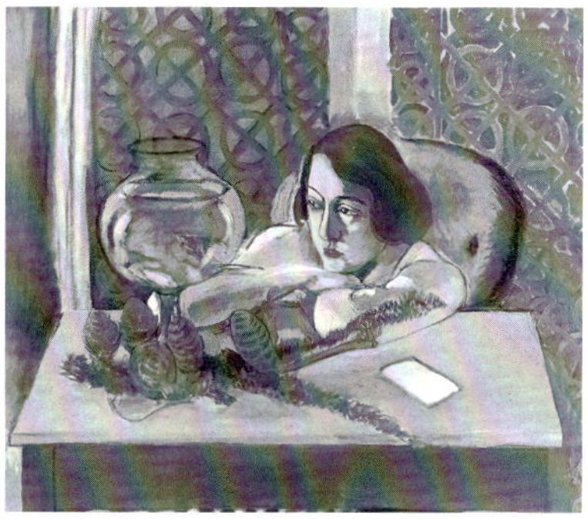

distinction between Matisse's painting and Lichtenstein's images. He has suggested of *Woman Before an Aquarium* that "the effect of the composition is to define a form of imaginary spectator who stands on the threshold of the pictorial space, but who has no power to enter it, or to interrupt the absorbed state of the woman represented."[10] If this is a fitting description of the work, then in comparing Matisse's painting with Lichtenstein's imagery it becomes clear that the terms of the reading have been extended even further. In *Good Morning . . . Darling!* and *Blonde Waiting* space has been compressed to an even greater degree. If the "imaginary spectator" was blocked from entering Matisse's composition by a tabletop that extends almost from one side of the painting to the other, in each of his images Lichtenstein has pressed the figure even closer to the picture plane. Although he provides us with rudimentary indications of foreground, middleground, and rearground they are on the point of utter collapse. A comparison between *Blonde Waiting* and its source only emphasizes such a reading; the artist cropped the image on all sides, tightly framing the figure and profoundly compressing the space of the picture.[11] In addition, while we may not be able to claim that Lichtenstein's figures are any more absorbed in the depicted act of contemplation than Matisse's woman, it is clear that in each case Lichtenstein, unlike Matisse, deprives us of the object of the figure's contemplative gaze. We saw much the same thing in *Vicki,* in which the female figure is shown looking at a face we cannot see. Form and subject seem to converge here; it is as if the absolute unyieldingness of the surface plane in Lichtenstein's paintings—with figures, objects, and interior spaces all pushed up to a veritable breaking point—finds its corollary in the refusal to grant the viewer visual access to the object of the depicted gaze. This kind of intense spatial pressure is only heightened by the even more claustrophobic closing-off of the picture from nature. In short, in Lichtenstein's work of this period there is a conflation between *psychological depth* and *spatial depth:* we are as unable to gain access to the interior state of the depicted figure as we are to enter the space of the painting. To put it another way: Lichtenstein pushes the scene to the surface of the image in much the same way as emotional states are written on the surface of his figures.

There is a term for this kind of treatment of form, in which emotions seem clearly written on the surface of the body: *melodrama.* A quote from Douglas Sirk, one of the most renowned purveyors of the filmic melodrama, is of use in understanding this characteristic of Lichtenstein's imagery. Critic Thomas Elsaesser begins an influential 1972 essay on filmic melodrama (referring particularly to the use of that genre in films from the 1950s and early 1960s) with reference to Sirk's conception of the form of his work:

> Asked about the colour in *Written on the Wind,* Douglas Sirk replied: 'Almost throughout the picture I used deep-focus lenses which have the effect of giving a harshness to the objects and a kind of enamelled, hard surface to the colours. I wanted this to bring out the inner violence, the energy of the characters which is all inside them and can't break through.'[12]

There is room here to make a historical argument about the appearance of Lichtenstein's decidedly melodramatic works so soon after that genre was taken up extensively by the Hollywood film industry. Moreover, the artist's tendency to magnify and closely crop his images could be connected to the extensive use of the close-up in filmic melodrama. Yet I am most struck by the fact that Sirk's account of his stylistic intentions for *Written on the Wind* comes remarkably close to describing the form of Lichtenstein's work. The harshness of objects to which the director refers finds its equivalence in the hard-edged outlines utilized in the artist's paintings. As we have already seen, Lichtenstein's canvases gradually lost almost all inflection (of pencil line or brushstroke) they contained when he began his Pop mode. Further, Sirk's own reference to colors with an "enamelled, hard surface" recalls the literally enameled surfaces of works like *Girl in Mirror* and *Vicki.*[13]

As noted earlier, it is tempting to create a clear distinction between Lichtenstein's war and romance comic images; in fact, that distinction has been made consistently in the critical literature on the artist's work. Yet in many ways it is easy to overemphasize the distinction between the two. Even though these works suggest a polarization between the exaggerated affects of masculinity and femininity, they all represent manifestations of the same impulse to melodrama. By the early 1960s, the whole comic book form itself—excluding particular exceptions like humor comics—was defined in large part by the melodramatic. Whether the battle between good and evil in the superhero comics, the "spine-tingling" tales of the horror comics, the emotional stories of love and loss in the romance comics, or the action-packed tales of heroic combat—all owed their narrative intensity, more or less, to the melodramatic. And it is melodrama—especially its consistent emphasis on moments of heightened tension—that ties together so many of Lichtenstein's works. This is true even in early Pop works, like the moment of suspense depicted in *The Engagement Ring* (fig. 88), through to the explosive battle scene of an image like *Okay, Hot-Shot* or the viewer's charged confrontation with the angry figure in *Image Duplicator.*

In describing melodrama as "a mode of high emotionalism and stark ethical conflict," Peter Brooks provides us with a useful list of some of the connotations of that term. "They include: the indulgence of strong emotionalism; moral polarization and schematization; extreme states of being, situations, actions; overt villainy,

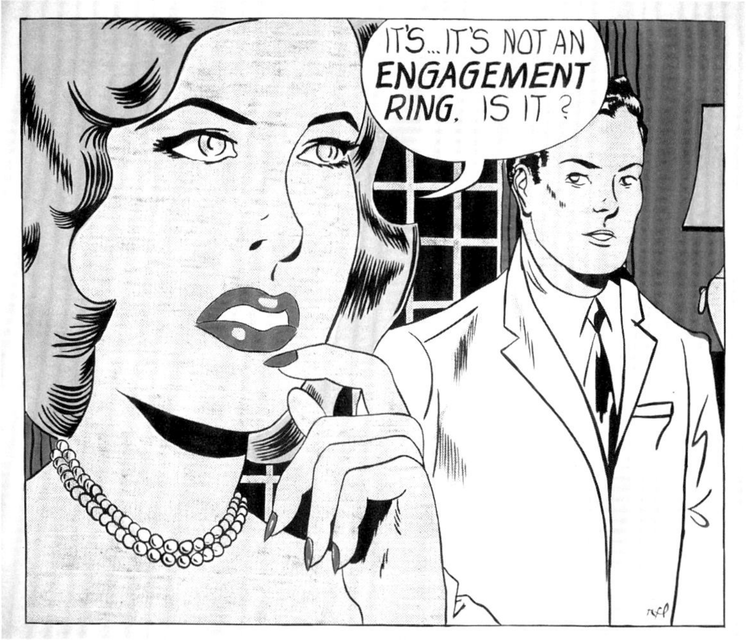

Figure 88.
The Engagement Ring, 1961.
Oil on canvas,
67¾ × 79½ in. (172 × 201.9 cm).
Private collection

persecution of the good, and final reward of virtue; inflated and extravagant expression; dark plottings, suspense, breathtaking peripety."[14] The comic book narratives from which Lichtenstein derived inspiration at this time contain many of these same elements, and his paintings exploit these qualities—emotionalism, expression, suspense—to their fullest. Moreover, as Thomas Elsaesser had done with his discussion of Sirk's films, Brooks foregrounds the role of *surface* in the melodramatic form. Time and time again he refers to the characteristic in melodrama of emotions and affect pushed to the surface:

> The desire to express all seems a fundamental characteristic of the melodramatic mode. Nothing is spared because nothing is left unsaid; the characters stand on stage and utter the unspeakable, give voice to their deepest feelings, dramatize through their heightened and polarized words and gestures the whole lesson of their relationship. They assume primary psychic roles, father, mother, child, and express basic psychic conditions. Life tends, in this fiction, toward ever more concentrated and totally expressive gestures and statements.[15]

As Brooks points out (in line with Elsaesser's quotation of Sirk), this quality—of expressiveness—gets worked out in the melodramatic text on the level of form as well. If characters in melodrama tend toward a state of complete expressivity—with their inner moral conflicts pushed to the surface—then the melodramatic text itself is often marked by that same kind of pressure. Brooks describes how in the opening pages of Balzac's *La Peau de chagrin* "we can observe the narrator pressuring the surface of reality (the surface of his text) in order to make it yield the full, true terms of his story."[16]

Herein lies the distinction between Lichtenstein's paintings and the common conventions of the melodramatic. Brooks suggests that the attention to surface in melodrama represents an attempt to "push through" that surface to something deeper behind it: a realm of emotional and spiritual reality to which the narrative always refers.

> We might say that the center of interest and the scene of the underlying drama reside within what we would call the "moral occult," the domain of operative spiritual values which is both indicated within and masked by the surface of reality. . . . The melodramatic mode in large measure exists to locate and to articulate the moral occult.[17]

By now it should be clear that Lichtenstein's images insistently call attention to surface, whether through the sheer physical flatness instantiated by a lack of paint texture and the visual patterning of dots, through the collapse of depicted space, or through visual scenarios that call attention to the act of looking at a surface. Yet the artist's removal of these images from their narrative contexts (in addition to his ever-closer cropping) removes the "meaning" of the melodramatic moment, that is to say the moral conflict to which it points. In other words, while his paintings depict emotionally charged or highly expressive moments, the emotional, moral, or psychological component of their original narrative contexts has been occluded.

So much is clear in Lichtenstein's well-known 1963 canvas *Drowning Girl* (fig. 89). It is not only that Lichtenstein removed the figure (the "Brad" to which the heroine's lament refers) that had appeared in the rear of the painting's comic book source panel, for the entire referential context of the heroine's emotional and moral condition has been cropped out as well. As viewers we no longer have access to the narrative at work in the original story: the heroine's difficulty in meeting men, her struggle with the male protagonist, her final abandoning of autonomy for heterosexual love. Lichtenstein's images are not simply closed off from the narratives from which they were taken; they seem to *perform* that very closing-off, as over and over again they make reference to objects inaccessible to us as viewers. We are insistently denied access on any number of levels: visual, spatial, psychological, even moral. It is as if his imagery intentionally frustrates us, repeatedly pointing to objects that lie outside the frames of his pictures. Even Pop works from as early as 1961—such as *The Engagement Ring, Emeralds,* and *Mr. Bellamy*—all refer ("off-stage," as it were) to such unseen objects. Over the course of his Pop mode

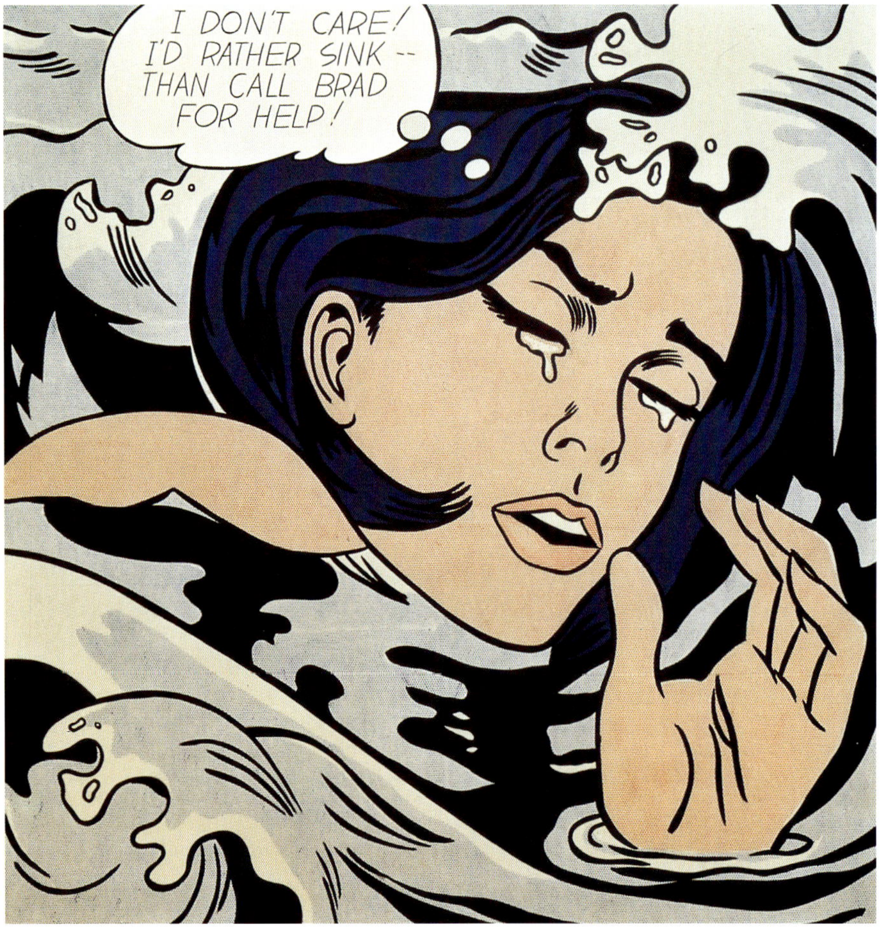

Figure 89.
Drowning Girl,
1963.
Oil and Magna on canvas, 67⅝ × 66¾ in. (171.6 × 169.5 cm). Museum of Modern Art, New York. Philip Johnson Fund and gift of Mr. and Mrs. Bagley Wright

the narrative information or supplied context in Lichtenstein's "melodramatic" works is reduced further and further until we are left with nothing but images of exaggerated—and isolated—affect: *Frightened Girl* (fig. 90), *Hopeless, Happy Tears* (fig. 91), *Crying Girl, Blonde Waiting.* The last case is particularly instructive, since there is no narrative context to explain the depicted waiting, and the turning of the clock face away from the viewer only emphasizes this refusal. It is significant as well that in most of these cases Lichtenstein excised the captions or thought balloons that in the comic books had expressed the figures' inner thoughts.[18] His images represent an extreme emotionalism without the "center" to which melodrama in other genres pointed: in other words, they proffer a world of surface without depth. As we have seen, it is at the very same moment that this distinctive imagery is more and more cut off from narrative (and hence moral or psychological meaning) that the collapse and flattening of depicted space becomes ever more severe.

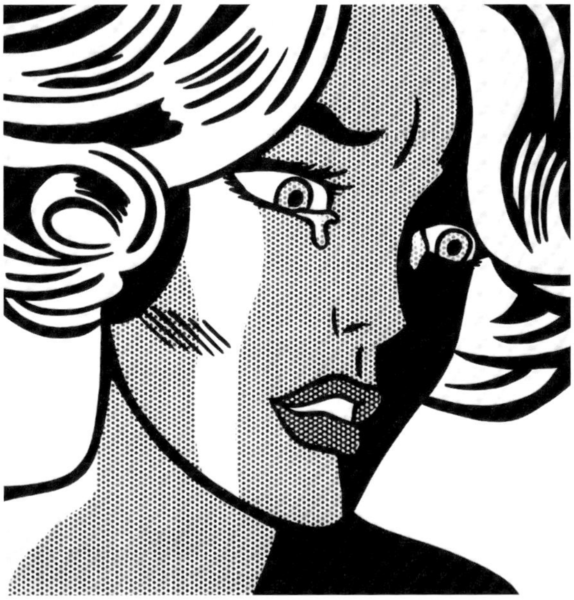

Figure 90.
Frightened Girl, 1964. Oil and Magna on canvas, 48 × 48 in. (121.9 × 121.9 cm). Private collection

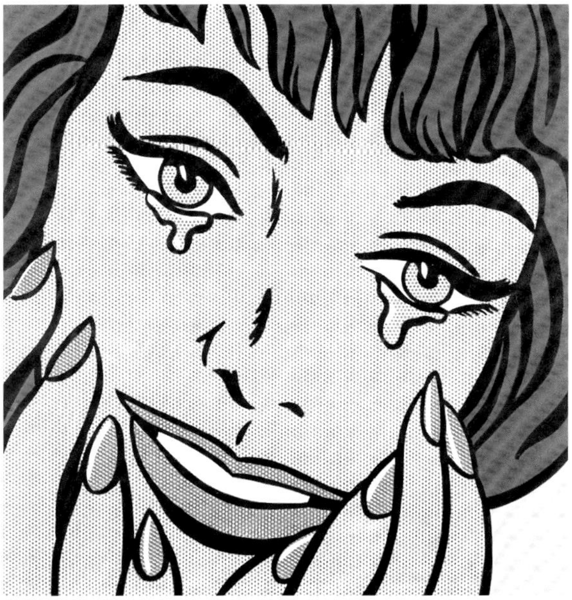

Figure 91.
Happy Tears, 1964. Magna on canvas, 38 × 38 in. (96.5 × 96.5 cm). Private collection

This development in the artist's work is undeniably gendered. Lichtenstein's war-comic derived paintings date almost exclusively from 1962 and into 1963, while *Hopeless* and *Drowning Girl,* both from 1963, will be followed by a long succession of close-up images like *Nurse, Frightened Girl,* and *Happy Tears* (all from 1964), even extending into 1965 with such works as *Girl with Hair Ribbon.*[19] Overwhelmingly, these figures of pure affect, enclosed in ever more tightly framed spaces and pushed up to the surface of the image, are depicted as feminine. Yet there is another gendered component of these images, one that is not so immediately visible—and this is precisely the point—but is no less significant. If the artist's isolation of individual panels from the comics cut these scenes off from the narratives in which they were originally embedded, we cannot say that narrative has been completely expunged from them. Wendy Steiner, for one, has discussed the ways in which Lichtenstein's imagery maintains a proto-narrative quality.[20] But what narrative they do retain consists largely in pointing to an unseen element—the "off-stage" or "out-of-frame" referent I described earlier—that is consistently identified as masculine. Take the case of the 1964 canvas *Oh, Jeff . . . I Love You, Too . . . But . . .* (fig. 92). Certainly, we might begin by taking note of the work's formal qualities: the sweeping bands of black and yellow that make up the figure's hair, the play of thick outlines against fields of regularized dots, the visual tension set up between the white background at left and the deep blue at right. We might also consider the undeniable play of an incipient narrative here, of a woman talking on the phone with her unseen male lover. The ellipsis at the end of the text adds to our sense of a story suggested but never fully revealed to us. But it is precisely that sense of an absent presence—the "Jeff" referred to in the word balloon—that I want to highlight here. This is only emphasized by the telephone receiver into which the figure speaks, which implies a connection to a presence—identified as male—unseen to us. This had been the case even in early Pop works like *Emeralds* or *Mr. Bellamy,* both of which make textual reference to a masculine term not imaged in the work. In this way Lichtenstein's paintings—particularly the images of women derived from the romance comics—set up an opposition between something offered to our gaze and something hidden from it, an opposition coded according to the terms feminine and masculine.

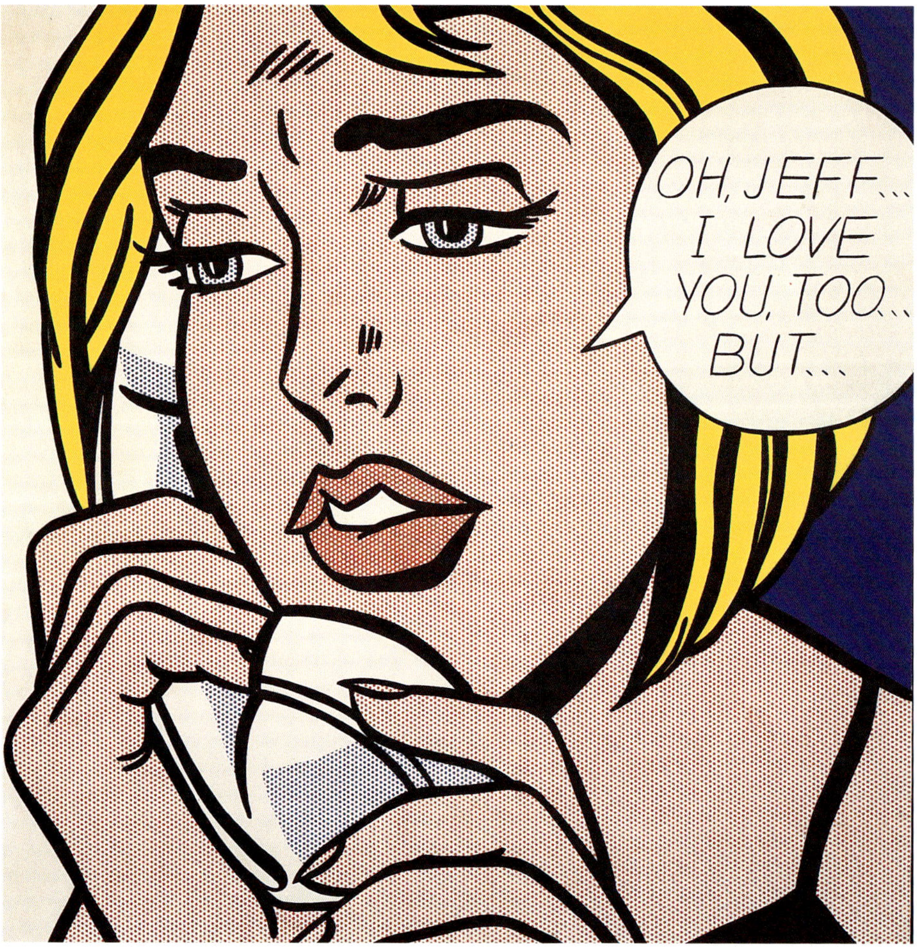

Figure 92.
Oh, Jeff . . . I Love You, Too . . . But . . . ,
1964.
Oil and Magna on canvas,
48 × 48 in.
(121.9 × 121.9 cm).
Simonyi collection

SEMIOLOGY AND SEXUAL DIFFERENCE

The 1963 canvas *In the Car* (fig. 93) presents us with yet another melodramatic moment—a scene of heightened emotional or psychological tension—cut free from narrative context. Two figures—a man and a woman—ride together in an automobile. She is locked in stiff profile, staring straight ahead, while at the wheel he turns to look at her. What exchange is occurring here? What went on just before this moment, and what will happen afterward? If the answers to these questions are unclear to us, we do know one thing: this painting must have been an important one for Lichtenstein. We know this because he did something decidedly rare

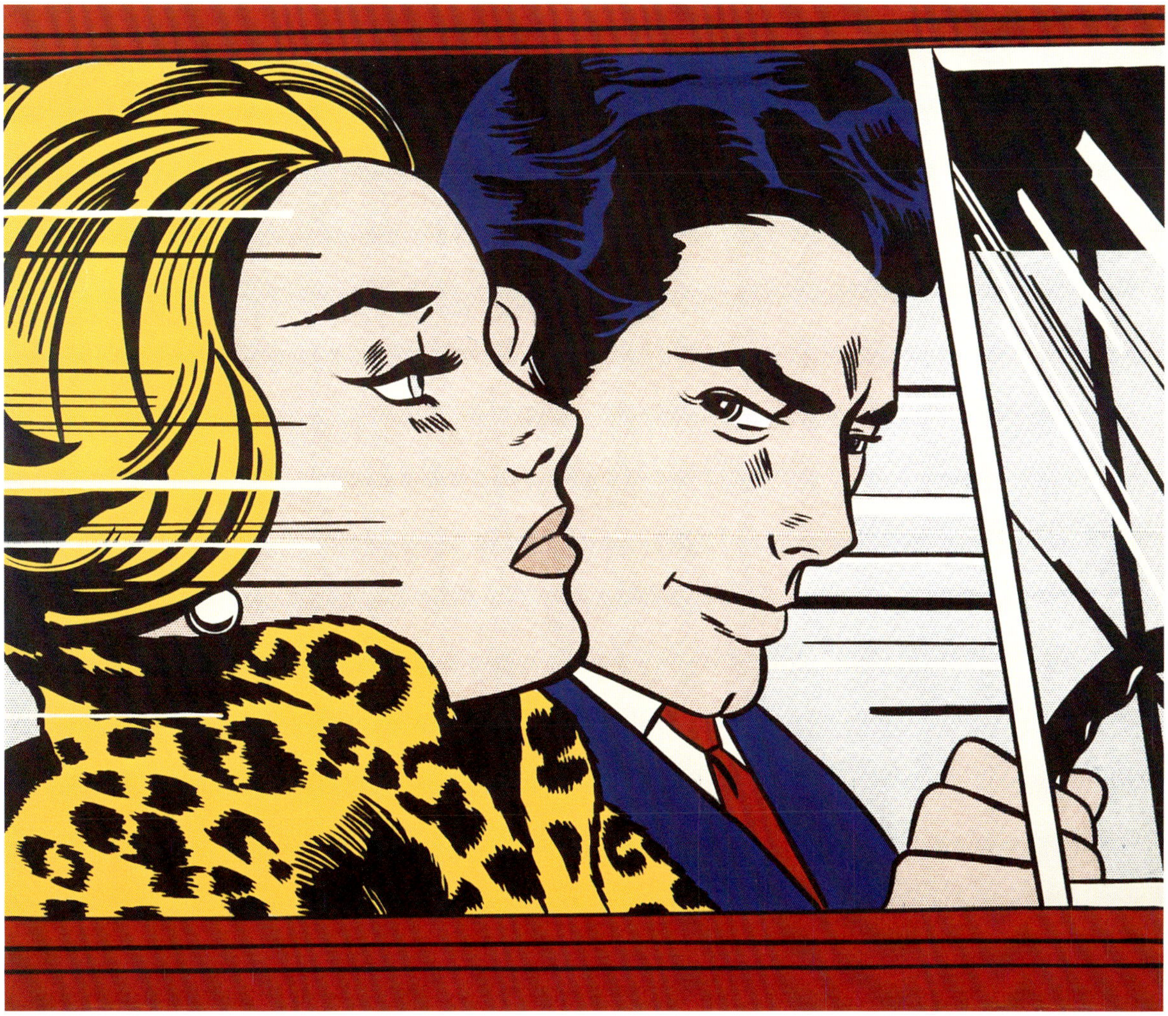

Figure 93. *In the Car,* 1963. Oil and Magna on canvas, 68 × 80 in. (172.7 × 203.2 cm). Scottish National Gallery of Modern Art, Edinburgh

in his practice: he repeated virtually the same image twice. There are two versions of the painting; a larger and more finished version—which I will refer to as *In the Car*—is in the collection of the Scottish National Gallery of Modern Art in Edinburgh. The other—which I will refer to as the preliminary version—is a significantly smaller image that has rarely been reproduced, as it remains in a private collection (fig. 94). My identification of the latter as an initial treatment of the motif is based in part on a comparison of the two paintings with the comic book panel on which they were based (fig. 95).[21] The preliminary version closely follows the original panel. In contrast, in *In the Car* Lichtenstein definitively altered the composition, and his drawing is tighter and more controlled.

We can track other changes—from the comic book panel through both of Lichtenstein's versions—to help us better understand the image's meaning. In both paintings, Lichtenstein removed the text that had appeared above the scene in the comic book panel ("I VOWED TO MYSELF I WOULD **NOT** MISS MY APPOINTMENT—THAT I WOULD **NOT** GO RIDING WITH HIM—YET BEFORE I KNEW IT. . ."). This in itself is a significant change, in that the thought balloon had provided the comic book reader a glimpse into the female protagonist's inner life. The removal of this element is in keeping with my earlier discussion, as Lichtenstein's removal of text again cuts the image off from the sense of inner life and conflict found in traditional melodramatic narratives. But if he removed what could be identified as a narrative frame for the scene, in *In the Car* he provided the image a more decisive visual frame. This is the long, roughly horizontal framing edge—ostensibly a section of a car door—that traverses the lower edge of the canvas. When compared with both the preliminary version and the comic book source panel, we can see how it acts precisely as a *framing* edge, particularly in conjunction with the similar red band that runs along the upper edge of the composition. Lichtenstein also gave greater visual weight to the panel of glass at right. For one, he extended the panel horizontally (that is, more of it is visible in the scene). He also called greater attention to it by framing it within three wide white bands. While the unnamed comic book artist had indicated the play of reflections on the glass with a series of quickly drawn diagonal lines, Lichtenstein applied a much more extensive series of diagonal bars to achieve the same effect.[22]

Those diagonal elements, in fact, point to the significance this image may have held for the artist, for they foreground a component of his work that would aptly be described as semiological. That is to say that they demonstrate the extent to which Lichtenstein recognized that the constitutive elements of an image might be structured like a language. Note how *In the Car* employs—and more significantly calls attention to—two very different instances of graphic notation: to the

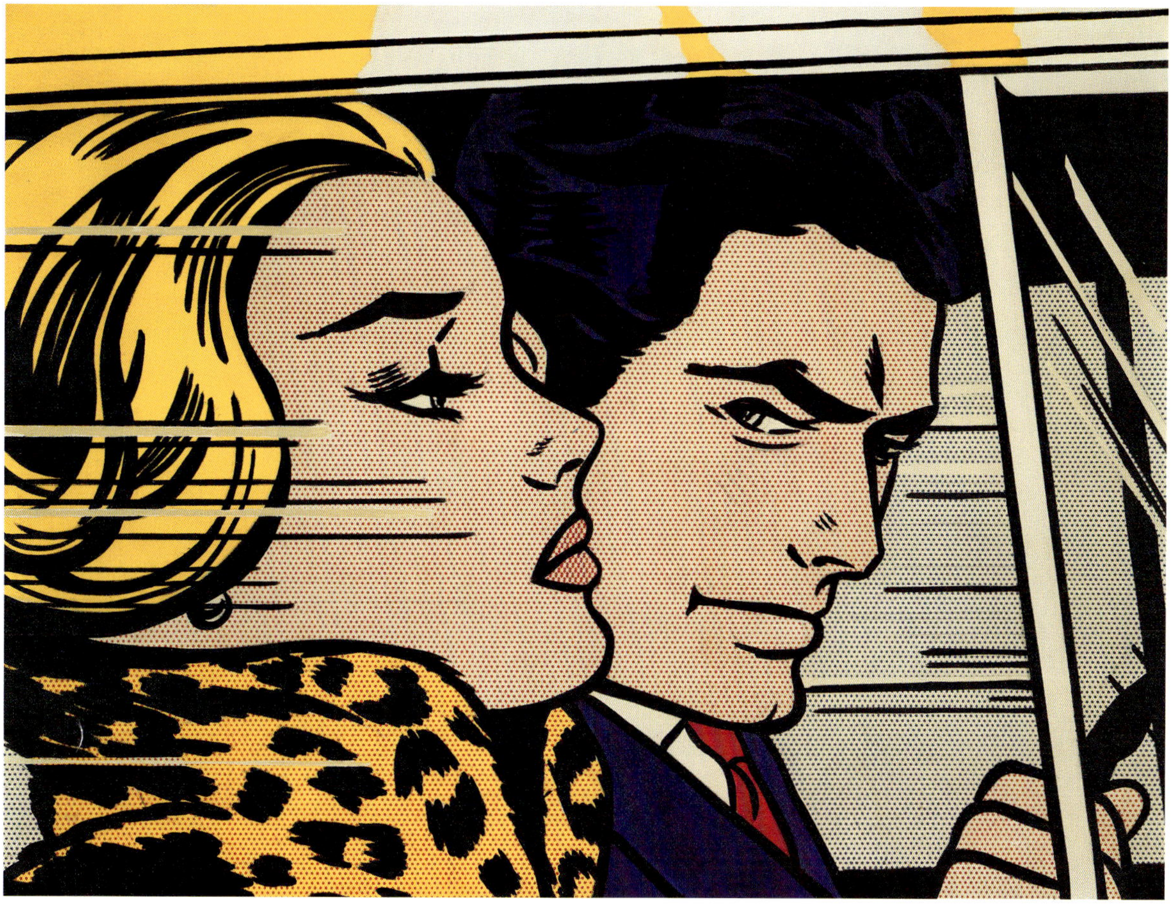

Figure 94. Preliminary version of *In the Car,* 1963. Oil and Magna on canvas, 30 × 40 in. (76.2 × 101.6 cm). Private collection

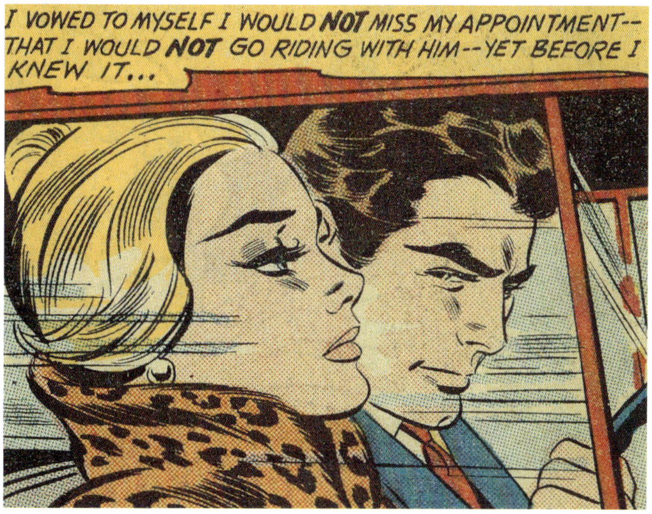

Figure 95. Panel from "Tomorrow and Tomorrow" in *Girls' Romances* no. 78 (September 1961)

right, the black and white bars are arrayed diagonally (and somewhat askew) to signify reflection off a pane of glass. In the center of the image, and to the left, almost identical marks—although here placed horizontally and exactly parallel to one another—signify the forward motion of the car. In this way the painting is almost a primer in the semiotic production of meaning. The juxtaposition of these elements demonstrates not only that the graphic sign is essentially arbitrary (those lines really don't, in the end, resemble either reflections or the visual effects of motion) but also that its meaning is produced through difference. In other words, it is precisely the differences between those bar-like notations—horizontal and parallel on the left versus diagonal and askew on the right—that produces the contrasting meanings of "motion" versus "reflection."[23]

Where would Lichtenstein have arrived at the recognition that such graphic devices could constitute something like a language? For one, through his engagement with commercial illustration itself. The kinds of notations used in *In the Car* represent just a few of the many techniques employed by cartoonists, comic book artists, and illustrators to produce a wide variety of visual effects using a limited system of graphic devices. As early as *Look Mickey* or perhaps even more with *Popeye* (in which he employed lines of motion and shooting stars to signify the impact of Popeye's powerful punch on Bluto's chin), Lichtenstein may very well have recognized the semiological implications of such techniques. In fact, in *In the Car* he did not merely transcribe those graphic notations, for their form is different from the thin lines that had been used by the comic book illustrator. One might suggest that this was merely a matter of aesthetics: that those thin lines would have appeared too fragile or delicate in a large canvas, and that the thicker black and white bars offered a visual heft that solved this problem. However, this does not seem a completely adequate explanation for the changes Lichtenstein made to them. For it is also the case that the use of two types of bars, black and white—a pairing that expresses one of the most basic forms of visual distinctiveness—calls attention to the broader concern with meaning and difference in the work.

If Lichtenstein's recognition that elements in a picture might be structured like a language came in part from his involvement with the codes of graphic illustration, it may have also been prompted by his interest in cubism.[24] Both Rosalind Krauss and Yve Alain-Bois have analyzed the ways in which cubism—especially in the form of Picasso's collages—engages with semiology, particularly in relation to the model of structural linguistics offered by Ferdinand de Saussure.[25] For instance, in her discussion of Picasso's 1912 collage *Violin* (fig. 96) Krauss points out the way the two utterly flat collage elements, scissored out of the same page of newsprint, are used to signify contrasting meanings: to the left and below, the

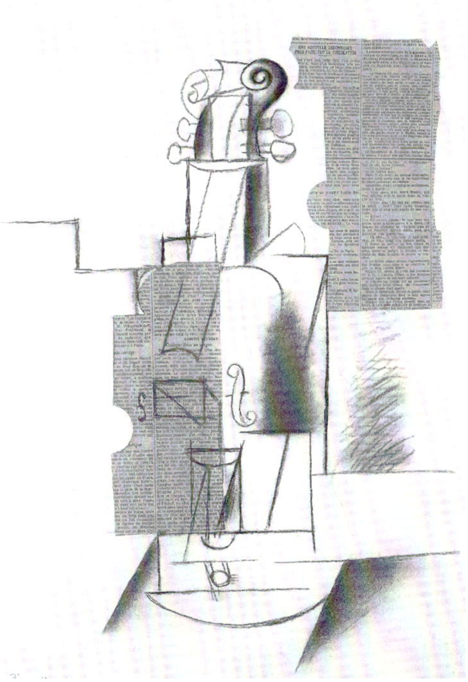

Figure 96. Pablo Picasso, *Violin,* 1912. Pasted papers and charcoal on paper, 24⅜ × 18½ in. (62 × 47 cm). Musée National d'Art Moderne, Paris

opaque wood graining of the violin itself; to the right and above, the atmospheric background of the scene. She explains:

> the magic of the whole collage, indeed the brilliance of the game it plays, is that the two opposite meanings—*light* on the one hand and *opacity* on the other—are generated from the "identical" scrap of paper, the "same" physical shape. Like Saussure's phonetic substance, this support is seen to take on meaning only within the set of oppositions that pits one against another, the implosive *p* of *up* against the explosive *p* of *put.* Picasso's sheet, sliced in two, is thus a paradigm, a binary couple married in opposition, each taking on a meaning insofar as it is *not* the other.[26]

There are notable differences between Picasso's work and that of Lichtenstein. Picasso's *Violin* is a collage of printed elements—shapes cut out of a newspaper—pasted to a sheet of paper (with additional drawing in charcoal). In contrast, *In the Car* forgoes actual printed matter to imitate the facture of mechanical printing in painted form. Yet in spite of these distinctions, when we compare the two (particularly in the context of Krauss' analysis), it is clear that the model of visual meaning produced through difference is at play in Lichtenstein's work as in Picasso's.

If Krauss locates the semiological effects of cubism particularly in the medium of collage—in that the utter flatness of the pasted elements for the most part prevents them from being read in illusionistic terms—we might consider Lichtenstein's transferal of this model back to painting as another example of the tendency toward pictorialization or aestheticization in his work. But there is another element in his painting we have to take into account: it draws a connection between the conventionalized language of graphic notation and sexual difference. This is registered in an easily overlooked distinction between *In the Car* and its comic book source. In the comic panel the horizontal "lines of motion" extend from the demarcated edge of the glass window panel and run across the figure of the male driver and the face (and leopard-patterned coat) of the female passenger. Yet Lichtenstein's painting evidences a curious change: those lines never mark the male figure (this is true of the preliminary version as well). While they extend from the edge of the depicted pane of glass, they abruptly stop at—and do not cross—the driver's face. In other words, those bar-like notational elements are inscribed only on the female figure.[27] And if, as I've noted, the painting plays with the semiotic difference between those "lines of motion" and the "lines of reflection" on the glass, then Lichtenstein has used the figure of the woman as a surface for semiological investigation.[28] In other words: *the painting establishes an equivalence between the figure of the woman and the flat plane of representation.*

The changes Lichtenstein made to the image emphasize this relation. For one, he changed the color of the man's hair, from the brown of the comic book to blue. This change effectively unifies the male figure (the blue of the hair now matching the blue of his jacket) and visually separates him from the woman at left. The cropping of the composition at left further flattens the female figure by cutting off spatial cues that had been present in the comic panel. This effect is only emphasized by the similar orientations of the woman's head and the pane of glass: note how they are tilted back at much the same angle. Lichtenstein's addition of the framing edge at the bottom of the canvas, and his lateral extension of the glass panel, further conflate female figure and representational surface. In the source image the orientation of that panel was somewhat ambiguous: was it supposed to be read as part of the car window and thus parallel to the plane of representation, or as a small segment of the windshield and thus perpendicular (or curved into) the depicted scene? His changes remove this ambiguity: that flat panel is locked in parallel to the picture plane, in much the same way as the woman's hard profile. Hence she does not look through it, as a passenger would with a windshield, for they are both in practically the same plane. They have been made in large part equivalent.

We see evidence in this work not only of Lichtenstein's investigation into the semiotic properties of graphic notation but also of a correlation between a surface (upon which graphic devices are arrayed) and the feminine. This would not have been the first time he had made such a connection. There is a prior instance of his refusal to interrupt the pictorial integrity of a male figure and the concurrent inscription of conventional notations onto a female figure. In fact, it brings us back to the example of Erle Loran. In each of the articles he published concurrently in *Art News* and *Artforum* in 1963, Loran chose to juxtapose a work by Lichtenstein with a diagram from his book *Cézanne's Composition.* In spite of the fact that the critic attacked Pop art for insufficiently "transforming" its sources (i.e., that it merely represented a fine-art form of copying), Loran ignored the rather significant changes the artist had made in the painting entitled *Man with Folded Arms* (fig. 97). Lichtenstein had removed all the elements—letters, arrows, dotted lines—that had served in Loran's drawing to diagram the movement of the viewer's eye through Cézanne's painting (fig. 98). Yet it was precisely these elements that had made Loran's diagram distinctive: it was these, more than anything else, that provided the viewer the means to decode the visual structure of the artist's work. Lichtenstein *had* included them in his *Portrait of Madame Cézanne,* for they were, to a large extent, the ostensive means for his critique of Loran's practice (fig. 99). When asked by John Coplans in a 1967 interview about using Loran's diagrams as sources for his paintings, the artist replied:

> The Cézanne is such a complex painting. Taking an outline and calling it Madame Cézanne is in itself humorous, particularly the idea of diagramming a Cézanne when Cézanne said, " . . . the outline escaped me." There is nothing wrong with making outlines of paintings. I wasn't trying to berate Erle Loran because when you talk about paintings you have to do something, but it is such an oversimplification trying to explain a painting by A, B, C and arrows and so forth.[29]

Why, then—if this was the substance of his critique—would he omit those elements ("A, B, C and arrows and so forth") from his own *Man With Folded Arms?* The answer becomes apparent only when Lichtenstein's two "Cézanne" (or perhaps more accurately, "Loran") paintings are examined as a pair. Taken together the paintings—one of a male figure, one of a female—again set out a particular relation between gender and visual representation.

Lichtenstein's *Man with Folded Arms* presents us with a male figure uninflected by the diagramming elements that had been present in Loran's illustration. Moreover, the artist made another change to the image: he added a field of regularized dots that gives the figure more visual weight (to use Lichtenstein's own language, "unifying" it) by separating it from the background. Loran was not completely

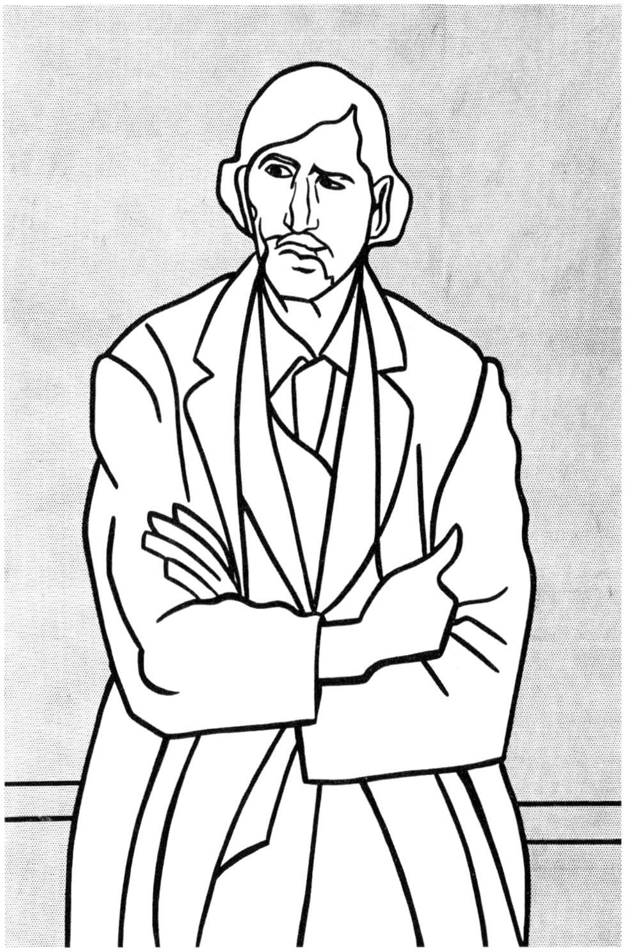

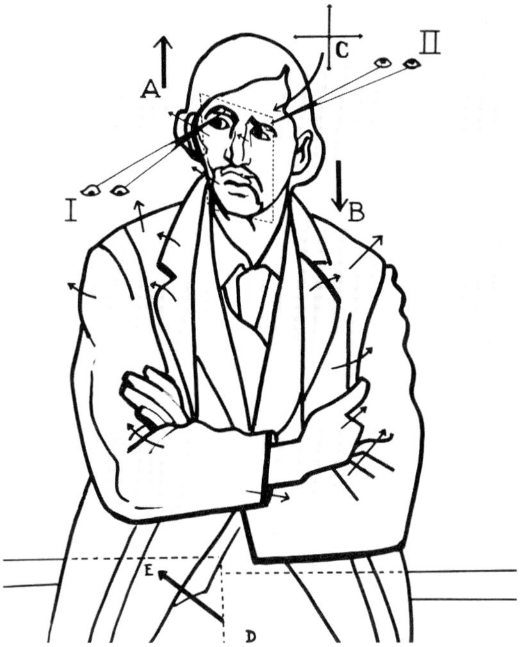

Figure 98. Erle Loran, diagram from *Cézanne's Composition* (1943)

Figure 97. *Man with Folded Arms,* 1962. Oil on canvas, 70 × 48 in. (177.8 × 121.9 cm). Museum of Contemporary Art, Los Angeles. Panza Collection

blind to the changes Lichtenstein had wrought on his image; he noticed the effect of the artist's addition of a background dot field, and called attention to—and criticized—it in his *Artforum* article:

> The Ben Day dots in the background of Lichtenstein's copy of my diagram of the great Cézanne portrait, Plates III and IV, which appears on p. 91 of "Cézanne's Composition," ruins the value of my original drawing. It pushes the background away from the figure of the man instead of integrating the two.[30]

Whether or not the "value" of his drawing had been ruined, Loran's estimation of the effect of those dots was accurate. The male figure is visually separated from that background, especially when contrasted with the female figure in *Portrait of Madame Cézanne*—a figure that has been completely dissolved into a tangle of lines and arrows arrayed across the surface of the picture. Although Lichtenstein

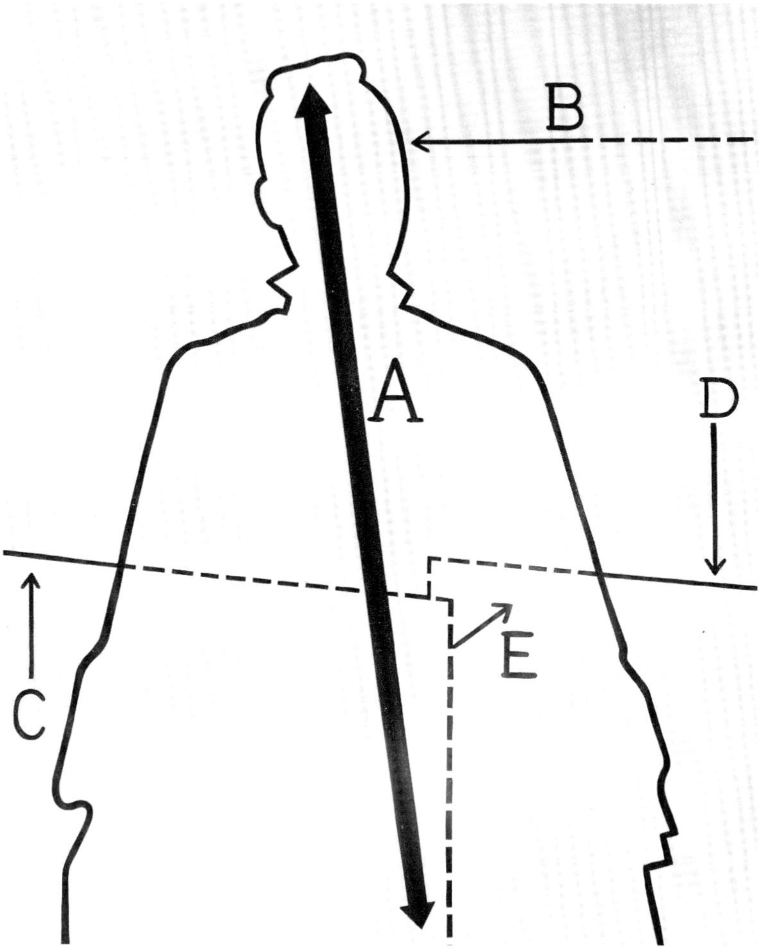

Figure 99.
Portrait of Madame Cézanne, 1962.
Magna on canvas,
68 × 56 in. (172.7 × 142.2 cm).
Private collection

had removed all such elements from that male figure, he retains them in *Portrait of Madame Cézanne,* thus describing the feminine as a veritable site for the inscription of diagramming elements, text, and graphic signifiers. In other words, the relation between these two figures is the same as that described by *In the Car,* which presents a male figure free of any markings and a female figure that—in contrast—serves as the site of inscription for graphic notation. Even Lichtenstein's titles reflect this gendered opposition. Whereas the image of the male figure is identified by the generic (*Man with Folded Arms*), the image of the female figure is given a name (*Portrait of Madame Cézanne*); not just any name, but that signifying the subsumption of the feminine by the male patronymic. In this way image and title correspond in that both represent the feminine as a site of inscription for masculine identity.

In the Car was an important work because it provided Lichtenstein the opportunity to investigate the semiology of graphic devices, and at the same time conflated that conventionalized language of notation with the feminine. It was also significant because it related to a painting he had produced a year earlier, namely *Masterpiece* (with which I began this chapter). If, as I've been suggesting, the gendered pairing of images—*Portrait of Madame Cézanne* and *Man with Folded Arms, Vicki* and *Girl in a Mirror*—was crucial to Lichtenstein's project at this time, then a comparison of *In the Car* and *Masterpiece* offers yet another instance of this type of pairing. In fact, such a comparison demonstrates that the figural groupings in the two works are effectively mirror reversals, with female and male figures transposed. In each a figure in profile is positioned at one edge of the composition; an element that stands for a flat surface of representation (whether windshield or canvas) is placed at the other; and a figure in the center is turned toward the one in profile. However, there is more to this pairing than a mere set of compositional reversals. If *In the Car* correlates a feminine figure with a flat surface for graphic notation, the equivalent positions in *Masterpiece* are taken up by a masculine figure and work of art. And not just a work of art, but more specifically a painting—one that has been turned away from us. The relation between the two works is given further meaning by the respective spaces in which the scenarios are set. One takes place in an automobile, the other in the painter's studio. The former is not only a mechanical device but also one of the most powerful symbols of postwar commercial culture—the epitome of the luxury good. The latter is the retreat of the fine artist, a space conventionally understood as bracketed off from the everyday in order for the artist to focus on the rarefied order of the aesthetic. In other words, their pairing plays off the arena of mass culture against the artist's studio, commercial culture against fine art. And in *Masterpiece* it is again the feminine figure—with her word-balloon reference to the market—that brings the world of commerce into the studio.[31]

On the one hand, we could read these two paintings as setting up a straightforward opposition: the feminine aligned with the commercial form of graphic notation, the masculine with the aesthetic form of the work of art. But if, as I've argued, *In the Car* conflates the feminine profile with a surface for graphic notation, what of the male artist in *Masterpiece,* depicted in equally flat, rigid profile? For one, this pairing again points to the semiological nature of Lichtenstein's project, in that it demonstrates the arbitrary and differential nature of the sign. In other words, *surface* can stand as much for the serious countenance of the male artist as for the woman's cosmetically enhanced features. Moreover, there is a developmental logic at work here: the move from *Masterpiece* (1962) to *In the Car* (1963) can be seen as marking the moment in which the relation between femininity and surface—and all its attendant meanings—came to be articulated in the artist's project.

We have seen throughout how Lichtenstein's work consistently returns to the articulation of difference, whether that between the trademark and the artist's signature, or between embodied perception and mechanically augmented vision. The distinctive gendering of imagery we have been examining here represents a related movement, an attempt by the artist to articulate difference in the face of the pictorial language he had incorporated into his practice at this time. Remember, it was not the act of appropriation that constituted a fundamental change in his project, for he had used borrowed images in his work since at least the early 1950s. Rather, his use of imagery from printed advertisements and the comics would have forced him to confront the implications of a pictorial syntax that utilized a conventional system of graphic devices. For instance, in the vocabulary of the commercial illustrator groupings of short lines could signify—depending on their placement—either the motion of an object or the reflection off a pane of glass. Early on Lichtenstein talked about the conventionality of illustration art:

> I had been interested in the comic strip as a visual medium for a long time before I actually used it in a painting. This technique is a perfect example of an industrial process that developed as a direct result of the need for inexpensive and quick color-printing. These printed symbols attain perfection in the hands of commercial artists through the continuing idealization of the image made compatible with commercial considerations. Each generation of illustrators makes modifications and reinforcements of these symbols, which then become part of the vocabulary of all. The result is an impersonal form. In my own work, I would like to bend this toward a new classicism.[32]

This account highlights the problem Lichtenstein confronted. He wanted to use visual devices borrowed from commercial illustration in order to develop a "new classicism." Yet he also recognized that such devices are "impersonal," that they belong to a "vocabulary of all." In other words, commercial illustration constitutes a language. But how does one personalize an essentially impersonal form? How could one possibly find originality in a set of techniques that ultimately lie outside the province of any particular individual?

Lichtenstein consistently asserted that there was a fundamental difference between his imagery and that of commercial artists. He resolutely maintained that his work exhibited a unified, aesthetic form that was lacking in the original. But how could he possibly incorporate such a common vocabulary into his work and at the same time maintain that it was fundamentally unique? Somehow, the very conventionality of graphic notation had to be marked as different from the work of art: it would be incorporated into his practice and yet at the same time bracketed off from within. Hence its equation in his work with the feminine, which is employed as the sign of difference itself. Significantly, Lichtenstein described women as veritable purveyors of what I have been calling the semiological; just as he talked above of the "idealization" of the comic book or printed image, he used similar language to describe the development of his distinctive imaging of women, particularly in about 1963 and 1964. When John Coplans asked him, in a 1967 *Artforum* interview, if his imagery "relates to the way women present themselves or the way they would like to be?" Lichtenstein responded: "Women draw themselves this way—that is what makeup really is. They put their lips on in a certain shape and do their hair to resemble a certain ideal."[33] Lichtenstein here describes the feminine *as* image; femininity is not a natural state but requires obedience to a pre-existing, conventionalized image or ideal. Moreover, his account conflates femininity (much as we've seen in his work) with *surface:* the woman cosmetically inscribes the idealized image of femininity onto the surface of her body.[34]

However, gendered terms are never defined in isolation. If the feminine in Lichtenstein's work is consistently assigned the qualities of *surface*—whether as surfaces exposed to the viewer's gaze or for the inscription of graphic notation—the masculine is repeatedly represented (or precisely *not* visually represented) as an unseen or hidden presence, refused to the viewer. Think of the out-of-frame "Brad" in *Drowning Girl,* or the turned-away picture frame in *Good Morning . . . Darling!* or the unseen face of the male figure in *Vicki.* In all these cases—as throughout the artist's imagery—the masculine is offered as an unmarked term in relation to the quite literally marked term of the feminine.[35] Lichtenstein's work incorporates the codes of commercial illustration, traffics in the very flatness that is the stuff of the printed image. Yet it maintains some faith in the possibility that there is some difference—some depth, some unseen or unseeable element—that might distinguish the work of art from the popular image.

Of course, the one-to-one mapping of the binary opposition of gender onto another set of oppositions—whether work of art versus commercial illustration, or original aesthetic form versus conventional graphic language—could be nothing more than a hopeful wish. The opposition between masculine and feminine itself must be repeatedly reiterated and reinscribed so as not to utterly collapse.[36] The difference between these terms is unsustainable, no matter how invested the artist's work might have been in maintaining it. Nevertheless, his imagery consistently returns to such distinctions in order to carve out some space for the work of art—and the artist—within the world of commercial culture and mechanical reproduction. We are again provided insight into the tension that veritably structured Lichtenstein's practice, specifically that accruing between two possibilities for comprehending the image: on the one hand, to understand it as articulated through a conventionalized set of rules or codes; on the other, to imagine it as the product of a unique, creating subject. These are two possibilities that might be termed, respectively, the semiotic and the aesthetic. As we have seen throughout this chapter—and the book as a whole—it was the very impossibility of adequately resolving the contradiction between these two versions of artistic activity that drove Lichtenstein's work in the early 1960s, and marked the practice we have come to know as Pop art.

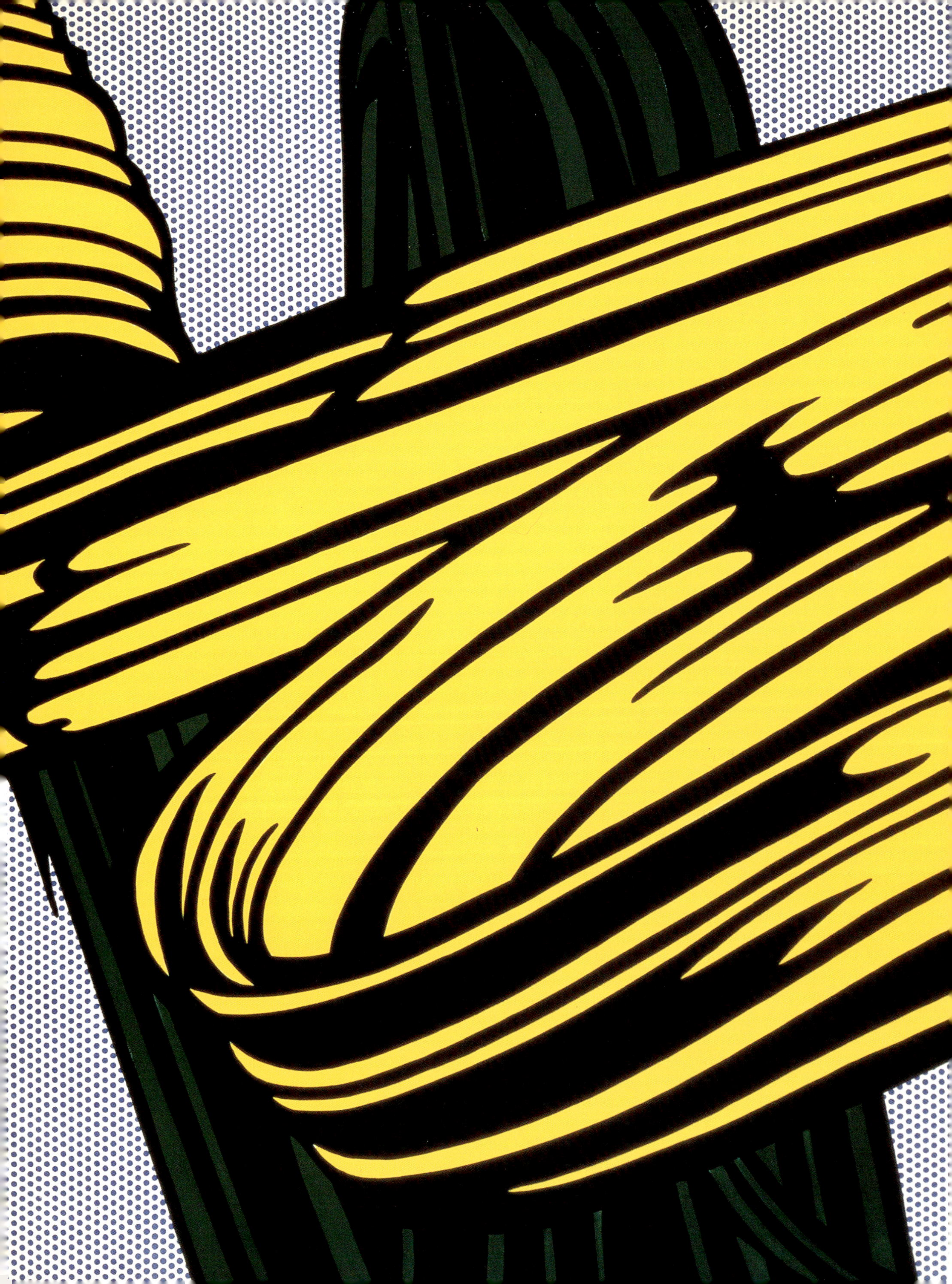

Conclusion

Lichtenstein faced the machine's threat to artistic practice by incorporating elements of the mechanical into his painterly idiom. His work preserved a traditional notion of the studio as a site of creative agency and aesthetic enclosure into which elements from industrial and consumer culture were brought in order to be transformed into fine art. His approach is reminiscent of those medical treatments in which the patient is given small doses of a poison in order to build up immunity. If he could incorporate elements of the mechanical into his practice perhaps he wouldn't destroy the privileged status of the work of art but rather extend its life.

A 1965 canvas by Lichtenstein brings together many of the concerns—the status of painting, the artist's investment in studio practice, the relation between the work of art and mechanical repetition—that we've identified as central to his project. It is a work that not only serves as something of an endpoint to his use of the appropriated comic book image in the early 1960s but that also inaugurated a series of some of his best-known paintings, works that cemented his reputation in the art world. These are the monumental *Brushstroke* canvases. In these paintings, images of wide, sweeping brushstrokes are splayed across fields of regularized dots (fig. 100). They mimic the signs of gestural painting—the distinctive texturing of paint, the strokes tracing the movement of the artist's hand across the canvas, the drips and dabs and splatters—while simultaneously parodying them in enlarged, flattened, and crisply delineated form. The *Brushstroke* paintings are often regarded as a culminating point in Lichtenstein's career because they allowed him to parody the painterly gesture even as he invented a series of distinctive, highly recognizable forms. And as a whole these are compelling paintings: the thick black outlines and looping bands of color, juxtaposed with fields of regularized dots, combine to wonderful visual effect. Yet the very means by which the artist produced these works bespeaks the same kind of radical ambiguity, even melancholy, that I have described throughout. Although they seem a moment of originality in

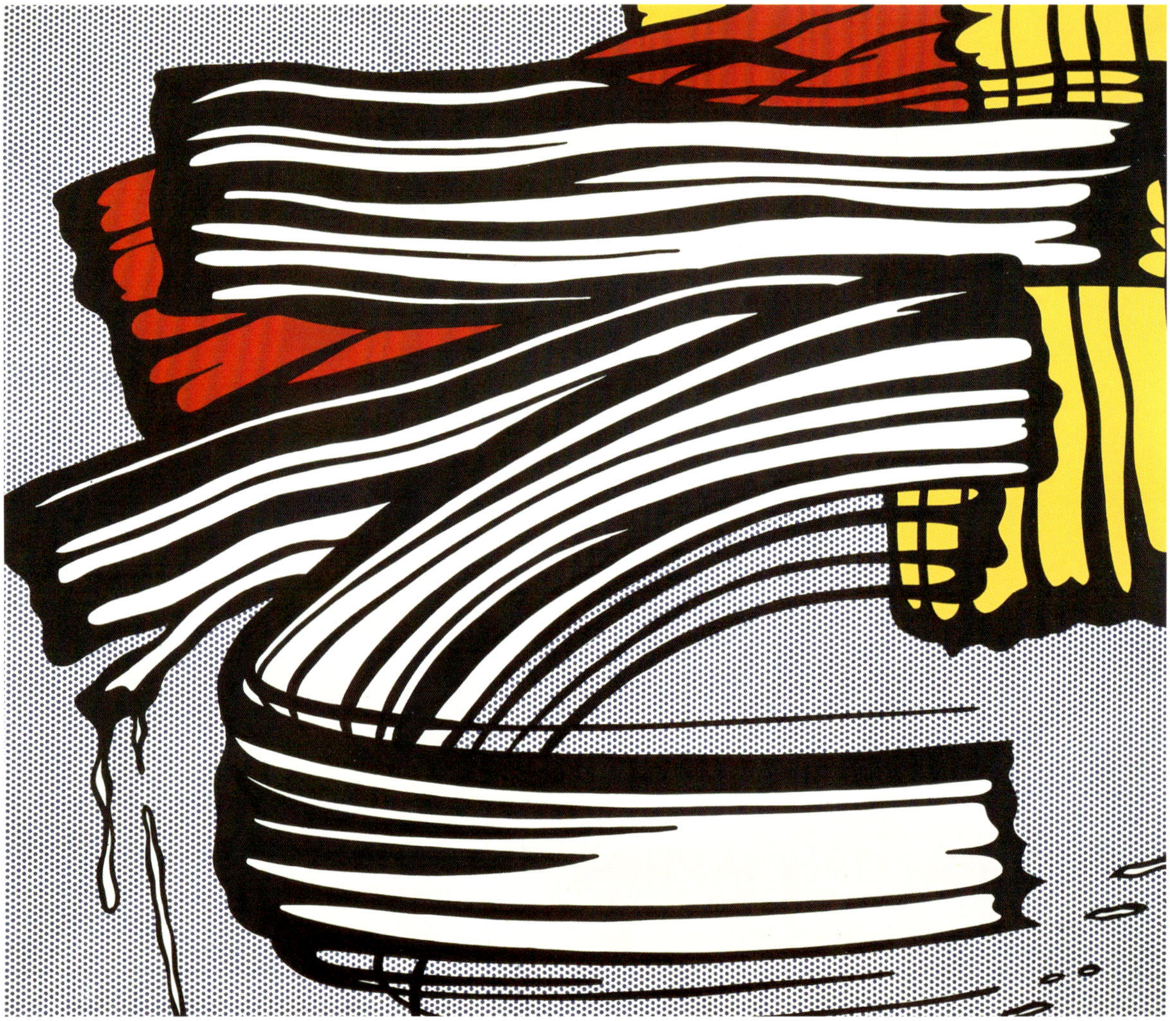

Figure 100. *Little Big Painting,* 1965. Oil and Magna on canvas, 68 × 80 in. (172.7 × 203.2 cm). Whitney Museum of American Art, New York. Purchase, with funds from the Friends of the Whitney Museum of American Art

which Lichtenstein was able to break free from his status as a veritable "image duplicator," the means by which he produced these works complicates such a view. Take Bernice Rose's account of the technique the artist used to create the *Brushstroke* paintings:

> He found the brushstroke difficult to create as a cliché. In fact he found he could not draw it at all, at first. He thought of brushstrokes as wide lines; evidently, it was difficult to draw a description of a line—to describe a line with a line. He finally discovered that if he painted an actual brushstroke as a small

study with ink or Magna on acetate, the acetate would repel the wet medium, forcing it to "crawl" back within its own contours, so that it looked like an imitation of itself. Projecting the study onto canvas enabled him to draw an outline around the brushstroke, creating it as a distinct formal unit, stylized as a cartoon.[1]

A studio shot by the photographer Ugo Mulas captures a scene set up to illustrate the process described by Rose (fig. 101). In the background one of the large paintings from the series, *Big Painting VI* (1965), has been propped against the wall of the artist's studio. A studio ladder encrusted with paint stands in front of it, centered in the frame. A collage of brushstroke studies—much like that described by Rose—has been fixed (perhaps taped) to the top of the ladder. If the *Brushstroke* paintings are conventionally interpreted as a means for Lichtenstein to get away from, and even mock, the painterly gesture, Rose's account—and Mulas' photograph—indicate the limits of such a view. For his method of making those paintings forced him right back into the practice of gestural painting, shadowed by another return to repetition. To produce each of the *Brushstroke* works (not necessarily the first one, but others in the series) he made a gestural painting on acetate and then transferred it, writ large, onto canvas. In order to parody the painterly gesture he was forced into repeating it again and again. At the very moment of seeming originality he returned, not unexpectedly, to repetition.

With the *Brushstroke* series the artist began to move away from direct appropriations of comics, advertising, and other printed sources, and—as with the landscapes and mirror works of the late 1960s and early 1970s—he began to more fully exploit the abstract qualities of his pictorial idiom. However, it is not widely recognized that the series began with a painting derived from a comic book source. That painting marks a moment of transition in Lichtenstein's work and provides a unique glimpse into his working process.

In the simplest terms *Brushstrokes* (fig. 102) images the act of painting. In the lower left of the canvas a hand—synecdoche for the artist's body—grasps a paintbrush that looks more like the wide brush of a house painter than the artist's fine-tipped instrument. From the upper right corner long bands of red and black—the brushstrokes of the work's title—spread downward and across the canvas, their ragged edges punctuated by oozing drips. Like the hand and paintbrush these brushstrokes are superimposed against a background of regularized blue dots. If this painting initiated an important series of works for the artist, he nevertheless seems to have had trouble depicting its central motif. We are even provided an account of Lichtenstein's struggle with the brushstroke before he came to incorpo-

Figure 101.
Ugo Mulas,
Roy Lichtenstein, New York, 1965

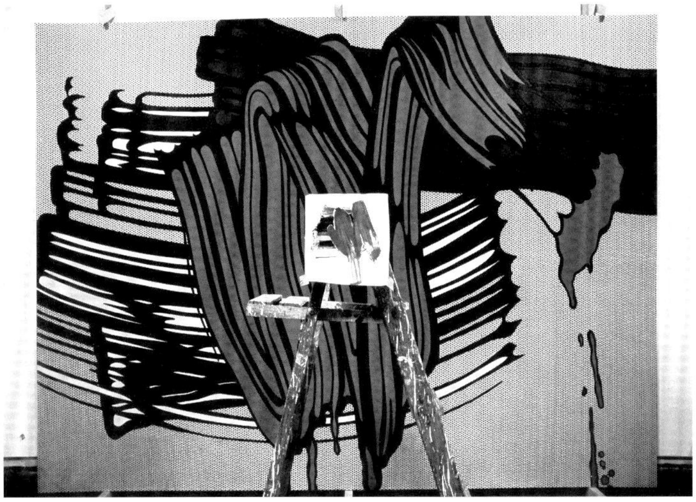

rate it into a finished work. Consider the following exchange from his wide-ranging 1964 interview with the collector Richard Brown Baker:

RBB: And you are, I take it, in rebellion against the brush stroke.

RL: Yes. I'm thinking of doing now something on Abstract Expressionism, since I've done Picasso ones, and there the problem will be to paint a brush stroke, a picture of a brush stroke which would . . .

RBB: That's interesting. I should invite you to my collection to go through to see if you can find any painting to parody. But totally . . .

RL: Mutilate.

RBB: That's an interesting problem. I wonder what artists would lend themselves . . .

RL: Purposely dripped paint and things, you know, where the drips are actually drawn as drips that look like drops of water drawn by a commercial artist.

RBB: I wonder if some of the Pollocks would lend themselves to this.

RL: They might.

RBB: You should go to the new exhibit and have a look around, maybe you'll find a clue. Or do you think de Kooning would, de Kooning's *Women* would they . . . ?

RL: That's a possibility. De Kooning probably comes closer. I've made some little sketches but most of the shapes look like wooden signs rather than brush strokes, they look like a lot of cartoon drawings of wooden signs, you know how the edges are zigzagged and they've got marks through them which look more like weathered wood than they do—I have to think of a way of representing . . . [2]

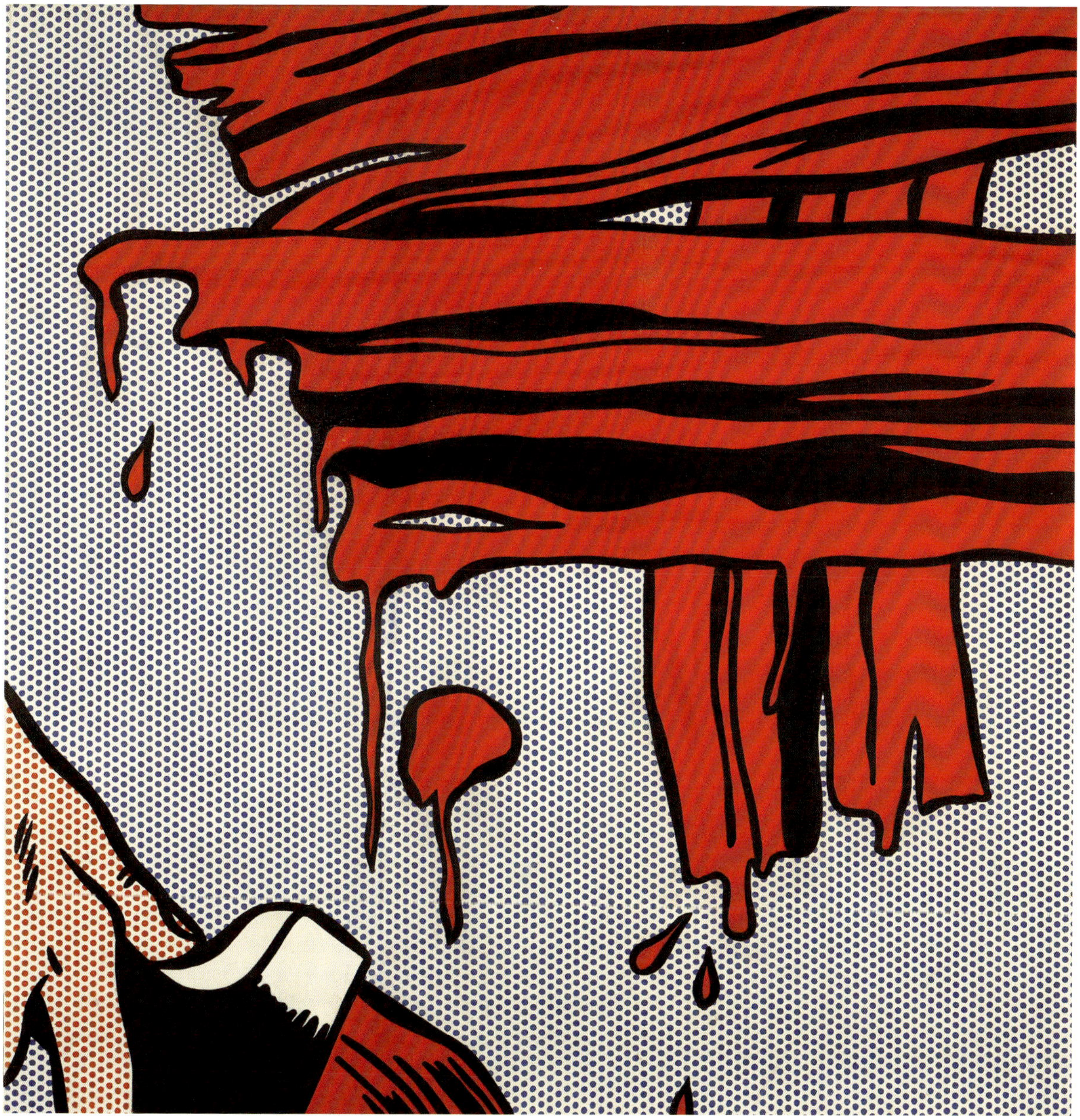

Figure 102. *Brushstrokes,* 1965. Oil and Magna on canvas, 48 × 48 in. (121.9 × 121.9 cm). Private collection

Considering my discussion of the semiological component of Lichtenstein's work—that is, his grappling with the implications of incorporating a conventional system of graphic notation into his painterly practice—it is significant that he talks here of confronting much the same problem: how to *re*-present a brushstroke, to turn it into an image that will read precisely as conventionalized. The above exchange indicates that this did not come easily to him. This is somewhat surprising, because many of the formal configurations he would go on to employ in the *Brushstroke* canvases had already appeared in his work. For example, as noted in the previous chapter, the treatment of the large expanse of blonde hair in *Girl in Mirror* is remarkably similar to the distinctive sweeping strokes used in a work like the 1966 canvas *Yellow and Green Brushstrokes* (fig. 103). Nevertheless, Lichtenstein needed a vehicle through which to depict the brushstroke, and he found it in a surprising place: the pages of a horror comic book.

"The Painting" is a story from a 1964 issue of Charlton Comic's *Strange Suspense Stories.*[3] Even though Charlton lacked the production values and more recognizable superhero characters of higher-end publishing houses like Marvel and DC Comics, "The Painting" would have stood out among the other stories with which it appeared.[4] This is due partly to its subject matter, partly to the quality of its rendering, and partly to the fact that it enjoyed pride of place on the comic book's cover. Lichtenstein seems to have favored sources from comics published by DC Comics, and he may have initially been drawn to another publisher's title because of the scene depicted on its cover (fig. 104). A young painter is compelled to paint the face of a male figure; once the picture is completed the mysterious figure begins to speak to the terrified artist. The last panel on the cover shows the painter brutally stabbing that figure—and the canvas—with a knife. A text panel asks the reader: "WHAT WAS THE STRANGE POWER OF . . . **'THE PAINTING'?**"

This cover may have proved irresistible to an artist who had spent the past several years grappling with the conjunction between painting and comic book illustration, and the story contained within would only have borne out that initial interest. "The Painting" tells the story of Jake Taylor, a young artist of great ability

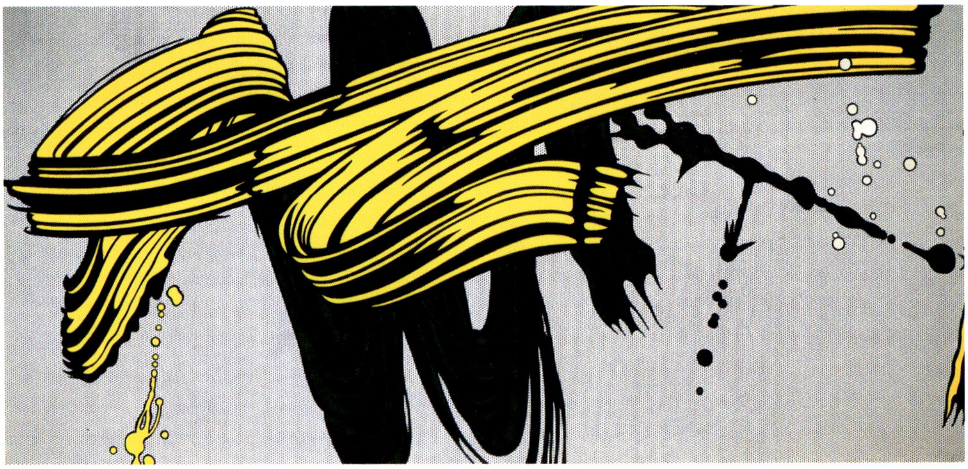

Figure 103.
Yellow and Green Brushstrokes,
1966.
Oil and Magna on canvas,
84 × 180 in.
(215 × 460 cm).
Museum für Moderne Kunst, Frankfurt.
Gift of the Ströher Family

who, in spite of encouragement from friends and teachers, refuses to exhibit his work because he believes that his talents are not yet fully developed. His refusal is so complete that he declines an offer of representation by a highly esteemed art dealer. Jake bemoans his lack of confidence: "I can't afford to show my paintings . . . what if the world doesn't like them? That would kill me! I can't! I need time!" Under the spell of a powerful compulsion, he picks up a brush and begins to paint the image of a sinister male figure. Late one night, soon after he has completed the picture, the figure speaks to him: "You call yourself an artist! Yet, you are afraid to face the world with your work and let them judge it!" Jake covers the painting in an attempt to silence it and return to his work yet finds himself inexorably drawn to the mysterious canvas. Each time he uncovers it the figure berates him for his failure to exhibit his work. Finally, in a rage Jake picks up a paintbrush loaded with red paint and, with a series of wide, slashing strokes, obliterates the painted figure. The caption above relates: "The painting was destroyed . . . the voice was silenced."

It was this panel—sans captioned text—that Lichtenstein appropriated for

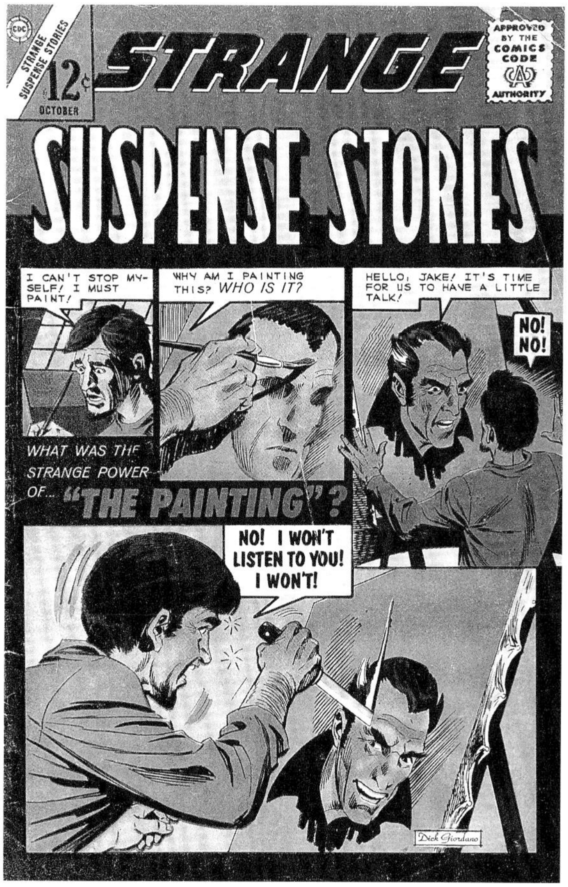

Figure 104. Dick Giordano, cover of *Strange Suspense Stories* no. 72 (October 1964)

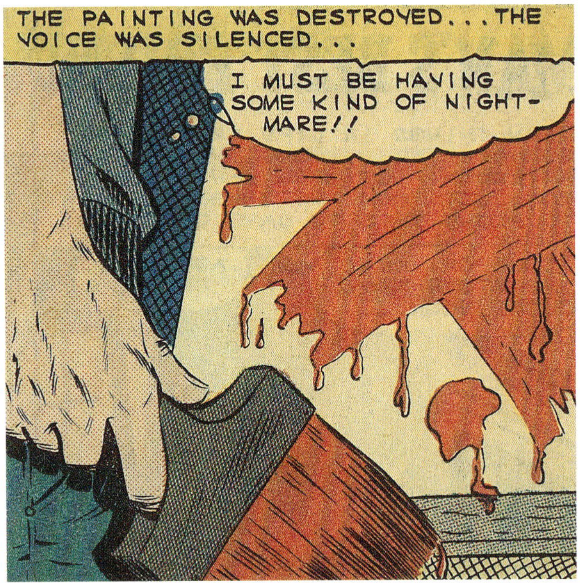

Figure 105.
Panel from "The Painting" in *Strange Suspense Stories* no. 72 (October 1964)

Brushstrokes (fig. 105).[5] Why did he need it to depict the brushstroke? The comic book narrative had taken up a longstanding theme in both art and literature: it imagined that the artist's mimetic duplication of reality could be so complete that the work of art might take on a life of its own.[6] The story, further, was specifically concerned with an artist's response to hostile criticism: in the source panel for *Brushstrokes* the artist has effectively silenced his critic. Finally, "The Painting" represents an ironic intersection of "high" and "low," although this was not a case of the avant-garde artist appropriating from mass culture but rather the opposite: the comic book writer and illustrator had constructed their story around the figure of the fine artist. Lichtenstein had probably already recognized the frequency with which artists were used as characters in comic books, especially in the romance comics; no doubt this allowed the creators of these stories to incorporate self-referential elements into their work.[7]

If these narrative elements were significant, Lichtenstein removed almost all traces of them from his finished painting. Moreover, in spite of his seeming need for a source that would provide the form for his brushstrokes, he radically altered their appearance in his finished canvas. He changed their orientation from diagonal X-es to more resolute horizontals and verticals, and he used thicker, undulating bands and black outlines to emphasize the thickness and striation of paint strokes. He also excised those elements that had signified the material supports of painting: the edges of a stretcher bar, the supporting cradle of an easel, even the shirt and pants worn by the painter. To signify the presence of the artist he left only the barest indications of two fingers and a thumb grasping the handle of the paint-

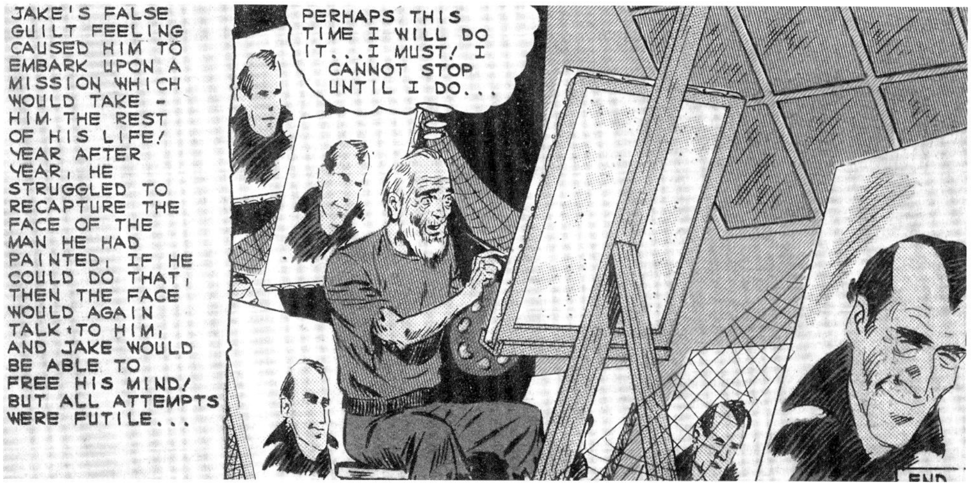

Figure 106. Final panel from "The Painting" in *Strange Suspense Stories* no. 72 (October 1964)

brush at lower left. The activity of that hand is thus made more ambiguous; in the comic book panel the caption and thought balloon made clear that the painter's act of destruction was completed. In Lichtenstein's painting the removal of supporting text, the absence of any signs of material support, and the formal similarity between the depicted brushstrokes and the red bristles on the end of the paintbrush allow us to read this as a scene of painting in process. In other words, it looks less like that hand is down at the painter's side (as it was in the comic book panel) than that it is pressing paintbrush against canvas in mid-stroke.

There is one aspect of the comic book narrative I have thus far omitted from my discussion, namely its ending. That ending provides a fitting conclusion to my own examination of Lichtenstein's project. In the comic book the young painter's violent crossing-out of the figure that haunted him is not without consequence; in the story's next panel he reads in the newspaper of the death of a man who looks just like the one who had appeared on his canvas. Fearing that he caused the man's death, Jake attempts to re-create that painted visage. The caption for the final panel reads: "Jake's false guilt feeling caused him to embark upon a mission which would take him the rest of his life! Year after year, he struggled to recapture the face of the man he had painted. If he could do that, then the face would again talk to him, and Jake would be able to free his mind! But all attempts were futile . . ." The final panel shows Jake, now a wizened old man, seated at an easel in a studio choked with cobwebs (fig. 106). He is surrounded by numerous canvases, each of which contains an identical image: the face of the man who had haunted him.

"The Painting," then, is the story of an artist's vain attempt to recapture a lost original. It suggests that the driving force behind painting is a compulsion to repeat in order to recapture something that will be forever out of reach. In short, it is the story Lichtenstein "needed" in order to paint the brushstroke because it was, to a certain extent, his own story as a painter. No doubt it is melodramatic and overblown, as befitting the genre. But it contains elements that would no doubt have prompted recognition for him. It presents the figure of an artist who confines himself to his studio, becoming nothing more than a literal image duplicator. The melancholy of "The Painting" is, finally, that of Lichtenstein himself, who sought originality only to find it—in distorted form—in repetition. Like so much of his work, *Brushstrokes* is haunted by the artist's attempt to yoke his painterly practice to the industrial and mechanical in the face of the profound sense of loss such a project inevitably evoked.

Notes

Introduction

1. Cécile Whiting has offered an extensive discussion of the reabsorption of Lichtenstein's imagery into the mass media. See Whiting, *Taste for Pop,* esp. 137–145.

2. This tendency is most evident in Stich, *Made in U.S.A.*, with such chapter headings as "American Food and American Marketing" and "Cities, Suburbs, and Highways—The New American Landscape," and Mamiya, *Pop Art and Consumer Culture,* with such chapter subheadings as "Automobiles" and "Processed Foods." Certainly, both authors discuss the distinct ways that the artists treat this shared subject matter. However, I would argue that this kind of overarching thematic categorization tends to generalize the work and to deemphasize the substantive distinctions between different artists' approaches.

3. Lichtenstein himself challenged this label in an early interview. Referring to the term Pop art, he stated in an aside: "I don't think it is a very good idea to group everybody together and think we are all doing the same thing." Glaser, "Oldenburg, Lichtenstein, Warhol," 22.

4. See Busche, *Roy Lichtenstein: Das Frühwerk.*

5. Most of this biographical information is culled from an indispensable chronology of the artist's life, compiled by Clare Bell, in Waldman, *Roy Lichtenstein* (1993), 364–375.

6. In fact, Johns and Rauschenberg were often identified as Pop artists along with others (such as Lichtenstein, Robert Indiana, and James Rosenquist) whose work became recognized somewhat later. To cite just one example, Johns was included by Gene Swenson in his series of landmark interviews, "What is Pop Art? Part II."

7. Coplans, "An Interview with Roy Lichtenstein," 31.

8. The activities of the Rutgers group have been amply documented and investigated in Marter, *Off Limits.*

9. Duchamp proposed that a common, industrially produced object—a snow shovel, a bottle rack—could be designated a work of art by the artist.

10. For Kaprow's account of his friendship with Lichtenstein, see *Lichtenstein at CalArts,* 23–36.

11. Kaprow, "Legacy of Jackson Pollock," 56–57.

12. "Neo-avant-garde" is the term used to describe a set of artistic strategies employed in the 1950s and 1960s that was modeled on the activities of early twentieth-century avant-garde movements like Dada and Surrealism. Hal Foster offers an analysis of the historical logic of such neo-avant-garde activities in *Return of the Real,* esp. Chapter One ("Who's Afraid of the Neo-Avant-Garde?"), 1–33.

13. Waldman, *Roy Lichtenstein, Riflessi-Reflections,* 19.

14. The best known of Lichtenstein's early hostile critics is Erle Loran; see Chapter Four for an extended discussion of Loran's attacks on the artist.

15. One of the earliest extended discussions of this is Boime, "Lichtenstein and the Comic Strip." See also Johnson, "Image Duplicators." Such juxtapositions can be found in any number of texts, including Waldman, *Roy Lichtenstein* (1993); Varnedoe and Gopnik, *High and Low;* and Whiting, *Taste for Pop.*

16. Seiberling, "Worst Artist in the U.S.?" 80.

17. Even though some of the text in the source is cropped out in the *Life* article, the remaining lettering seems to indicate that Lichtenstein substituted "image duplicator" for what had been in the original "stones of babylon."

18. The source files in Lichtenstein's New York studio contained loose clippings of panels from the *X-Men* comic book. His treatment of source materials in those files seems to have been rather haphazard; he had pasted some clippings into ordinary composition notebooks, had left others loose, and had also kept several stacks of comic books from the period and after. He seems to have been decidedly uninterested in maintaining a record of his sources.

19. Boime, "Lichtenstein and the Comic Strip," 158.

20. See Busche, *Roy Lichtenstein: Das Frühwerk,* 58.

21. My use of certain terms to describe the tension in Lichtenstein's work—particularly that of originality versus repetition—is indebted to the work of Rosalind Krauss, especially her essay "The Originality of the Avant-Garde" in *Originality of the Avant-Garde,* 151–170.

22. Seiberling, "Worst Artist in the U.S.?" 80.

23. The first sentence of O'Doherty's article reads: "One of the worst artists in America has raised some of the most difficult problems in art." O'Doherty, "Triumph of the Banal," 21.

24. The status of the later article as a repetition of the earlier one is not only due to the similarity of their respective titles. For one, although the Pollock profile was uncredited, Seiberling was the author of both articles. Further, the article on Pollock included photographs that documented the painter's famous "drip" technique; as I've already described, the later article provided similar photographic documentation of Lichtenstein's working process. See "Jackson Pollock: Is He the Greatest Living Painter in the United States?"

25. Seiberling, "Worst Artist in the U.S.?" 80.

26. Fried, *Courbet's Realism,* 3.

27. A 1962 exhibition at the Sidney Janis Gallery in New York, which included work by Lichtenstein, Oldenburg, Rosenquist, Dine and Warhol (among others), was titled "The New Realists."

28. Fried, "New York Letter," 66.

Chapter One. The Emergence of Pop Art

1. Ratcliff, "Work of Roy Lichtenstein," 112.

2. Glaser, "Oldenburg, Lichtenstein, Warhol," 22.

3. Warhol and Hackett, *POPism,* 20.

4. Hughes, "Pop's Most Popular," 101.

5. A list of the most important of these would include Thomas Crow's groundbreaking "Saturday Disasters," which argues that the artist's most significant work reveals, through images of suffering and death, the breakdown of commodity exchange; Richard Meyer's "Warhol's Clones," which interprets Warhol's imagery in relation to modes of repetition within homosexual male subcultures; and Hal Foster's consideration, in *Return of the Real,* of Warhol's approach to representation in light of theories of traumatic experience and the modern subject.

6. Stein, *Edie,* 245–246.

7. On the back of the contact sheet someone has written: "Idelle and Julian Weber's party, October 1964." However, this date, which was probably written at a later time, seems to be incorrect. Warhol did not meet Sedgwick until early 1965, and she did not come to wide public recognition until the summer of that same year. See Stein, *Edie.*

8. I would like to thank Andrew Perchuk for making this suggestion to me.

9. The former could be said of Hal Foster's analysis of Warhol's work as a type of "traumatic realism"; see Foster, *Return of the Real,* esp. 130–136. Robert Hughes, on the other hand, is probably the harshest critic of Warhol's seeming capitulation to the excesses of consumer and spectacular culture. See Hughes, "Rise of Andy Warhol."

10. Hughes, "Image Duplicator," 83.

11. *Andy Warhol and Roy Lichtenstein* (1966), produced and directed by Lane Slate and written and narrated by Alan Solomon, is

contained in the archives of the Museum of Television and Radio, New York City. It was part of the *USA: Artists* series, and according to Caroline Jones was originally broadcast Tuesday, March 6, 1966, on the public television station (W)NET. See Jones, *Machine in the Studio*, 91.

12. Warhol, interviewed by Alan Solomon in *Andy Warhol and Roy Lichtenstein* (1966); I have taken this quotation from Caroline Jones' own transcription of the interview in *Machine in the Studio*, 92.

13. Transcribed by the author from a videotape of the documentary.

14. Kozloff, "New Vulgarians," 36.

15. "The reason I'm painting this way is that I want to be a machine, and I feel that whatever I do and do machine-like is what I want to do." Swenson, "What Is Pop Art? Part I," 26.

16. Livingstone, "Do It Yourself," 66.

17. "Warhol alone set the terms of employment in the Factory workshop, seeking for himself the position of a manager rather than line worker." Jones, *Machine in the Studio*, 264.

18. Coplans, "Talking with Roy Lichtenstein," 34.

19. See Goldman, *James Rosenquist*, esp. 60–81.

20. For my account of the continuing tradition of painting as manual craft in Rosenquist's work, see Lobel, "Rosenquist's Craft."

21. Tomkins, "Brushstrokes," 11–12.

22. Filler, "Pop's Granddad," 150.

23. Ibid., 151.

24. Schjeldahl, "His Royness," 101.

25. Ratcliff, "Work of Roy Lichtenstein," 112.

26. Whiting, *Taste for Pop*, 1.

27. The fact that the term Pop has this meaning in the American vernacular but not in the British may explain the historical evolution of that term. Although the term Pop art was coined in the context of the work of the Independent Group in London in the 1950s, the term itself did not gain widespread critical and popular acceptance until it crossed the ocean and was used to describe the common imagery of a range of American artists in the early 1960s. Perhaps this is due in part to the different meanings of the word in Britain and the United States. This may also explain why, in an essay in which he cites numerous dictionary definitions of the word Pop, the British critic Dick Hebdige overlooks this one crucial, gendered meaning of the term. See Hebdige, "Fabulous Confusion." For more on the Independent Group, see *Modern Dreams*.

28. Warhol, quoted in Swenson, "What Is Pop Art?" 61.

29. Clipping from *Home Furnishings Daily*, May 10, 1967 (Joan Kron Papers, Archives of American Art, Smithsonian Institution, Washington, D.C.), reel 4224, frame 1146.

30. Swenson, "What Is Pop Art? Part I," 27.

31. For the intersection between Pop and gay male identity, see Silver, "Modes of Disclosure." For an analysis of Indiana's work in relation to homosexual identity, see Plante, "Truth, Friendship, and Love." For an interesting (albeit homophobic) early reading of Pop as emerging from a homosexual camp sensibility, see Gornick, "It's a Queer Hand."

32. In addition to the essays by Kenneth Silver and Richard Meyer that I have already cited, 1996 saw the publication of a whole volume devoted to the "queerness" of Warhol's practice. See Doyle et al., *Pop Out*.

33. Whiting, *Taste for Pop*, 132.

34. For instance, Whiting asserts that the "art and persona of Lichtenstein thus together came to figure a form of masculinity that finessed many of the threats perceived in the late 1950s and early 1960s to men and to high art." Ibid., 137.

35. See Busche, *Roy Lichtenstein: Das Frühwerk*, esp. 201–222.

36. Esterow, "Conversation," 91.

37. In 1954, at the age of twenty-four, Johns destroyed all of his works (at least those that were in his possession). However, it is not clear whether Lichtenstein would have known at this time of Johns' own act of destruction. See Crichton, *Jasper Johns*, 26.

38. For Busche's account of this transition, see *Roy Lichtenstein: Das Frühwerk,* Chapter Six, 223–261.

39. Glaser, "Oldenburg, Lichtenstein, Warhol," 21.

40. This information was obtained through the author's correspondence with the keepers of the Walt Disney Archives (including an April 1998 letter from archivist Dave Smith), and correspondence in the curatorial files of the National Gallery of Art, Washington, D.C. In the early 1960s both Mickey Mouse and Donald Duck appeared separately in their own newspaper comic strips. Lichtenstein's recollection of a bubble gum comic as the source for *Look Mickey* might have been informed by memory of another event, a conversation with his colleague Allan Kaprow. Kaprow is supposed to have pointed to the cartoon on a bubble gum wrapper and asserted—with characteristic bravado—that one could not teach color from a Cézanne but had to start with a simpler example, like the cartoon. For Kaprow's account of this exchange, see *Roy Lichtenstein at CalArts,* 27–28.

41. Filler, "Pop's Granddad," 152.

42. Lichtenstein, interview with the author, March 6, 1997. Lichtenstein had earlier stated that "I'd done pictures of Mickey Mouse and Donald Duck for the kids, but whether that has any relationship to drawing. . . . Deciding to do it straight is hard to tell, it may have had some influence, but probably hundreds of people have drawn Mickey Mouse for their children and . . . I don't think there's much relationship between that and my changing to Pop, really."

43. "About Face from the Abstract," 10.

44. Richter, *Dada: Art and Anti-Art,* 204.

45. Rose, *Drawings of Roy Lichtenstein.*

46. Okun, "Surrealist Object," 14. There are significant differences between Breton's and Lichtenstein's projects, most notably in that Breton's had a much more emphatically historical dimension. Breton's searching through the flea markets was, as Hal Foster has noted, a consequence of the artist's investment in the *outmoded,* in that the objects he found there were evidence of past modes of production. Lichtenstein's images are nostalgic inasmuch as the comics inevitably refer to youth or childhood, yet during this period he always used images from current comic books and advertisements; at the most his sources were two or three years old. In this way his practice is significantly different not only from Breton's, but also from that of other Pop artists; for example, Thomas Crow has called attention to Warhol's use, in his *Marilyn* paintings, of an almost decade-old photograph of the celebrity. Similarly, in a 1964 interview James Rosenquist noted: "In 1960 and 1961 I painted the front of a 1950 Ford. I felt it was an anonymous image. I wasn't angry about that, and it wasn't a nostalgic image either. Just an image. I use images from old magazines—when I say old, I mean 1945 to 1955—a time we haven't started to ferret out as history yet." Swenson, "What Is Pop Art? Part II," 41. For Warhol see Crow, "Saturday Disasters"; for Breton see Foster, *Compulsive Beauty,* esp. 157–161.

47. There is still a great deal to be done with the relations between Pop art and surrealism. There is in fact a 1966 article of that name that would provide a fortuitous entry for one who wished to consider that relation. See Irwin, "Pop Art and Surrealism." Hal Foster also emphasizes the connections between Pop art and surrealism in *Return of the Real,* especially when he outlines his theory of Warhol's work as a type of traumatic realism (see esp. 130–136). As I've suggested, however, I think that such a reading could be extended in various ways to the work of other Pop artists.

48. My attention was first drawn to *Look Mickey*'s significance as a joke in a talk given by Terry R. Myers at the 1996 College Art Association annual conference.

49. Freud, *Jokes and Their Relation to the Unconscious,* 118.

50. "The fateful process of civilization would thus have set in with man's adoption of an erect posture. From that point the chain

of events would have proceeded through the devaluation of olfactory stimuli and the isolation of the menstrual period to the time when visual stimuli were paramount and the genitals became visible, and thence to the continuity of sexual excitation, the founding of the family and so to the threshold of human civilization." Freud, *Civilization and Its Discontents,* 54. Rosalind Krauss makes use of this model to describe the effect of horizontalization in Jackson Pollock's work; see Krauss, *Optical Unconscious,* esp. 246–248.

51. Mikhail Bakhtin, for one, sets out this distinction in articulating his theory of grotesque realism in *Rabelais and His World.* Considering that Bakhtin's study is concerned with the incorporation of elements of folk humor into Rabelais' work, it bears some affinity with our investigation of Lichtenstein's incorporation of humorous popular materials into the work of fine art (although we would want to distinguish between the folk humor discussed by Bakhtin and the twentieth-century mass cultural forms treated in Lichtenstein's work). Bakhtin's discussion of degradation is much in keeping with our analysis of the humor of Donald's position: "To degrade also means to concern oneself with the lower stratum of the body, the life of the belly and the reproductive organs." Bakhtin, *Rabelais,* 21.

52. The difference between the two is reminiscent of the distinction, discussed by Peter Stallybrass and Allon White, between the classical and grotesque body: "The classical statue has no openings or orifices whereas grotesque costume and masks emphasize the gaping mouth, the protuberant belly and buttocks, the feet and the genitals." Stallybrass and White, *Politics and Poetics of Transgression,* 22.

53. Esterow, "Conversation," 90.

54. Swenson, "What Is Pop Art? Part I," 25.

55. *The Oxford English Dictionary,* 2nd ed., vol. 4, prepared by J. A. Simpson and E. S. C. Weiner (Oxford: Oxford University Press, 1989), 529.

Chapter Two. Trademark Lichtenstein

1. "New Paintings of Common Objects" was a 1962 exhibition at the Pasadena Art Museum curated by Walter Hopps. "Six Painters and the Object," curated by Lawrence Alloway, appeared in 1963 at the Guggenheim Museum in New York.

2. The inclusion of certain works in this category is ambiguous. There is the case of a painting and drawing, both titled *Keds,* which I discuss later in this chapter. There is also one exception that may define the rule; in 1964 Lichtenstein produced an image—entitled *Duridium*—of a single, magnified razor blade displayed against a field of regularized dots. For one, it is not clear whether that word refers to the name of the object or the type of metal from which it is made. It is also an exception in that most of Lichtenstein's images of common objects date from at least two years earlier, and that he seems to have experimented with a new technique—airbrushing—in producing the canvas.

3. Lichtenstein, interviewed by Richard Brown Baker (Archives of American Art, Smithsonian Institution,Washington, D.C.), tape 2, side 2, 41.

4. For Mickey Mouse's position within the field of copyright, patent, and trademark law, see Buskirk, "Commodification as Censor."

5. Varnedoe and Gopnik, *High and Low,* 206.

6. Ibid., 199.

7. In this way their argument could almost be seen as an extension of Clement Greenberg's famed dictum that the modernist artist's task was to isolate the ostensibly "pure" properties of the individual medium: "Guiding themselves, whether consciously or unconsciously, by a notion of purity derived from the example of music, the avant-garde arts have in the last fifty years achieved a purity and a radical delimitation of their fields of activity. . . . The arts lie safe now, each within its 'legitimate' boundaries, and free trade has been replaced by autarchy" (Greenberg, "Newer Laocoon," 32). Green-

berg himself rejected the Pop approach exemplified by Lichtenstein's work, yet it may be useful to consider Varnedoe and Gopnik's account as a kind of extension of the Greenbergian paradigm to mass cultural forms.

8. Ratcliff, "Work of Roy Lichtenstein," 115.

9. Lichtenstein, interviewed by Richard Brown Baker (Archives of American Art, Smithsonian Institution, Washington, D.C.), tape 1, side 1, 49.

10. Waldman, *Roy Lichtenstein* (1971), 25.

11. Ernst Busche provides extensive formal analysis of Lichtenstein's pre-Pop work, and compares it with an array of earlier artistic idioms, including cubism and that of Klee. See Busche, *Roy Lichtenstein: Das Frühwerk.*

12. For the source image for *The Explorer,* see Waldman, *Roy Lichtenstein* (1993), 9.

13. Public Opinion Index for Industry, *Language of Corporate Trademarks,* 5.

14. Capitman, *American Trademark Designs,* ix.

15. Jacobson, *Trademark Design.*

16. Jones, *Machine in the Studio,* 164–165.

17. Girardot, "Can Package Design Be Evaluated?" 24–25.

18. For the classic, contemporary account of (and attack on) motivational research in advertising, see Packard, *Hidden Persuaders.*

19. Jacobson, "Some Principles of Visual Communication," in *Trademark Design,* 171.

20. Johnson, *American Artists on Art,* 103.

21. Rosenblum, "Lichtenstein and the Realist Revolt," 39.

22. Swenson, "What Is Pop Art? Part I," 62.

23. Rose, *Drawings of Roy Lichtenstein,* 22.

24. Waldman, *Roy Lichtenstein* (1993), 33.

25. *What You Should Know About Du Pont Trademarks,* 6.

26. *How to Use the General Electric Signature and Monogram,* 1.

27. Lichtenstein, quoted in Coplans, "Talking with Roy Lichtenstein," 34.

28. McClellan, "Roy Lichtenstein, Ferus Gallery," 47.

29. Barthes, "Death of the Author." In a late essay on Pop Barthes made this claim directly: "The Pop artist does not stand *behind* his work, and he himself has no depth: he is merely the surface of his pictures: no signified, no intention, anywhere." Barthes, "That Old Thing, Art . . . ," 372.

30. See the Museum of Modern Art Library artist's file on Lichtenstein, folder 2.

31. Lichtenstein did not discard the signature altogether; he moved it to the back of his canvases. It also appeared in the margins of prints (coupled with the conventional numbering of successive impressions or proofs) and drawings. The signature, of course, has its uses—it is still an important marker of authenticity in the art gallery, museum, and auction house. Yet in that context the artist's signature can just as effectively be placed on the back of a canvas as the front. I want to draw attention to something different: the signature as a kind of rhetorical device, as a mark of identity that occupies—and becomes a distinct element within—the compositional field of the painting itself.

32. These were the cover of a 1967 Lichtenstein exhibition at the Pasadena Art Museum, and the cover for a 1971 *Untitled* portfolio by Equipo Crónica, a group comprised of the Spanish artists Rafael Solbes and Manolo Valdes. See Maharaj, "Framing Roy Lichtenstein," 14.

33. Ibid., 14.

34. In an interview with the author, Lichtenstein commented, "Of course I couldn't copyright Popeye anyway." Lichtenstein, interview with the author, March 6, 1997.

35. Waldman, *Roy Lichtenstein* (1993), 37.

36. I am referring to Derrida's essay "Signature Event Context," in which he writes: "In order to function, in order to be legible, a signature must have a repeatable, iterable, imitable form; it must be able to detach itself from the present and singular intention of its production." Derrida, *MARGINS of Philosophy,* 328.

37. Bob Colacello records a humorous exchange that points to Warhol's interest in the power of branding, in which the artist repeatedly urges Colacello to change his

name from Robert Colacello to Bob Cola. See *Holy Terror,* 47–48.

38. Shiff, "Performing an Appearance," 103.

39. Ibid., 116.

40. The term Ben Day refers to a type of half-tone technology used in mechanically printed images. Although it is abundantly clear that Lichtenstein derived the dot-fields in his work from the example of mechanical printing, it is important to recognize that these are fundamentally not printed dots. They are regularized dots painted on the surface of a canvas to simulate, represent, or recall such printed screens. If this seems like a banal or obvious point, I make it only because there is a tendency in the critical literature to refer to the dots in Lichtenstein's paintings as Ben Day dots, and thus to conflate the material status of the artist's paintings with that of printed images. One writer has even suggested—again, erroneously—that Lichtenstein used silkscreens in his work (Steiner, *Pictures of Romance,* 157, 175). For a thorough discussion of these issues—including an extended footnote on the origin and working process of the Ben Day printing technique—see Nesbit, "Lichtenstein: Birth of a Style."

41. Krauss, *Originality of the Avant-Garde,* 210.

42. Ibid., 212.

43. One could cite, for instance, Robert Rauschenberg as one example of a roughly contemporaneous artist whose work more fully embraced the mechanical implications of indexical marking. This is evident in such work as the photograms on blueprint paper that he produced in collaboration with Susan Weil. And if Lichtenstein produced an image of a tire with its tread, Rauschenberg executed a work in 1951 which consisted of the actual—that is to say, indexical—imprint of a tire on a scroll-like length of paper. For Rauschenberg's work, see Hopps and Davidson, *Robert Rauschenberg: A Retrospective.*

44. Lichtenstein, in Coplans, "Talking with Roy Lichtenstein," 34.

45. Kozloff, "Art," 284.

46. See, for example, Frow, "Signature," and Gaines, *Contested Culture.*

47. Waldman, *Roy Lichtenstein* (1971), 9.

48. Barthes, "That Old Thing, Art . . . ," 371.

49. It is impossible to date the images in these source notebooks in any consistent way, because Lichtenstein seems to have assembled them haphazardly. When I visited his studio in the spring and summer of 1997 his accumulated source materials included several notebooks, files of loose clippings, and stacks of comic books. I suspect that in part the notebooks may have even been compiled retrospectively, in the sense that at some later date Lichtenstein may have pasted loose clippings into the notebooks without regard to their original date of use.

Chapter Three. Technology Envisioned

1. Reinhardt produced canvases painted primarily in tones of black from 1954 until his death in 1967, while Stella painted his landmark series of so-called *Black Paintings* between 1958 and 1960.

2. As a teenager Lichtenstein had some early but not extensive training in art. He took watercolor classes at Parsons School of Design, and he attended a painting class taught by Reginald Marsh at the Arts Students League in New York; see Clare Bell's indispensable chronology in Waldman, *Roy Lichtenstein* (1993), 364–375. The most exhaustive critical account of Hoyt Sherman's project is presented in Deitcher, "Teaching the Late Modern Artist." Deitcher offers a condensed version of that account in his essay "Unsentimental Education." In *Roy Lichtenstein: Das Frühwerk,* Ernst Busche provides yet another extended account of Lichtenstein's training.

3. See Sherman, *Visual Demonstration Center.*

4. Deitcher, "Unsentimental Education," 102.

5. See Sherman, *Drawing by Seeing.*

6. Bruce Breland, e-mail correspondence with the author June 2, 1998.

7. *Roy Lichtenstein at CalArts,* 27.

8. Lichtenstein, interview with the author, March 6, 1997.

9. Swenson, "What Is Pop Art? Part I," 25, 62.

10. Deitcher, "Unsentimental Education," 105.

11. Tomkins, "Brushstrokes," 14.

12. Sherman, *Drawing by Seeing,* 66.

13. For a sustained analysis of the history of the *camera obscura* as both a device and a philosophical concept, see Crary, *Techniques of the Observer.*

14. Of course, *camera* is Latin for "room" (as in *I Can See the Whole Room*).

15. Discussing the work of two students trained in the flash lab, Sherman wrote: "Both students were able freely to express their personalities through their drawing at the level at which their personalities would allow, *and this is one of the prized achievements the teacher is after.*" Sherman, *Drawing by Seeing,* 29.

16. Even before his move into Pop, Lichtenstein had treated mechanical themes, producing a series of canvases with mechanical diagrams as their subject matter. Ernst Busche links these to Lichtenstein's studies in basic engineering in Columbus, and to a short period during which the artist was employed as a mechanical draftsman in Cleveland. Significantly, in these works the machine is isolated; in other words, there is no depicted interaction between human body and machine. There are, however, certain pre-Pop works that image the interaction between human figures and machines, including Lichtenstein's 1951 version of Charles Willson Peale's *Exhuming the Mastodon* (which places more emphasis on the central mechanism than had Peale's canvas). See Busche, *Roy Lichtenstein: Das Frühwerk,* 172–182.

17. Baer, "Photography and Hysteria," 67.

18. Ibid., 53–55.

19. Sherman, *Drawing by Seeing,* 11.

20. For the Surrealist strategy of automatism, see Foster, *Compulsive Beauty.*

21. See Ruskin, *The Elements of Drawing,* 5.

22. Sherman, *Cézanne and Visual Form,* 64.

23. I can't help but see in the rhetoric of Sherman's program a move from the monocular as an idealized representation of a religious deity (whether in depictions of the Holy Trinity or as expressed in the great oculus of the Roman Pantheon) to the monocular as an idealized representation of the machine (i.e., the camera).

24. Sherman, *Drawing by Seeing,* 2.

25. Sherman, *Cézanne and Visual Form,* 81.

26. My reading is indebted to the work of Rosalind Krauss, who has described modernist visuality in precisely these terms—that is to say, as structured by the repression of the corporeality of vision. See Krauss, *Optical Unconscious,* esp. Chapter One.

27. Lichtenstein, quoted in Tomkins, "Brushstrokes," 15.

28. One could also suggest that the red-and-white textual element—the final "o" of "Live Ammo" that strays from the left panel into the right—is almost eyelike, an element calling further attention to the ocular thematic in Lichtenstein's painting.

29. Wassenaar, "Strong to the Finich."

30. Ibid., 23.

31. In describing this quality of monocularity in Lichtenstein's work I do not mean any figure depicted with a single eye visible, as in the case of a figure shown in profile. I refer specifically to a figure that is depicted frontally in such a way as to expose both eyes to the viewer, yet which has one eye closed or otherwise obscured.

32. *Crying Girl* measures 18 × 24 inches; *CRAK!* measures 19¼ × 27⅝ inches. For more information on these prints, see Corlett, *Prints of Roy Lichtenstein,* 254–255.

33. For instance, in an early review Max Kozloff referred to the artist's images of women as the "lachrymose girls from *True Romance.*" Kozloff, "Dissimulated Pop," 418.

34. See Waldman, *Roy Lichtenstein* (1993), 241–249.

35. Waldman, *Roy Lichtenstein* (1993), 97.

36. One of the first recorded uses of the

term is in Clynes and Kline, "Cyborgs and Space."

37. I have derived this information on reflector gun sights from archival materials in the National Air and Space Museum Library, Smithsonian Institution, Washington, D.C. These include Goldberg, "Reflector Gun Sights," and Clarke, "Drawing a Bead," Parts Three and Four.

38. Wendy Steiner has discussed the status of narrative in Lichtenstein's work at length; I will explore this question further in Chapter Five. See Steiner, *Pictures of Romance.*

39. "Robot Plane Sight Adapted," *New York World-Telegram* October 18, 1944 (National Air and Space Museum Library, Smithsonian Institution, Washington D.C.).

40. Kaprow, quoted in *Roy Lichtenstein at CalArts,* 25.

41. Lichtenstein, interview with the author, March 6, 1997.

42. Much of this information on Lichtenstein's military service is culled from Clare Bell's chronology in Waldman, *Roy Lichtenstein* (1993), 365. Additional details are taken from Richard Brown Baker's 1963 interview with Lichtenstein in the collection of the Archives of American Art, Smithsonian Institution, Washington, D.C.

43. In contrast, many of the artists who illustrated war comics seem to have been military buffs who took care to faithfully render airplanes, guns, and other military equipment. In a similar vein, the war comic books often included letters pages that functioned as a kind of clearinghouse for information on military history and weaponry. For example, "Sgt. Rock's Combat Corner" in *All American Men of War* (from which Lichtenstein appropriated many source images) printed exchanges like this one: "Dear Sgt. Rock: Did the German Junkers carry any other armament besides its machine gun?—Bobby Stone, Toledo, Ohio. *Dear Bobby: The Junker also carried a 20-mm. cannon.—Sgt Rock.*" *All American Men of War* no. 95 (January–February 1963), n.p.

44. Lichtenstein, interviewed by Richard Brown Baker (Archives of American Art, Smithsonian Institution, Washington, D.C.): tape 2, side 1, 16.

45. Lichtenstein, interviewed by Richard Brown Baker (Archives of American Art, Smithsonian Institution), tape 2, side 2, 38. I must note, however, that even though I offer this account its veracity remains unclear to me. As we have seen with the case of *Look Mickey,* Lichtenstein does not seem to have been averse to offering anecdotes of questionable factuality.

46. "Then I know that I made my own metal stencil out of a piece of aluminum and graph paper. . . . I drilled through and it came out relatively uneven [laughing]. . . . I can tell which were done that way." Lichtenstein, interview with the author, March 6, 1997.

Chapter Four. The Image Duplicators

1. See, for instance, Busche, *Roy Lichtenstein: Das Frühwerk,* 248.

2. Gombrich, *Art and Illusion,* 39.

3. Tuchman, "POP!: Interviews," 27.

4. "An Interview with Roy Lichtenstein," Whitney Museum of American Art Independent Study Program, 1981, n.p.

5. Loran, "Pop Artists or Copy Cats?" 48.

6. Robert Nelson has called attention to the use of such rhetorical devices in the discourse of art history, and their inextricable connection to the mechanically reproduced image. See Nelson, "Slide Lecture."

7. "The important thing in the word is not the sound alone but the phonic differences that make it possible to distinguish this word from all others, *for differences carry signification*" (emphasis added). de Saussure, *Course in General Linguistics,* 118.

8. Loran, "Problems of 'Transformation,'" 35.

9. It is important to note that not all critics at the time embraced the possibilities afforded by the photomechanical reproduction of images. In his introduction to *Art and Objecthood* Michael Fried recalls a series of lec-

tures that Clement Greenberg delivered at Princeton University in 1958. According to Fried, Greenberg refused to use slides—thus depriving his audience of visual reference—"on the grounds that they misrepresented the works they ostensibly reproduced." Fried, *Art and Objecthood,* 4.

10. For a discussion of Loran's diagrams in the context of the larger modernist project, see Krauss, *Optical Unconscious,* 98–103.

11. Loran, *Cézanne's Composition,* 1.

12. Linda Nochlin has explored and thematized this aspect of the art historical project as the search for a lost original in an analysis of Courbet's painting *L'origine du monde.* See Nochlin, "Origin Without an Original."

13. Benjamin, "Work of Art."

14. Lichtenstein, interviewed by Richard Brown Baker (Archives of American Art, Smithsonian Institution, Washington, D.C.), tape 1, side 1, 63.

15. Wendy Steiner discusses extensively the narrative or proto-narrative elements in Lichtenstein's work. See Steiner, *Pictures of Romance.*

16. Moreover, *Step-On Can with Leg* is yet another imaging of the interaction between human body and machine, albeit a simple one. The same is true of a work such as the 1963 canvas *Trigger Finger,* a close-up view of a finger curled around the trigger of a gun.

17. Swenson, "What Is Pop Art? Part I," 62.

18. At the time of this writing I have been unable to determine whether the artist's library contained a copy of *Art and Illusion.*

19. These include the "Fraser spiral" on page 220 of *Art and Illusion,* which is also illustrated on page 60 of Sherman's *Visual Demonstration Center.*

20. Equating cartooning with techniques used in modern art, Gombrich writes: "The modern sculptor is free to grope for a global, physiognomic form in shapes which are sisters under their skin to Al Capp's motherly Shmoo. The modern painter may use what he calls 'automatic painting,' the creation of Rorschach blots, in order to stimulate the mind—his own and those of others—toward fresh inventions." Gombrich, *Art and Illusion,* 358.

21. Lichtenstein may have derived the motif of a cleaning hand from the source for *The Refrigerator,* or from a wristwatch ad. In a book that documents the creation of the artist's 1986 *Mural with Blue Brushstroke,* Bob Adelman provides a diagram of the "sources" for various motifs in the mural; it suggests that Lichtenstein based the cleaning hand on a 1950s ad for Elgin watches. Adelman, *Art of Roy Lichtenstein,* 30. As for the artist's use of the motif from Gombrich, it is tempting to consider that Lichtenstein knew of Gombrich's role in the so-called National Gallery Cleaning Controversy at that time, and that his two *Sponge* paintings make reference to it. There was a debate, extending back at least a decade, concerning the cleaning of pictures in the National Gallery of London, a debate at the center of which Gombrich found himself. In fact, the section of *Art and Illusion* in which the poster under discussion is reproduced makes reference to the debate about varnishes and the cleaning of paintings. See Gombrich, "Dark Varnishes."

22. Deitcher has suggested that Sherman's approach to art instruction "found its artistic complement in the work of Roy Lichtenstein." Deitcher, "Unsentimental Education," 105.

23. Lichtenstein, interview with the author, March 6, 1997.

24. For his own part, Bryson wants to see Gombrich's perceptual model replaced with a more appropriately semiotic one. He writes that "the work of Gombrich amounts to a transitional aesthetics that recognises but cannot yet theorise in depth the material nature of the painterly sign." Bryson, *Vision and Painting,* 22.

25. George Tuska, *Buck Rogers* Sunday newspaper comic strip, July 23, 1961.

26. The original text had read: "EXCEPT SOMETHING WENT WRONG . . . AND GROOT ENDED UP *DEAD* IN A SWAMP!" The text in *The Engagement Ring* reads "IT'S . . . IT'S

NOT AN *ENGAGEMENT RING*, IS IT?" and that of *Mr. Bellamy* reads "I AM SUPPOSED TO REPORT TO A MR. BELLAMY. I WONDER WHAT HE'S LIKE."

27. This is true as well of the small copyright symbol that appears at lower right, which further confuses the status of the various inscriptions on the picture plane.

28. Steinberg, "Other Criteria."

Chapter Five. Engendering Difference

1. Whiting, *Taste for Pop,* esp. 102–117.

2. "Web of Heartbreak," *Girls' Love Stories* number 92, January 1963.

3. "Tomorrow and Tomorrow," *Girls' Romances* number 78, September 1961.

4. Steiner, *Pictures of Romance,* 157.

5. *Mad Scientist* was based on a panel in *Justice League of America* number 12, June 1962.

6. In a later image, the 1974 *Artist's Studio (with Model and Explosion),* a hand grasping a pencil appears at the same point in the composition. Here it signifies the presence of an artist engaged in the act of sketching a model, literalizing the activity of drawing that is only suggested in *Mad Scientist.* Although it dates to a decade later than *Mad Scientist* it is one of Lichtenstein's many retrospective images, in which he assembled motifs from earlier works (including the explosion at left and the background friezes from his *Entablature* series).

7. See Koerner, *Caspar David Friedrich,* and Fried, *Courbet's Realism.* Fried analyzes a similar tendency in the work of Thomas Eakins in *Realism, Writing, Disfiguration.*

8. This is not to say that the two weren't derived from comic book sources, but that like so many of Lichtenstein's images they have multiple references.

9. Charles Harrison, *Modernism,* 64.

10. Ibid., 64.

11. The source for *Blonde Waiting* is from "Give Me an Hour" in *Girls' Romances* number 81, January 1962. The panel is reproduced in Varnedoe and Gopnik, *High and Low,* 197.

12. Elsaesser, "Tales of Sound and Fury," 43.

13. Lichtenstein experimented with other ways to produce a painting with an utterly smooth surface; in one case he painted in reverse on the back of a sheet of plexiglass, so that the plexiglass becomes the smooth, uninflected surface through which the image is seen.

14. Brooks, *Melodramatic Imagination,* 11–12.

15. Ibid., 4.

16. Ibid., 1–2.

17. Ibid., 5.

18. This is true of *Blonde Waiting, Happy Tears, Good Morning . . . Darling!* and *Oh, Jeff,* among others.

19. Alberto Boatto has described this ever-closer framing of Lichtenstein's comic-book imagery, noting that the artist was "obliged to give up the dispersing distant views of the first characters of 1961 and to enclose the image within a progression of framings from the knee upwards that finally ceases before exaggerated close-ups and before any unusual detail in the face or the hands." Boatto, "Comicstrip [sic] Under the Microscope," 56. Further, Cécile Whiting has commented on the gendering of these depictions of closely-framed figures cut free from narrative context: "These canvases of overwrought emotion frequently eliminate from the comic-book sources parts of text, incidental characters, and features of the setting in such a way as to highlight the tense, anxious female face alone while dispensing with narrative context or resolution." Whiting, *Taste for Pop,* 110.

20. Steiner, *Pictures of Romance,* 156.

21. The source panel for *In the Car* is from "Tomorrow and Tomorrow" in *Girls' Romances* number 78, September 1961.

22. A note about my reference to the "unnamed comic book artist" here. While some comic books in this period provide the name of writer and artist, this was not the case for the romance comics from which Lichtenstein appropriated in the early 1960s.

Moreover, according to the conventions of comic book illustration there may have been several artists whose work is represented in a finished story: the penciller, the inker, the colorist, as well as the individual who lettered the text.

23. For these characteristics of the sign—arbitrariness and difference—see Saussure, *Course in General Linguistics*. Yve-Alain Bois offers a condensed explanation of the Saussurean formulation of the sign in his discussion of cubism; see Bois, "Semiology of Cubism," esp. 173–174.

24. In interviews Lichtenstein often talked about the connections between cubism and cartooning: "There is a relationship between cartooning and people like Miró and Picasso which may not be understood by the cartoonist, but it definitely is related even in the early Disney." Lichtenstein, quoted in Coplans, "Talking with Roy Lichtenstein," 36. Although the artist is referring here mainly to the formal similarities between the two modes, it's conceivable that he recognized on some level that both approaches might also foreground the semiotic component of visual representation.

25. See, for instance, Bois, "Semiology of Cubism," and Krauss, *Picasso Papers*.

26. Krauss, *Picasso Papers*, 28.

27. It may be that in the comic book panel the reading of the horizontal elements as "lines of motion" is somewhat ambiguous, in that they can also be read, like the diagonal lines at right, as "lines of reflection." In other words, one could take them to signify reflections off a window interposed between the viewer and the figures inside the car. However, I would argue that the changes Lichtenstein made in his painting—including the way that the horizontal notations repeat the shape of the woman's profile, as if they describe her forward motion—remove this ambiguity.

28. A curious feature of the preliminary version of *In the Car* points both to the canvas' status as an experimental version, and to Lichtenstein's grappling with the semiotic play of meaning produced through difference. The white bars on the face of the female figure seem to have been filled in—rather roughly—with tan- or flesh-colored paint (because the painting remains in a private collection it has not been possible to inspect the painting firsthand). This is not true of any of the other white bars—horizontal or diagonal—in the rest of the painting. Such treatment is also not evident in version II. Whatever the reason, I take this as further evidence of the importance of the image for Lichtenstein, in that he was clearly experimenting with possible approaches to the motif.

29. Lichtenstein, in Coplans, "Talking with Roy Lichtenstein," 36. Note that when Lichtenstein discusses the possibility of diagramming a Cézanne he may again be invoking—consciously or not—the example of his teacher, Hoyt Sherman; Sherman had published his own diagrams of Cézanne's paintings (Sherman, *Cézanne and Visual Form*). One could suggest that Lichtenstein's appropriation of Loran's diagrams was yet another way to engage with (or even attack) Sherman's teachings.

30. Loran, "Problems of 'Transformation,'" 35.

31. Andreas Huyssen has perceptively analyzed the longstanding conflation of mass culture with the feminine; see Huyssen, "Mass Culture as Woman."

32. Lichtenstein, quoted in Rublowsky, *Pop Art*, 43.

33. Lichtenstein, interviewed by John Coplans, "Talking with Roy Lichtenstein," 39. Significantly, Lichtenstein goes on to say: "I've always wanted to make up someone as a cartoon. That's what led to my ceramic sculptures of girls. I was going to do this for some fashion magazine. I was going to make up a model with black lines around her lips, dots on her face, and a yellow dyed wig with black lines drawn on it, and so forth. This developed into the ceramic sculpture heads. I was interested in putting two-dimensional symbols on a three-dimensional object." The art-

ist is referring here to a group of sculptures he produced in 1965, in which his trademark dot-fields and black outlines were applied to the three-dimensional forms of women's heads. In this way they might be seen as further extending the graphic inscription of the female form I have identified in his paintings. For more on these sculptures, see Waldman, *Roy Lichtenstein* (1993), 315–321.

34. This reading of the feminine as surface (and as image) prefigures the appearance of similar readings in later feminist theory, such as Laura Mulvey's analysis of the feminine within the conventions of Hollywood film. See Mulvey, "Visual Pleasure and Narrative Cinema." However, while Mulvey is invested in critiquing or deconstructing such conventions, Lichtenstein's work maintains them in order to strategically (and one might say problematically) mark off difference within his work.

35. Semiotic theory often makes use of such distinctions between marked and unmarked terms: "A mark is a distinguishing sign: to be marked is to be differentiated from a class of otherwise similar items by means of some token. The presence of a mark creates a binary opposition between the marked and the unmarked, establishing the unmarked as primary, original, and genuine, and the marked as secondary, derived, and deviant." Bouissac, ed., *Encyclopedia of Semiotics*, 385. Further, the relation between feminine and masculine in language often accrues as that between marked and unmarked.

36. Judith Butler provides one of the most incisive analyses of the cultural reinscription of gender as a binary form; see Butler, *Gender Trouble*.

Conclusion

1. Rose, *Drawings of Roy Lichtenstein*, 27.

2. Lichtenstein, interviewed by Richard Brown Baker (Archives of American Art, Smithsonian Institution), tape 2, side 2, 70.

3. "The Painting," *Strange Suspense Stories* number 72, October 1964.

4. Typically such a comic book would contain four or five separate stories, representing the work of several artists and writers. This is generally true of the romance and war comics of the time, although by this time many superhero comics contained one full-length story.

5. Diane Waldman provided the source for *Brushstrokes* in the catalogue for Lichtenstein's 1993 Guggenheim Museum retrospective. However, it has also been misidentified in print; in a 1983 article David Deitcher wrote that "*Brushstrokes* was derived from a specific comic-book panel in which a woman, while painting the picket fence in front of her new suburban house, splatters paint all over the boy next door, making fun of the suburban '60s tuxedo he wears to impress the other woman in his life." Deitcher, "Lichtenstein's Expressionist Takes," 85.

6. This theme—which speaks to the notion of the artist having almost magical powers, as well as to the mimetic power of the work of art itself—is found both in art and literature (including Oscar Wilde's *Picture of Dorian Gray* and Edgar Allan Poe's "The Oval Portrait").

7. The use of artists as characters in comic book stories is true of "Julian, My Love!" in *Girls' Romances* no. 92 (June 1963), from which Lichtenstein borrowed for the 1964 painting *Happy Tears;* "Don't Kiss Me Again!" in *Girls' Romances* no. 105 (December 1964), which contained a panel that he appropriated for *M-Maybe (A Girl's Picture);* and "Listen to Love!" in *Heart Throbs* no. 79 (August–September 1962), which provided the source for the 1964 canvas *The Sound of Music.*

Bibliography

"About Face from the Abstract." *St. Louis Post-Dispatch* (December 31, 1961): 10–11.

Adelman, Bob. *The Art of Roy Lichtenstein: Mural with Blue Brushstroke* (New York: Harry N. Abrams, 1988).

Alloway, Lawrence. *Roy Lichtenstein* (New York: Abbeville, 1983).

Baer, Ulrich. "Photography and Hysteria: Toward a Poetics of the Flash," *Yale Journal of Criticism* 7, no. 1 (Spring 1994): 41–77.

Bakhtin, Mikhail. *Rabelais and His World*, trans. Helen Iswolsky (Cambridge, Mass.: MIT Press, 1968).

Barthes, Roland. "The Death of the Author," trans. Stephen Heath, in *Image, Music, Text* (New York: Hill and Wang, 1977): 142–48.

———. "That Old Thing, Art . . . ," trans. Richard Howard, in Madoff, *Pop Art*, 370–74.

Benjamin, Walter. "The Work of Art in the Age of Mechanical Reproduction," trans. Harry Zohn, in *Illuminations* (New York: Schocken, 1969): 217–51.

Boatto, Alberto. "The Comicstrip Under the Microscope," in *Lichtenstein*, ed. Alberto Boatto and Giordano Falzoni, special issue of *Fantazaria* (Rome) 1, no. 2 (July–August 1966): 52–61.

Boime, Albert. "Roy Lichtenstein and the Comic Strip," *Art Journal* 28, no. 2 (Winter 1968–69): 155–59.

Bois, Yve-Alain. "The Semiology of Cubism," in *Picasso and Braque: A Symposium*, ed. Lynn Zelevansky (New York: Museum of Modern Art, 1992): 169–208.

Bouissac, Paul, ed. *Encyclopedia of Semiotics* (Oxford: Oxford University Press, 1998).

Brooks, Peter. *The Melodramatic Imagination: Balzac, Henry James, Melodrama, and the Mode of Excess* (New Haven: Yale University Press, 1995).

Bryson, Norman. *Vision and Painting: The Logic of the Gaze* (New Haven: Yale University Press, 1983).

Busche, Ernst. *Roy Lichtenstein: Das Frühwerk, 1942–1960* (Berlin: Gebr. Mann, 1988).

Buskirk, Martha. "Commodification as Censor: Copyrights and Fair Use," *October* 60 (Spring 1992): 82–109.

Butler, Judith. *Gender Trouble: Feminism and the Subversion of Identity* (New York: Routledge, 1990).

Capitman, Barbara Baer. *American Trademark Designs: A Survey with 732 Marks, Logos, and Corporate-Identity Symbols* (New York: Dover, 1976).

Clarke, R. Wallace. "Drawing a Bead," pt. 3, *Aeroplane Monthly* (April 1983): 200–204.

———. "Drawing a Bead," pt. 4, *Aeroplane Monthly* (May 1983): 279–83.

Clynes, Manfred, and Nathan Kline. "Cyborgs and Space," *Astronautics* 5, no. 9 (September 1960): 26–27, 74–76.

Colacello, Bob. *Holy Terror: Andy Warhol Close Up* (New York: HarperCollins, 1990).

Coplans, John. *Roy Lichtenstein* (New York: Praeger, 1972).

Corlett, Mary Lee. *The Prints of Roy Lichtenstein: A Catalogue Raisonné, 1948–1993* (New York: Hudson Hills, 1994).

Crary, Jonathan. *Techniques of the Observer: On Vision and Modernity in the Nineteenth Century* (Cambridge, Mass.: MIT Press, 1990).

Crichton, Michael. *Jasper Johns* (exh. cat.) (New York: Harry N. Abrams in association with the Whitney Museum of American Art, 1977).

Crow, Thomas. "Saturday Disasters: Trace and Reference in Early Warhol," in *Modern Art in the Common Culture* (New Haven: Yale University Press, 1996): 49–65.

Deitcher, David. "Lichtenstein's Expressionist Takes," *Art in America* 71, no. 1 (January 1983): 84–88.

———. "Teaching the Late Modern Artist: From Mnemonics to the Technology of Gestalt," 2 vols. (Ph.D. diss., Graduate Center, City University of New York, 1989).
———. "Unsentimental Education: The Professionalization of the American Artist," in *Hand-Painted Pop: American Art in Transition, 1955–62* (exh. cat.), ed. Russell Ferguson (Los Angeles: Museum of Contemporary Art, 1992): 95–118.
Derrida, Jacques. "Signature Event Context," trans. Alan Bass, in *MARGINS of Philosophy* (Chicago: University of Chicago Press, 1982).
"Don't Kiss Me Again!" *Girls' Romances* no. 105 (December 1964).
Doyle, Jennifer, Jonathan Flatley, and José Esteban Muñoz, eds. *Pop Out: Queer Warhol* (Durham, N.C.: Duke University Press, 1996).
Elsaesser, Thomas. "Tales of Sound and Fury: Observations on the Family Melodrama," *Monogram* no. 4 (1972); reprinted in *Home Is Where the Heart Is: Studies in Melodrama and the Woman's Film,* ed. Christine Gledhill (London: British Film Institute, 1987): 43–69.
Ferguson, Russell, ed. *Hand-Painted Pop: American Art in Transition, 1955–62* (exh. cat.) (Los Angeles: Museum of Contemporary Art, 1992).
Filler, Martin. "Pop's Granddad," *Vanity Fair* 56, no. 8 (August 1993): 128–35, 149–53.
Foster, Hal. *Compulsive Beauty* (Cambridge, Mass.: MIT Press, 1993).
———. *The Return of the Real: The Avant-Garde at the End of the Century* (Cambridge, Mass.: MIT Press, 1996).
Freud, Sigmund. *Civilization and Its Discontents,* trans. and ed. James Strachey (New York: W. W. Norton, 1961).
———. *Jokes and Their Relation to the Unconscious,* trans. and ed. James Strachey (New York: W. W. Norton, 1960).
———. "The Uncanny," in *The Standard Edition of the Complete Psychological Works of Sigmund Freud,* vol. 17, trans. and ed. James Strachey (London: Hogarth, 1955): 219–56.
Fried, Michael. *Absorption and Theatricality: Painting and Beholder in the Age of Diderot* (Berkeley: University of California Press, 1980).
———. *Art and Objecthood* (Chicago: University of Chicago Press, 1998).
———. *Courbet's Realism* (Chicago: University of Chicago Press, 1990).
———. "New York Letter," *Art International* 7, no. 9 (December 5, 1963): 66.
———. *Realism, Writing, Disfiguration: On Thomas Eakins and Stephen Crane* (Chicago: University of Chicago Press, 1987).
Frow, John. "The Signature: Three Arguments About the Commodity Form," in *Aesthesia and the Economy of the Senses,* ed. Helen Grace (Kingswood, NSW, Australia: UWS Nepean, 1996): 151–200.
Gaines, Jane M. *Contested Culture: The Image, the Voice, and the Law* (Chapel Hill: University of North Carolina Press, 1991).
Girardot, Norman. "Can Package Design Be Evaluated?" *Planning Package Development,* Packaging Series Number 24 (Papers presented at the Packaging Conference and Exposition of the American Management Association, Philadelphia, April 8–11, 1947) (New York: American Management Association, 1947): 22–28.
Glaser, Bruce. "Oldenburg, Lichtenstein, Warhol: A Discussion," *Artforum* 4, no. 6 (February 1966): 20–24.
Goldberg, H. S. "Reflector Gun Sights," *Army Air Forces Technical Report* no. 5179, Wright Field, Dayton, Ohio (January 2, 1945) (National Air and Space Museum Library, Smithsonian Institution, Washington, D.C.).
Goldman, Judith. *James Rosenquist: The Early Pictures, 1961–1964* (New York: Rizzoli, 1992).
Gombrich, E. H. *Art and Illusion: A Study in the Psychology of Pictorial Representation* (Princeton, N.J.: Princeton University Press, 1989).

———. "Dark Varnishes: Variations on a Theme from Pliny," *Burlington Magazine* 104, no. 707 (February 1962): 51–55.
Gornick, Vivian. "It's a Queer Hand Stoking the Campfire," *Village Voice* 11, no. 25 (April 7, 1966): 1, 20.
Greenberg, Clement. "Avant-Garde and Kitsch," reprinted in *Pollock and After: The Critical Debate,* ed. Francis Frascina (New York: Harper and Row, 1985): 21–33.
———. "Towards a Newer Laocoon," reprinted in *Clement Greenberg: The Collected Essays and Criticism, Volume I: Perceptions and Judgments 1939–1944,* ed. John O'Brian (Chicago: University of Chicago Press, 1986): 23–38.
Harrison, Charles. *Modernism* (Cambridge: Cambridge University Press, 1997).
Haskell, Barbara. *Blam!: The Explosion of Pop, Minimalism, and Performance, 1958–1964* (exh. cat.) (New York: Whitney Museum of American Art, 1984).
Hebdige, Dick. "Fabulous Confusion! Pop Before Pop?" *Hand-Painted Pop: American Art in Transition 1955–62* (exh. cat.), ed. Russell Ferguson (Los Angeles: Museum of Contemporary Art, 1992): 205–41.
Hopps, Walter, and Susan Davidson. *Robert Rauschenberg: A Retrospective* (New York: Solomon R. Guggenheim Museum, 1997).
How to Use the General Electric Signature and Monogram (New York: Marketing Services Division, General Electric Company, c. 1953).
Hughes, Robert. "The Image Duplicator," *Time* 142, no. 19 (November 8, 1993): 83–84.
———. "Pop's Most Popular," *Time* 150, no. 15 (October 13, 1997): 101.
———. "The Rise of Andy Warhol," in *Art After Modernism: Rethinking Representation,* ed. Brian Wallis (New York: New Museum of Contemporary Art, 1984): 45–57.
Huyssen, Andreas. "Mass Culture as Woman: Modernism's Other," in *After the Great Divide: Modernism, Mass Culture, Postmodernism* (Bloomington: Indiana University Press, 1986): 44–62.
Irwin, David. "Pop Art and Surrealism," *Studio International* 171, no. 877 (May 1966): 187–91.
"Jackson Pollock: Is He the Greatest Living Painter in the United States?" *Life* 27, no. 6 (August 8, 1949): 42–45.
Jacobson, Egbert, ed. *Seven Designers Look at Trademark Design* (Chicago: Paul Theobald, 1952).
Johnson, Ellen H., ed. *American Artists on Art from 1940 to 1980* (New York: Harper and Row, 1982).
———. "The Image Duplicators—Lichtenstein, Rauschenberg, and Warhol," *Canadian Art* 23, no. 1 (January 1966): 12–19.
Jones, Caroline. *The Machine in the Studio: Constructing the Postwar American Artist* (Chicago: University of Chicago Press, 1996).
D[onald] J[udd]. "Roy Lichtenstein," *Arts* 36, no. 7 (April 1962): 52–53.
"Julian, My Love!" *Girls' Romances* no. 92 (June 1963).
Kaprow, Allan. "The Legacy of Jackson Pollock," *Art News* 57, no. 6 (October 1958): 24–26, 55–57.
Koerner, Joseph Leo. *Caspar David Friedrich and the Subject of Landscape* (New Haven: Yale University Press, 1990).
Kozloff, Max. "Art," *Nation* 197, no. 14 (November 2, 1963): 284–87.
———. "Dissimulated Pop," *Nation* 199, no. 17 (November 30, 1964): 417–19.
———. "'Pop' Culture, Metaphysical Disgust, and the New Vulgarians," *Art International* 6, no. 2 (March 1962): 34–36.
Krauss, Rosalind. *The Optical Unconscious* (Cambridge, Mass.: MIT Press, 1993).
———. *The Originality of the Avant-Garde and Other Modernist Myths* (Cambridge, Mass.: MIT Press, 1985).
———. *The Picasso Papers* (Cambridge, Mass.: MIT Press, 1999).
"The Last Case of the Justice League." *Justice League of America* no. 12 (June 1962).
Lichtenstein, Roy. "An Interview with Roy Lichtenstein," Whitney Museum of

American Art Independent Study Program, 1981, n.p.

———. Interviewed by Richard Brown Baker, November 15 and December 6, 1963 (Archives of American Art, Smithsonian Institution, Washington, D.C.).

———. Interviewed by John Coplans, "An Interview with Roy Lichtenstein," *Artforum* 2, no. 4 (October 1963): 31.

———. Interviewed by John Coplans, "Talking with Roy Lichtenstein," *Artforum* 5, no. 9 (May 1967): 34–39.

———. Interviewed by Milton Esterow, "Conversation," *Art News* 90, no. 5 (May 1991): 85–91.

———. Interviewed by Gene R. Swenson, "What Is Pop Art? Answers from Eight Painters, Part I," *Art News* 62, no. 7 (November 1963): 25, 62–63.

———. Talk given at College Art Association annual meeting, Philadelphia, January 1964, reprinted in *American Artists on Art from 1940 to 1980,* ed. Ellen H. Johnson (New York: Harper and Row, 1982): 102–4.

Lichtenstein's Picassos: 1962–1964 (exh. cat.) (New York: Gagosian Gallery, 1988).

"Listen to Love!" *Heart Throbs* no. 79 (August–September 1962).

Livingstone, Marco. "Do It Yourself: Notes on Warhol's Techniques," in *Andy Warhol: A Retrospective,* ed. Kynaston McShine (New York: Museum of Modern Art, 1989): 63–78.

Lobel, Michael. "Rosenquist's Craft: Painting and the Limits of the Machine." *Parkett* no. 58 (2000): 60–61.

Loran, Erle. "Cézanne and Lichtenstein: Problems of 'Transformation,'" *Artforum* 2, no. 3 (September 1963): 34–35.

———. *Cézanne's Composition: Analysis of His Form with Diagrams and Photographs of His Motifs* (Berkeley: University of California Press, 1943).

———. "Pop Artists or Copy Cats?" *Artnews* 62, no. 5 (September 1963): 48–49, 61.

McClellan, Doug. "Roy Lichtenstein, Ferus Gallery," *Artforum* 2, no. 1 (July 1963): 44, 47.

McLuhan, Herbert Marshall. *The Mechanical Bride: Folklore of Industrial Man* (New York: Vanguard, 1951).

McShine, Kynaston, ed. *Andy Warhol: A Retrospective* (exh. cat.) (New York: Museum of Modern Art, 1989).

Madoff, Steven Henry, ed. *Pop Art: A Critical History* (Berkeley: University of California Press, 1997).

Maharaj, Sarat. "Framing Roy Lichtenstein: A Mickey Mimesis Mimicked, Also Mimed?" in *Roy Lichtenstein* (exh. cat.) (London: Tate Gallery, 1993): 13–20.

Mamiya, Christin J. *Pop Art and Consumer Culture: American Supermarket* (Austin: University of Texas Press, 1992).

Marter, Joan, ed. *Off Limits: Rutgers University and the Avant-Garde, 1957–63* (exh. cat.) (Newark: Newark Museum, and New Brunswick: Rutgers University Press, 1999).

Meyer, Richard. "Warhol's Clones," *Yale Journal of Criticism* 7, no. 1 (Spring 1994): 79–109.

Modern Dreams: The Rise and Fall and Rise of Pop (exh. cat.) (New York: Institute for Contemporary Art, and Cambridge, Mass.: MIT Press, 1988).

Mulvey, Laura. "Visual Pleasure and Narrative Cinema" (1975), reprinted in *Visual and Other Pleasures* (Bloomington: Indiana University Press, 1989): 14–26.

Napoles, Veronica. *Corporate Identity Design* (New York: Van Nostrand Reinhold, 1988).

Nelson, Robert S. "The Slide Lecture, or The Work of Art *History* in the Age of Mechanical Reproduction," *Critical Inquiry* 26 (Spring 2000): 414–34.

Nesbit, Margaret S. "Roy Lichtenstein: Birth of a Style, 1961–63," in *Richard Brown Baker Collects! A Selection of Contemporary Art from the Richard Brown Baker Collection* (exh. cat.) (New Haven: Yale University Art Gallery, 1975): 62–71.

Nochlin, Linda. "Courbet's *L'origine du monde:* The Origin Without an Original," *October* 37 (Summer 1986): 76–86.

O'Doherty, Brian. "Lichtenstein: Doubtful but Definite Triumph of the Banal," *New York Times* (October 27, 1963), sec. 2, p. 21.
Okun, Henry. "The Surrealist Object" (Ph.D. diss., Institute of Fine Arts, New York University, 1981).
Owens, Craig. *Beyond Recognition: Representation, Power, and Culture* (Berkeley: University of California Press, 1992).
Packard, Vance. *The Hidden Persuaders* (New York: David McKay, 1957).
"The Painting," *Strange Suspense Stories* 1, no. 72 (October 1964).
Plagens, Peter. "Infinite Gesture," *Bookforum* (Summer 1997): 3, 32.
Plante, Michael. "Truth, Friendship, and Love: Sexuality and Tradition in Robert Indiana's Hartley Elegies," in Patricia McDonnell, *Dictated by Life: Marsden Hartley's German Paintings and Robert Indiana's Hartley Elegies* (exh. cat.) (Minneapolis: Frederick R. Weisman Art Museum, 1995): 57–87.
Public Opinion Index for Industry. *The Language of Corporate Trademarks and Symbols* (Princeton, N.J.: Opinion Research, 1960).
Ratcliff, Carter. "The Work of Roy Lichtenstein in the Age of Walter Benjamin's and Jean Baudrillard's Popularity," *Art in America* 77, no. 2 (February 1989): 111–22, 177.
Richter, Hans. *Dada: Art and Anti-Art,* trans. David Britt (New York: Harry N. Abrams, 1965).
"Robot Plane Sight Adapted," *New York World-Telegram* October 18, 1944 (National Air and Space Museum Library, Smithsonian Institution, Washington, D.C.).
Rose, Bernice. *The Drawings of Roy Lichtenstein* (exh. cat.) (New York: Museum of Modern Art, 1987).
Rosenblum, Robert. "Roy Lichtenstein and the Realist Revolt," *Metro* no. 8 (March 1963): 38–45.
Roy Lichtenstein at CalArts: Drawings and Collages from the Artist's Collection (exh. cat.) (Valencia: California Institute of the Arts, 1977).
Roy Lichtenstein: Drawings and Prints (Secaucus, N.J.: Wellfleet, 1988).
Rublowsky, John. *Pop Art* (New York: Basic Books, 1965).
Ruskin, John. The Elements of Drawing in Three Letters to Beginners (London: George Allen, 1904).
de Saussure, Ferdinand. *Course in General Linguistics,* ed. Charles Bally and Albert Sechehaye, trans. Wade Baskin (New York: McGraw-Hill, 1966).
Schjeldahl, Peter. "His Royness: Roy Lichtenstein, 1923–1997," *Village Voice* 42, no. 42 (October 21, 1997): 101.
Seiberling, Dorothy. "Is He the Worst Artist in the U.S.?" *Life* 56, no. 5 (January 31, 1964): 79–81, 83.
Sherman, Hoyt. *Drawing by Seeing: A New Development in the Teaching of the Visual Arts Through the Training of Perception* (New York: Hinds, Hayden and Eldredge, 1947).
———. *The Visual Demonstration Center, Part 1: A Manual for Operation with an Emphasis on Vision in the Fine Arts* (Columbus: Institute for Research in Vision, Ohio State University, 1951).
———. *The Visual Demonstration Center, Part 2: Cézanne and Visual Form* (Columbus: Institute for Research in Vision, Ohio State University, 1952).
Shiff, Richard. "Performing an Appearance: On the Surface of Abstract Expressionism," in *Abstract Expressionism: The Critical Developments,* ed. Michael Auping (exh. cat.) (New York: Harry N. Abrams, and Buffalo: Albright-Knox Art Gallery, 1987): 94–123.
Silver, Kenneth E. "Modes of Disclosure: The Construction of Gay Identity and the Rise of Pop Art," in *Hand-Painted Pop: American Art in Transition 1955–62* (exh. cat.), ed. Russell Ferguson (Los Angeles: Museum of Contemporary Art, 1992): 179–203.

Stallybrass, Peter, and Allon White. *The Politics and Poetics of Transgression* (Ithaca, N.Y.: Cornell University Press, 1986).
Stein, Jean. *Edie: An American Biography*, ed. with George Plimpton (New York: Knopf, 1982).
Steinberg, Leo. "Other Criteria," in *Other Criteria: Confrontations with Twentieth-Century Art* (London: Oxford University Press, 1972): 55–91.
Steiner, Wendy. *Pictures of Romance: Form Against Context in Painting and Literature* (Chicago: University of Chicago Press, 1988).
Stich, Sidra. *Made in U.S.A.: An Americanization in Modern Art, the '50s & '60s* (exh. cat.) (Berkeley: University Art Museum, University of California, 1987).
Swenson, Gene R. "What Is Pop Art? Answers from Eight Painters, Part I," *Art News* 62, no. 7 (November 1963): 24–27, 59–64.
———. "What Is Pop Art? Part II," *Art News* 62, no. 10 (February 1964): 40–43, 62–67.
Tomkins, Calvin. "The Antic Muse," *New Yorker* 57, no. 26 (August 17, 1981): 80–83.
———. "Brushstrokes," in Bob Adelman, *The Art of Roy Lichtenstein: Mural with Blue Brushstroke* (New York: Harry N. Abrams, 1988): 7–29.
"Tomorrow and Tomorrow." *Girls' Romances* no. 71 (September 1961).
Tuchman, Phyllis. "POP!: Interviews with George Segal, Andy Warhol, Roy Lichtenstein, James Rosenquist and Robert Indiana," *Art News* 73, no. 5 (May 1974): 24–29.
Varnedoe, Kirk, and Adam Gopnik. *High and Low: Modern Art and Popular Culture* (exh. cat.) (New York: Museum of Modern Art, 1990).
Waldman, Diane. *Roy Lichtenstein* (exh. cat.) (New York: Solomon R. Guggenheim Museum, 1969).
———. *Roy Lichtenstein* (New York: Harry N. Abrams, 1971).
———. *Roy Lichtenstein* (exh. cat.) (New York: Solomon R. Guggenheim Museum, 1993).
———. *Roy Lichtenstein, Riflessi-Reflections* (exh. cat.) (Rome: Chiostra del Bramante, 1999).
Warhol, Andy. *The Philosophy of Andy Warhol (From A to B and Back Again)* (New York: Harcourt Brace Jovanovich, 1975).
———, and Pat Hackett. *POPism: The Warhol Sixties* (New York: Harcourt Brace Jovanovich, 1980).
Wassenaar, Michael. "Strong to the Finich: Machines, Metaphor, and Popeye the Sailor," *Velvet Light Trap* 24 (Fall 1989): 20–32.
Weiss, Jeffrey. *Mark Rothko* (exh. cat.) (Washington, D.C.: National Gallery of Art, 1998).
What You Should Know About Du Pont Trademarks (Wilmington, Del.: Du Pont de Nemours [E.I.] and Company, c. 1960).
Whiting, Cécile. *A Taste for Pop: Pop Art, Gender, and Consumer Culture* (Cambridge: Cambridge University Press, 1997).

Index

Page numbers in italics refer to illustrations.

Credits

Photograph © 2001, The Art Institute of Chicago (fig. 87); Photo by Burckhardt (figs. 26, 97, 99); The Butler Institute of American Art, Youngstown, Ohio (fig. 21); © 1943 Regents of the University of California (figs. 70, 98); CNAC/MNAM/Dist Réunion des Musées Nationaux/Art Resource, New York (fig. 96); © 1961 DC Comics, All rights reserved, Used with permission (fig. 95); © 1962 DC Comics, All rights reserved, Used with permission (figs. 54, 56, 65, 78); © 1963 DC Comics, All rights reserved, Used with permission (fig. 82); © 2001 King Features Syndicate, reprinted with special permission of North American Syndicate (figs. 43, 76); Kröller-Müller Museum (fig. 33); © Estate of Roy Lichtenstein (figs. 1, 2, 3, 4, 9, 11, 12, 13, 14, 15, 16, 18, 19, 20, 21, 23, 24, 25, 26, 27, 28, 29, 30, 31, 34, 35, 37, 38, 39, 40, 41, 42, 50, 51, 52, 53, 55, 57, 58, 59, 60, 61, 64, 66, 67, 71, 73, 74, 75, 77, 79, 80, 81, 83, 84, 85, 86, 88, 89, 90, 91, 92, 93, 94, 97, 99, 100, 102, 103); © John Loengard/TimePix (figs. 7, 8); TM & © 2001 Marvel Characters, Inc., Used with permission (fig. 6); © 1943, 1971 Erle Loran (fig. 69); © 2001 Succession H. Matisse, Paris/Artists Rights Society (ARS), New York (fig. 87); The Robert B. Mayer Family Collection, Chicago, Photographed by Dorothy Zeidman, Courtesy The Museum of Modern Art (fig. 29); Photo by Robert McKeever (figs. 2–4, 13, 25, 28, 52, 58, 61, 74, 94); © Ugo Mulas Estate, All rights reserved (fig. 101); Photograph © 2001 The Museum of Modern Art, New York (image reproduced on right); National Air and Space Museum, Smithsonian Institution (SI Neg. No. 2000–7995) (fig. 62); Wright-McCook Field Photo Collection (Ref. No. 90848), National Air and Space Museum, Smithsonian Institution (fig. 63); Photograph © 2001 Board of Trustees, National Gallery of Art, Washington, D.C./photo by Dean Beasom (fig. 57); The Ohio State University Photo Archives (figs. 44, 46, 49); ©2001 Estate of Pablo Picasso/Artists Rights Society (ARS), New York (figs. 32, 96); © 1988 Van Nostrand Reinhold Company, Inc., reprinted by permission of John Wiley & Sons, Inc. (fig. 22); © Scottish National Gallery of Modern Art (fig. 93); Norton Simon Museum Archives, Pasadena, California (fig. 27); Charles Simonyi/photos © Eduardo Calderon (figs. 1, 53, 61, 92); The Andy Warhol Foundation/Art Resource, NY (fig. 10); © 2001 Andy Warhol Foundation for the Visual Arts/Artists Rights Society (ARS), New York (figs. 10, 17, 68); Photograph © Whitney Museum of American Art (figs. 17, 68, 100); Harvey Cushing/John Hay Whitney Medical Library, Yale University (fig. 47)

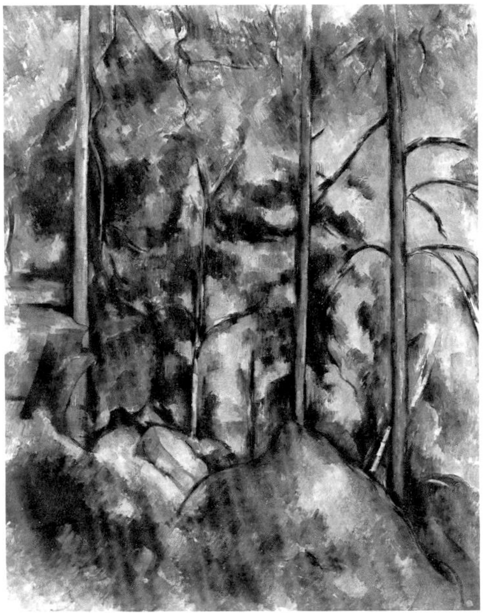

Paul Cézanne, *Pines and Rocks (Fontainebleau?)*, 1896–99. Oil on canvas, 32¾ × 25¾ in. (81.3 × 65.4 cm). The Museum of Modern Art, New York. Lillie P. Bliss Collection. Photograph © 2001 The Museum of Modern Art, New York (see fig. 49)